READING RASMUSSEN AND DEN UYL

READING RASMUSSEN AND DEN UYL

Critical Essays on *Norms of Liberty*

Edited by Aeon J. Skoble

LEXINGTON BOOKS

A Division of Rowman & Littlefield Publishers, Inc.
Lanham • Boulder • New York • Toronto • Plymouth, UK

LEXINGTON BOOKS

A division of Rowman & Littlefield Publishers, Inc.
A wholly owned subsidiary of The Rowman & Littlefield Publishing Group, Inc.
4501 Forbes Boulevard, Suite 200
Lanham, MD 20706

Estover Road
Plymouth PL6 7PY
United Kingdom

British Library Cataloguing in Publication Information Available

Library of Congress Cataloging-in-Publication Data

Reading Rasmussen and Den Uyl : critical essays on Norms of liberty / [edited by] Aeon J. Skoble.
p. cm.
Includes bibliographical references and index.
ISBN-13: 978-0-7391-2692-9 (cloth : alk. paper)
ISBN-10: 0-7391-2692-X (cloth : alk. paper)
1. Rasmussen, Douglas B., 1948- Norms of liberty. 2. Liberty. 3. Liberalism. 4. Natural law. 5. Political science—Philosophy. I. Skoble, Aeon J.
JC585.R423 2008
323.44'01--dc22 2008012057

Printed in the United States of America

∞™ The paper used in this publication meets the minimum requirements of American National Standard for Information Sciences—Permanence of Paper for Printed Library Materials, ANSI/NISO Z39.48-1992.

Contents

Preface

When I was an undergraduate, it seemed as though liberal political theory, and indeed ethics generally, came in two flavors: consequentialist and deontological. Kant or Bentham? Locke or Mill? Happily, the renaissance of interest in Aristotle which got started in the 1970s had spillover effects in moral and political philosophy: virtue ethics, and the use of virtue ethics as a possible groundwork for liberalism. Entering graduate school in the mid-1980s, I had already studied Locke, Mill, Rawls, and Nozick. I had also studied Aristotle, although at the time I could not see how he could have any connection to liberal political theory, and I couldn't articulate why I was uncomfortable with the appeal to Aristotle in such thinkers as MacIntyre. As I began pursuing independent research projects, however, I came across two anthologies of classical liberal theory, one edited by Tibor Machan, *The Libertarian Reader*, and one edited by Jeffrey Paul, *Reading Nozick: Essays on* Anarchy, State and Utopia. The essays in these volumes greatly expanded my horizons in a number of ways, not the least of which was introducing me to the neo-Aristotelian approach to grounding classical liberalism, and the two most articulate proponents of this approach, Douglas B. Rasmussen and Douglas J. Den Uyl. I immediately gravitated towards their work, finding it to be both technically impressive and substantively right, and by 1990 I was privileged to have made their acquaintance.

In 1991, they produced *Liberty and Nature: An Aristotelian Defense of Liberal Order*, which I found to be a persuasive and coherent argument. But Rasmussen and Den Uyl continued to work on the project: responding to critics, reformulating and strengthening parts of the argument, reevaluating methodological issues. They wrote many short pieces, both separately and together, and participated in conferences devoted to the themes they helped bring to the foreground. This continued work reached its apex in the 2005 release of *Norms of Liberty: A Perfectionist Basis for Non-Perfectionist Politics*. This book turned out to be even more comprehensive, and it struck me as having the potential to be hugely influential and important. I therefore organized a symposium on it, to meet at the December 2005 meeting of the American Philosophical Association in New York City. The symposiasts raised a variety of interesting questions, to which Rasmussen and Den Uyl replied, and there was lively interplay with the audience. I learned shortly thereafter that there were also symposia on *Norms of Liberty* planned for the 2006 meetings of the American Political Science Association and the American Catholic Philosophical Association, partly confirming my suspicion that the book was as important as I thought it was. I contacted the organizers of those symposia, and the result is this book. What follows are, revised for publication of course, the proceedings of all three symposia, and then an omnibus reply essay from Rasmussen and Den Uyl. The contributors range from highly sympathetic to highly critical. If you have already read *Norms of Liberty*, I hope you find these essays interesting and illuminative. If you have not read *Norms of Liberty*, I hope they pique your interest enough to drive you to do so.

The symposium at the APA featured an introduction from Fred Miller and papers by myself, Edwin England, David Thunder, and Charlotte Thomas. From the APSA symposium we have here papers by Ken Grasso, Elaine Sternberg, and Sue Collins. The ACPA symposium featured papers by Denis Sullivan, Timothy Fuller, James S. Taylor, William Kline, and Peter Vedder. I would like to thank all of them for the careful thought and hard work they have put into this. In addition, I would like to express my gratitude to Patrick Dillon, Jessica Bradfield, Jonathan Sisk, Kia Westwood, and everyone at Lexington Books. I am also grateful to the following people for the many discussions which have helped me think about these themes over the years: Nick Capaldi, Mark Conard, Allan Gotthelf, Lester Hunt, Jonathan Jacobs, David Kelley, Irfan Khawaja, Loren Lomasky, Roderick Long, Tibor Machan, Eric Mack, James Otteson, John Pappas, Jeffrey Paul, Chris Sciabarra, Danny Shapiro, Tara Smith, and David Steele. I would like to thank my wife Lisa and our daughters Lydia and Madeleine for their support, including their toleration of my frequent conference travel. I am also very grateful to Brian Adam and Milo Schield for their generous support and encouragement.

The last and heartiest expression of gratitude, of course, is to Doug Rasmussen and Doug Den Uyl. Their support, encouragement, counsel, and friendship over the years have been invaluable, and I am deeply grateful for those things. I would also like to thank them for all the work they have done for moral and political philosophy over the last thirty years, and especially for writing *Norms of Liberty*.

Aeon J. Skoble

An Introduction to *Norms of Liberty*

Fred D. Miller Jr.

This collection of essays is devoted to critical reflection about *Norms of Liberty: A Perfectionist Basis for Non-Perfectionist Politics*, co-authored by Douglas B. Rasmussen and Douglas J. Den Uyl, and published by the Pennsylvania State University Press in 2005.[1] *Norms of Liberty* is, unquestionably, one of the most original and interesting works on liberal political philosophy in recent years. The book advances a neo-Aristotelian defense of liberalism, which Rasmussen and Den Uyl understand in its classical sense as a political theory deeply committed to individual liberty.

Rasmussen and Den Uyl make a convincing case that liberalism is very much in need of defense. Recent proponents of liberalism have commonly eschewed any commitment to a substantive theory of the objective good for two reasons: they sought to erect a "big tent" which will accommodate as many liberal partisans as possible, and they feared that a substantive theory of the objective good might serve as a basis for infringements by the state on the freedom of the individual. Rasmussen and Den Uyl, however, contend that this neutralist strategy has backfired and resulted in a "crisis of liberalism." Adversaries from both sides of the political spectrum complain that liberalism is a sterile and implausible doctrine based on atomism, instrumentalism, subjectivism, relativism, and skepticism. The deep divide between welfare liberals such as John Rawls and libertarians such as Robert Nozick shows that liberals have trouble agreeing among themselves on important issues such as the relative importance of liberty and equality, and the nature and extent of individual rights to self-ownership, personal assets, and external property. The very poverty of a liberalism without moral foundations has led paradoxically, Rasmussen and Den Uyl contend, to a tendency on the part of many recent liberals to politicize morality, by advocating political correctness and liberal virtues. Rasmussen and Den Uyl seek to remedy this deficiency by providing a neo-Aristotelian, perfectionist justification for liberal political theory.

The book's argument is distinctive in the first place in that it seeks to justify liberalism (non-perfectionist political theory) on neo-Aristotelian (perfectionist) foundations. As Rasmussen and Den Uyl recognize, Aristotle himself upheld a virtue ethics and inferred that the best system of laws would promote the moral virtue of the citizens, even if this entailed significant limitations on individual liberty. Rasmussen and Den Uyl avoid this implication by distinguishing between the functions of *ethical theory* (which is concerned with the values and duties of individuals) and those of *political theory* (concerned with the values and obligations of states). Even if moral virtue is the end of the individual (the view of many ancient ethical theorists), it does not follow that virtue is the end of the political state (the view of many ancient political theorists). The fundamental problem of the modern polity—which Rasmussen and Den Uyl call "liberalism's problem"—is that different individuals are evidently able to flourish and realize moral virtue in very different ways (a possibility recognized by many modern political theorists). How can we establish a political and legal order that allows for this possibility?

Rasmussen and Den Uyl's neo-Aristotelian argument for liberalism involves two main points: First, human flourishing is an inclusive end which includes different kinds of intrinsic goods, for which there is no preset weighting pattern. They reject an aggregationist "maximizing" approach to human flourishing. Different individuals will value different intrinsic goods to a different extent, thus allowing for great diversity in authentic forms of human flourishing. Second, Rasmussen and Den Uyl argue that the state should instead be concerned with self-direction, which is necessary for all forms of human flourishing. This will permit different forms of the good life to coexist and will afford each individual the latitude to realize a distinctive form of flourishing.

To some extent their argument has been anticipated by earlier political philosophers such as Spinoza, Kant, Mill (following Humboldt), and T. H. Green. However, Rasmussen and Den Uyl draw a further important distinction between *normative* principles (which should guide personal conduct) and *metanormative* principles (which should guide legislation, i.e., the framing of laws regulating personal conduct). A political philosophy of metanorms, they argue, "seeks not to guide individual conduct in moral activity, but rather to regulate conduct so that conditions might be obtained where moral action can take place" (pp. 38–39). From the fact that normative principles are perfectionist (e.g. aim at virtue or flourishing) it does not follow that metanormative principles must also be perfectionist. But Rasmussen and Den Uyl make an even stronger argument than this, which may be summed up in the following syllogism:

1. Normative principles (those which should guide individual conduct) are perfectionist.
2. Non-perfectionist metanormative principles (those which should guide legislation) are required in order to protect perfectionist normative principles.
3. Therefore, metanormative principles should be non-perfectionist.

Thus Rasmussen and Den Uyl argue not only that liberalism is not necessarily connected to moral minimalism or skepticism but also (as the book's subtitle suggests) that non-perfectionist (i.e., liberal) political theory has a perfectionist basis.

In summary, *Norms of Liberty* is one of the most important works on liberalism in recent years. The fact that individuals have different views of the good life poses a fundamental problem for modern political philosophy. Rasmussen and Den Uyl present a brilliant solution by distinguishing between normative principles guiding individual moral conduct and metanormative principles that govern legislation. They argue on this basis that neo-Aristotelian perfectionist ethics can support non-perfectionist politics. The essays in this volume have all recognized the points I have emphasized above, and in their reflections we can see areas for further discussion.

Note

1. Throughout this book, references to *Norms of Liberty* will be given as in-line parenthetical citations.

1

Assessing the Prospects for *Norms of Liberty*

Aeon J. Skoble

The subject of this essay, and this volume, is the 2005 book *Norms of Liberty* by Douglas B. Rasmussen and Douglas J. Den Uyl. The book offers a neo-Aristotelian ethic of human flourishing as a basis for a liberal conception of human rights.[1] One of the authors' central contentions is that a key problem for any (liberal) political philosophy is how to establish a political/legal order which in principle does not require that any one person or group's well-being be given structured preference over that of any other. This paper is mostly a discussion of the prospects facing their argument. I partly discuss what I see as the merits of their case, with which I'm in agreement, and examine their methodology in replying to critics. I particularly focus on their distinction between normative principles guiding individual conduct and "metanormative" principles that concern legislation.

The Argument

Liberty can be defended on various grounds. Although there are several others, people tend to be most familiar with the natural-rights defense in Locke, the rule-utilitarian defense offered by Mill, or the economic approaches in Smith, and later in Hayek and Friedman. Less well known, but I think ultimately more successful, is the approach that has been called "neo-Aristotelian": the idea that human flourishing requires a sphere of liberty in order to be realized. Rasmussen and Den Uyl have pioneered and articulated this conception extremely thoroughly, and I fail to see how the theory fails to answer any objection which might be put by non-liberals, although I shall turn to this matter shortly. Rasmussen and Den Uyl conceive of rights as being "metanormative" principles, as opposed to normative, in that they do not specify ends as such, but merely the conditions under which pursuit of ends is legitimate. This is, for them, a foundation from which to derive a regime of liberty. Recognition of others as rights-bearing produces a social order in which all are free to pursue their ends, to the extent that they are not violating the rights of others. They argue, following Aristotle, that human flourishing depends on the excellent use of practical reason in the development of virtue, and then go on to show that this requires a political culture of freedom. This strategy avoids both radical moral subjectivism and the tendency towards political totalitarianism. It is a "natural rights" approach, but not in the Lockean sense of the rights being some thing in nature. The rights are natural in the sense of "derived from a conception of human nature."

This is a very important book, for several reasons. First of all, the mere fact that Rasmussen and Den Uyl are offering another attempt to defend natural rights liberalism is significant in a time when liberalism is under increasing attack from both the left and the right, but this particular defense has the virtue of actually doing what many critics of liberalism claim is lacking in liberal theory—grounding the concept of natural rights in a coherent account of human nature. Of course, most political theories that derive from a conception of human nature are anti-liberal, such as theocracy, communitarianism, fascism, and communism. Rasmussen and Den Uyl argue convincingly that an Aristotelian understanding of human flourishing as an ultimate moral standard can be used to generate a theory of natural rights.

First of all, I take Aristotle to be arguing something like the following:

All living things seek their flourishing through their natural activity.
Humans are living things.
So, humans seek their flourishing through their natural activity.
(Where "flourishing" is read as positive growth and development; living well.)
A thing flourishes best by its excellence or virtue (that characteristic by which it excels at its activity).
So, to flourish *qua* X requires excellent activity particular to X, or excellent activity for Xs.
So, humans will flourish through human excellence or virtue.
In other words, (call this A1) The good life for a human is achieved through human excellence or virtue.
Nothing reaches its most excellent state except through the use of all its powers or potential.
So, the good life for a human is attained through the full use of those powers available to a human.
The range of human potentiality extends to include what Aristotle calls rational activity, construed broadly as involving theoretical and practical reason, conceptualization, abstraction.
So, (A2) the good life for a human is only attained through rational activity.

Now, A1 and A2 are *generic* accounts of activities that constitute the human good. They are claims about what all humans need to do in order to flourish, that is to say, use practical reason well (among other things) to develop virtues that are conducive to living well. But as Rasmussen and Den Uyl note, the human good has individualizing components as well as generic components. In other words, the fact that we are all humans means that there will be generic necessary conditions of our flourishing, but the fact the we are all different people means that there will be more than one possible way to flourish, or, that the generic necessary conditions of flourishing are not the sufficient conditions for this or that human's flourishing. There is a diversity among people layered on top of the generic sameness. So the human good should be understood as objective yet also individualized. As they put it, the human good is objective but plural—inclusive, individualized, agent-relative, self-directed, and social. While some liberals (and some critics of liberalism) claim to be allowing for "different conceptions of the good life," the neo-Aristotelian approach cashes out more accurately in terms of "different good lives." Agent-relativity is not the same thing as subjectivism. Consider the sliding fee scale of dues for membership in the American Philosophical Association: while the "right dues" may differ for Smith and for Jones, it is objectively determinable in each case what the right dues are, and in neither case is it a matter of subjective preference or opinion. So, there isn't really "human flourishing" except in the generic sense—rather, there is the flourishing of this or that human. It is plural, yet not subjective.

Furthermore, A2 above implies that autonomy or self-directedness is another necessary condition of human flourishing. The outline of the argument is growing clearer: coercion interferes with flourishing because it inhibits self-development and self-directedness. Coercion interferes with flourishing because it conflicts with A2 by not allowing choice-making. One cannot exercise or develop practical wisdom without freedom. The generic goods of "human nature" are the understructure of the reality of each life being distinct, and thus realizable only through individual, self-directed action.

But what about Aristotle's observation that we are social creatures?[2] This is true—so, Rasmussen and Den Uyl argue, we need norms for social order that allow for the realization of our flourishing, in its objective, individualized, agent-relative senses. The social construct of "rights" is what allows all of these to come to be. Rights should not be conceived of as exhaustive guides to moral conduct, but as the precondition for moral activity—the precondition of self-directed development of the person. Rights protect the possibility of self-directedness in a social setting. If the human good is plural and agent-relative, rights protect that diversity. The social dimension of human flourishing is not an argument against individual rights—it's why we need individual rights. This creates a space for each to develop and pursue projects subject to the constraint of allowing the same space for others. A social order of rights respects both individuality and sociality. The neo-Aristotelian conception of human flourishing is not "atomistic" in a Hobbesian way—our well-being typically requires relationship with others.[3]

Rasmussen and Den Uyl argue that humans cannot flourish *qua* humans "except through the actualization of those individuative potentialities that make the person the unique person he is . . . whose own insight and judgment is absolutely crucial to knowing what is the right thing. . . ."[4] Human flourishing thus isn't "the common good" because one person's flourishing isn't identical with another's. "The common good" must instead be that social order which has a political/legal structure that protects the possibility of individual pursuit of human flourishing, that is to say a right to liberty. In short, there's more to moral philosophy than rights, but a social order of rights is the necessary precondition of moral action, of human self-development. It is what allows for the possibilities of different flourishings without creating moral conflict, which we might call the "compossibility" of good lives.[5]

"Human nature" as a generic rubric provides generic parameters for flourishing, but the plural and agent-relative nature of human flourishing make it the sort of thing that can only be realized in a context of freedom to act, not in a coercive environment.

If the application of practical reason to self-directed action is a necessary condition of human flourishing, then people need to be free to develop and pursue their ends. This pursuit will be bounded by the compossibility criterion, that such pursuits do not infringe on others' attempts to do the same. A social order of individual rights is what translates this into practice: "The individual right to liberty allows each person a sphere of freedom whereby self-directed activities can be exercised without being invaded by others. This translates socially into a principle of maximum compossible and equal freedom for all" (p. 90). Maximizing the opportunities for self-directed action means minimizing the opportunities for coercion, hence (negative) liberty will be a necessary condition for human flourishing—or, more precisely, it's not so much that rights are necessary conditions of human flourishing, it's that rights *make possible* and *protect* the necessary conditions of human flourishing. Rights protect the possibility of self-directedness in a social setting. Thus the conception of rights as "metanorms" as opposed to norms, and thus the "natural" in "natural rights."

The Prospects for Persuasion

It's hard to understate the significance of the way Rasmussen and Den Uyl connect classical-liberal political theory and neo-Aristotelian ethical theory. Many political theorists who try to argue for minimal government and free markets often find themselves beset by critics who bemoan the "thin theory of human nature" presupposed by laissez-faire economics or the lack of any convincing basis for rights in strictly deontological theories. Interpreting rights as teleological necessary conditions for human flourishing and self-development is a strategy for defending liberalism that avoids both of these objections. Conversely, many ethicists sympathetic to the character-centered, Aristotelian approach to virtue find themselves saddled with an archaic and oppressive communitarianism that many have argued follows from Aristotle's views about community. Rasmussen and Den Uyl's argument avoids this objection also by showing how a eudaimonist conception of the human good which is plural yet objective is best served by liberal (non-perfectionist) politics.

It is difficult to defend a position that gets attacked from more than one side. Rasmussen and Den Uyl are offering a theory that is subject to attack from many sides, although as Plato noted in the *Gorgias*, the truth is never refuted.[6] Here is a schematic:

Ethical basis: neo-Aristotelian eudaimonism
Chief critics: Kantians, Utilitarians, Marxists, subjectivists (potentially also natural law Thomism)

Outcome: robust defense of classical-liberal rights theory
Chief critics: welfare-liberals, communitarians, Marxists, natural-law conservatives, traditionalist conservatives—and consequentialist libertarians.[7]

In other words, the liberal rights theory they develop is likely to be criticized by the right, the left, and what is misleadingly known as the center. Some conservatives will object to the pluralist conception of the good life, even though there's an objective basis to underwrite the pluralism. For instance, despite the Aristotelian influence on Thomism, a natural-law conservative who might otherwise be attracted to the teleology of Rasmussen and Den Uyl's account might balk at the idea that this *telos* isn't a single absolute for all. How can there be a "right" to make wrong choices? They address this concern in chapter 10 of *Norms of Liberty*—this is one of the strategic uses of the norm-metanorm distinction—the idea that there might be *political* or *legal* right to make choices (that are at most *self*-destructive) is necessary to allow self-directedness and moral development. It doesn't speak to the normative wrongness of any particular choice. (A Burkean conservative will also balk at the idea of "rights to do wrong," although this distaste will be motivated by a more fundamental rejection of the teleological approach.) Rasmussen and Den Uyl also anticipate a eudaimonist conservative criticism of their view—in a way a kind of Platonism about the human good. Since we need to bring about our own good, and our own good is bound up with the social good, a robust liberal rights theory won't do because people will err. (Note that this argument has a twin on the left.) But, they reply, what concretely ought to be done in a given case will vary from individual to individual. While Platonic rulers might have some sort of insights here, real-world rulers aspiring to Platonic Knowledge of the Just will necessarily lack sufficient information to make the call.[8]

Communitarian criticisms come in left- and right-flavors. MacIntyre's conception of the community, like Gray's or Etzioni's, presupposes the priority of community good over individual autonomy largely on the grounds that the community is said to be *constitutive* of the individual. But Rasmussen and Den Uyl note many times that they agree with Aristotle that humans are social creatures, and indeed that the human good is "profoundly social," but this "suggests no theory of collective action whatsoever. It is precisely because we are such social beings that the case for strong collective action is weakened" (p. 239). They note with a soupçon of irony that it is really on an atomistic conception of individualism that communitarianism would be necessitated, wherein the need to override individual choice-making to achieve coordination would be much greater.

The Marxist left will reject the project out of hand: liberalism being the product of the false consciousness of bourgeois society, it scarcely matters whether the putative justification is Aristotelian, Lockean, Kantian, or Rule-Utilitarian. The center-left, or welfare-liberalism, for example Rawlsians, will object that this robust individualistic libertarianism won't allow for social justice to be implemented, where social justice is understood as anything from egalitarianism to Rawlsian maximin redistributivism. Rasmussen and Den Uyl reply that justice in the social sense is not the major virtue in the self-perfecting life (practical wisdom is), and justice cannot be followed at the price of destroying other constituent virtues (like self-directedness). Rawls' justice-as-fairness presupposes an impersonalism that Rasmussen and Den Uyl have argued will not adequately account for the conditions of human flourishing.[9]

The poor might be said to lack the means for self-directedness, thus necessitating a less minimal liberalism, one in which the needs of the poor were supplied by the state. But, Rasmussen and Den Uyl reply, first of all, this is incompatible with equal respect for the self-directedness of all, and second of all, it confuses *protecting the possibility* of self-direction with *securing the exercise* of self-direction. "The exercise of the innate capacity of self-direction by individuals is not something that can be secured or guaranteed by others" (p. 308; see also pp. 303-311 generally).

The postmodernist left might object on the grounds that there is no human telos in the first place, so the underwriting metaethic is mistaken. But if there is no fixed human nature at all, so much stronger the argument for individuality-respecting liberalism. There are many other objections one might encounter, and Rasmussen and Den Uyl anticipate and reply to them (most specifically in chapter 7 and chapter 12, though in another sense throughout the entire book). While this book is their most thorough and systematic argument yet, they have been making a similar argument since at least 1991 (arguably since 1978). If the arguments are as compelling as I have been making them out to be (since the early 1990s), why hasn't the argument had more traction?

I began this section of my remarks by noting Plato's claim that what's true is never refuted, but the *Gorgias* is a dialogue about the differences between real persuasion and rhetoric. What he means is that objective rational argument cannot conclusively demonstrate the falsehood of that which is true. Obviously, fallacious arguments can *appear* to have refuted truths. More to the point, consider another famous passage in Plato, from the first page of *Republic* [paraphrasing 327d-e]: Socrates says "couldn't we persuade you to let us go?" And Polemarchus replies "Not if we won't listen." Some of the resistance to any argument for a non-status-quo politics is the inertial sense that "well, *that* just *can't* be right." One reason Rawls' argument is so successful is that his argument, however carefully constructed and however well grounded in Kantian ethics, is a defense of the society we pretty much already live in: a democratic system of equal political rights, with strong respect for civil liberties, and with a modicum of respect for economic liberties that may be overridden to accomplish redistributive goals as determined by experts. I think Rasmussen and Den Uyl have an effective (i.e., logically compelling) rebuttal to Rawls, but then again Nozick's 1974 rebuttal to Rawls was effective also.[10] Much critical response to Rasmussen and Den Uyl in 2008 will be, I'm afraid, like much of the critical response to Rasmussen and Den Uyl in 1991, or to Nozick in 1974: either to ignore it entirely, or to say, well that just can't be right. If their argument implies that the function of the state isn't to promote one particular conception of the good life, then one side will reject the argument a priori, then look for reasons to support that rejection. If it means that individual liberty cannot be violated to make one a means to further the ends of another, then the other side will reject the argument a priori, and then look for reasons to support that rejection. Also, if one holds a contrary position on the basis of what one sees as revealed truth, that's a reason to reject it a priori.[11]

I don't mean to suggest that all criticisms of Rasmussen and Den Uyl's position are intentionally dishonest, although surely some are: classical liberalism is more frequently caricatured than engaged.[12] But political philosophy more than any other subfield is prone to intuitionistic arguments where, even if unconsciously, one has become Polemarchus. It is hard to imagine anything more frustrating to the specialist in political philosophy to have spent years working out an argument, only to have one's metaphysics or epistemology colleagues dismiss it with a wave of the hand: "well *of course* the state has to do X, otherwise Y." Imagine how the political philosopher's reputation would suffer were she to enter an analogous argument on metaphysics: "well of course there's such a thing as knowledge—there are . . . things, and we know about them!" She'd be laughed at for offering an unresearched and underjustified opinion, yet the metaphysicians feel as though they're entitled to a political view, since after all, this is a democracy. The metaphysician will regard his colleague's poorly-researched, intuitionist hand-waving about, say, whether the mind and brain enjoy a supervenience relationship with a sense of entitlement ("I've written three books on the mind-body problem, so don't tell *me*!") that they think illegitimate when claimed by the political philosopher ("This is a democracy, so I am just as entitled to my theory of rights as you are."). Of course, this is a problem for political philosophers of all stripes, whether natural-law conservative, anarchist, Marxist, or libertarian. The fundamental premise of a democratic society is that everyone gets a say, but it is too easy (and very common) to proceed from this premise to the non-sequitur conclusion that any political theory is as good as any other, and that arguments do not matter as much as convictions.

Besides the intuitionistic objections from those who simply cannot conceive of a world without the progressive income tax, there is the infallibilism of the ideologue: since I'm right, no argument can prove me wrong! This is far more common in political philosophy than in other subfields—in some quarters, *Norms of Liberty* will be poorly received simply because its conclusions just "have to be" wrong. (And in some quarters, of course, the book will simply be ignored.[13])

Again, though, there will also be honest and thoughtful objections, for example the ones that follow in the present volume. I think that Rasmussen and Den Uyl can answer those objections (and they will of course endeavor to do so), but one strength of *Norms of Liberty* is that it shows them taking those objections seriously and grappling with them respectfully, not trading in the caricature and hand-waving that they may themselves frequently receive.

The bottom line, then, is that I think that *Norms of Liberty* will be less persuasive than it deserves to be, but that Rasmussen and Den Uyl couldn't hope to do better than they have done, for the ones they cannot persuade are not really open to persuasion anyway. However, the book's prospects for success among those who are open to rational persuasion are quite good. The arguments are sound, and what's true is never refuted.

Notes

1. Fred Miller defines "neo-Aristotelian" as "modern theorizing which incorporates some central doctrines of Aristotle" (*Nature, Justice, and Rights in Aristotle's* Politics (Oxford: Clarendon Press, 1995).

2. For example, at *Nicomachean Ethics* 1097b10. Aristotle's use of the word "polis" doesn't clearly differentiate society and state, so his claim that we are "naturally political" doesn't actually make a claim about forms of government, it just stipulates that we are social creatures.

3. For one thing, if we did not live among others, there would be no division of labor, and it would be impossible to achieve any great things. But more to the point, Aristotle discusses the value of friendship in the development of the good life in books 8 and 9 of the *Nicomachean Ethics*.

4. This formulation is from their *Liberty and Nature: An Aristotelian Defense of Liberal Order* (Chicago: Open Court, 1991), 114.

5. Following the usage of that word in rights theory to describe a set of non-conflicting rights.

6. 473b10

7. Potentially also anarchists, although I've argued elsewhere that Rasmussen and Den Uyl's argument is not logically incompatible with anarcho-capitalism (in *Deleting the State: An Argument about Government* (Chicago: Open Court, 2008); also in "Rasmussen on Teleology and Politics," paper presented at the American Philosophical Association meeting Dec. 28, 2000).

8. See, e.g., *Norms of Liberty* pp. 263–64.

9. See, e.g., *Norms of Liberty* pp. 297–299.

10. *Anarchy, State, and Utopia* (New York: Basic Books, 1974).

11. I am deliberately suggesting a phenomenon analogous to that described by the proponents of "legal realism" jurisprudence, the theory that legal arguments are constructed after the fact to justify conclusions one is predisposed to have based on prior ethical or religious commitments. See John Hasnas, "The Myth of the Rule of Law," *Wisconsin Law Review* (1995, no. 1).

12. For instance, that it's atomistic or anti-social, or based on selfishness, or a thin theory of human nature. See my "Another Caricature of Libertarianism," *Reason Papers* no. 17, Fall 1992.

13. I speculated at the 2005 APA symposium about whether it would receive any reviews at all from the same places where one might see a review of books by Gray, Sen, Walzer, Nussbaum, Dworkin. None were forthcoming. Arguably, it shows greater contempt to have no review than to have a negative review. But contemptuous indifference is not a philosophical stance.

2

A Liberal Defense of Liberalism

Edwin England

This essay focuses on the structure of the overall argument of *Norms of Liberty*. I argue that its defense of metanormative rights as a solution to liberalism's problem need not persuade anyone who is not already sympathetic to liberalism's problem on other grounds, or unless she concurs with the authors' theory of the good, that is, Individualistic Perfectionism. All arguments must start somewhere, so I spend little time criticizing their fundamental assumptions. Instead, I hope merely to elucidate the rational scope of the authors' argument.

Despite the complexity of *Norms of Liberty*, extraordinary care was taken to lay bare the structure of its central argument. That structure, as I understand it, is this:

The authors begin by developing a philosophical anthropology. We must know whether humans have a nature and a *telos*, and if so, what they are. Their neo-Aristotelian view—Individualistic Perfectionism—holds human flourishing to be the telos of human conduct. A correct account of human flourishing depends in part on our biological natures, and it also depends on the capacities, circumstances, interests, beliefs, and desires we have and on our individual nexus of past choices and socializing influences. Their account is not merely scientific. It looks to *endoxa*, established opinions concerning the requirements and conditions for human volition and action, for cultural and social practices, and to common sense judgments about *eudaimonia* (see, e.g., pp. 115–16). A close study of our biology, and these endoxa, reveals a relatively unchanging set of basic goods and virtues, generic goods that every human needs in some measure to flourish. However, the account leaves open the evaluative ranking of these goods. If so, not only is it possible that individuals will rank these goods differently on the basis of their own nexus, it is also *necessary* for the good of these individuals that they do so. Individualistic perfectionism rejects subjectivism, existentialism, and Platonic essentialism, but embraces the good as individualized, objective, inclusive (pleasure, virtue, friendship, etc.), agent-relative, and profoundly social. The good is for individuals, it is neither abstract nor a universal *summum bonum*; rather, there are *summa bona*, a variety of ways for humans to flourish. We each actualize our telos (self-perfection—our own individualized brands of human flourishing) through self-direction and through our dispositions for the *proper* desires and actions and through our *right* use of reason (practical wisdom) which integrates and orders the virtues in accordance to our individual nexus.

The authors argue that a problem arises from some of the features of Individualistic Perfectionism. According to their account, our sociality is a constituent part of human flourishing. To say human flourishing is profoundly social means that the maturation of our potentialities requires a life with others. For example, these potentialities are sometimes other-directed, as in friendship. And to say our social natures are open-ended means they "impose no *a priori* limitation regarding with whom one may have a relationship" (p. 82). If human flourishing is highly individualized, agent-relative *and* profoundly social, we face the problem of finding an ethical basis for our political and legal institutions that is not structurally prejudiced for or against some forms of human flourishing, a principle that leaves the social context open-ended and does not, as a matter of principle, prefer one form of self-perfection over others. This problem is what Rasmussen and Den Uyl call "liberalism's problem."

To anticipate for just a moment, on their view Lockean rights of mutual non-interference mediate between and correctly reconcile an individual's moral code and the legal code of a society. In other words, the negative right of liberty solves liberalism's problem. However, if rights are understood normatively (as most defenders of liberalism have thus far understood them), their value as a solution to liberalism's problem will be missed. Let me briefly explain why.

In *Democracy's Discontents*, Michael Sandel offers a devastating critique of liberalism's alleged neutrality. Minimalist liberalism, as he calls it, demands that the political order not affirm in law any particular vision of the good life and it enjoins citizens to set aside their "encumbrances" (those duties and loyalties which stem from one's particular conception of the good life) whenever we enter the public realm. Typically it is the fact of reasonable pluralism which justifies this demand. When reasonable disagreement persists on some matter, that matter should be "bracketed off" by the state and left for individuals to decide privately.

The problem with this strategy, as Sandel argues, is that:

> [a]t least where grave moral questions are concerned, whether it is reasonable to bracket moral and religious controversies for the sake of political agreement partly depends on which of the contending moral or religious doctrines is true. Minimalist liberalism wants to separate the case for toleration from any judgment about the moral worth of the practices being tolerated. But this separation is not always defensible. We cannot determine whether toleration is justified in any given case without passing moral judgment on the practice in question.[1]

So, when the liberal demands that opponents and defenders of abortion "bracket off" abortion as a private matter, the defender of abortion has much less at stake than her opponent. As Sandel says, "there is little difference between believing that abortion is morally permissible and agreeing that, as a political matter, women should be free to decide the moral question for themselves." However, if, say, the Catholic church is correct about the moral status of the fetus, it becomes a matter of serious normative reflection to determine whether, in this case, the values of tolerance and liberty and women's equality should trump the value of respect for the fetus for the sake of political peace. Sandel concludes, "[t]he case for abortion rights cannot be neutral with respect to the underlying moral and religious controversy. It must engage rather than avoid the substantive moral and religious doctrines at stake."

I suspect that Rasmussen and Den Uyl would agree that Sandel's argument is sound and that its broader conclusion is true, namely, that minimalist liberalism is not neutral between competing conceptions of the good. According to liberalism, morality demands that states defend the negative right to liberty as fundamental while not favoring any particular conception of morality. Yet, if the right to liberty is conceived as the same type of principle as those it allegedly trumps, then liberalism is guilty of favoring its own conception of morality by holding liberty to be fundamental and it begs the question against rival ethics. The force of Sandel's argument stems from the normative conception of rights that liberals have presumed. Rasmussen and Den Uyl diagnose the ailment in this way: "Our view, therefore, is simply that the malaise of liberalism is largely the result of treating it as an equinormative system. Liberalism is both more vulnerable to its critics and subject to its own "tensions" when understood in this way. . . It is quite possible . . . that the exclusive focus upon liberal values has led people to ignore other significant moral virtues and has thereby impoverished morality in the process" (p. 35).

Instead, they say we should conceive of rights as metanormative principles, as principles concerned to create the political/legal conditions that make moral action possible. Rasmussen and Den Uyl believe they can solve liberalism's problem and remove the question-begging character of political liberalism by following that sage medieval advice: when one runs into a puzzle or paradox or contradiction, draw a relevant philosophic distinction. In their view the right to liberty and those rights that can be derived from it (rights to life and property, for example) mark out the principles that found and properly circumscribe the sphere of political and legal activity. *Norms of Liberty* begins by staking out an Aristotelian anthropology and ethics, and ends up defending the central tenets of classical liberalism, namely:

(1) We have a basic negative moral right to liberty; that is, we have a right not to be used without our consent, and (2) this right is of fundamental importance, i.e., it trumps all other moral claims.[2] No doubt, it would be a significant achievement if the introduction of the metanormative/normative distinction can defend classical liberalism while avoiding the question-begging character of minimalist liberalism.

To be sure, the authors believe the right of liberty is a kind of ethical principle, but its purpose is not normative, it is not intended to directly regulate human conduct. Rather, as a metanormative ethical principle, the right to liberty and its attendant derivative rights "regulate the conditions under which [moral] conduct could take place" (p. 39). The right of liberty trumps all other ethical claims because it is a metanormative principle and, as such, it solves liberalism's problem.

Now I have an interest in solving liberalism's problem. It resonates with me and perhaps with many readers. However, one should worry about the source of the problem and how that bears on the effectiveness and scope of Rasmussen and Den Uyl's defense. They say: "We are very careful to say that these [metanormative] principles aren't derived from, or themselves reducible to, claims about the good, or human flourishing" (p. 317). Fine, but how are they *justified*?

Earlier on they say:

> Though our justification for individual rights arises from the nature and character of human self-perfection, it by no means follows that the aim of the political/legal order is to be understood in terms of such self-perfection. . . . The necessity and need for individual rights does presuppose an account of human flourishing, but that does not mean that individual rights are justified in terms of either achieving or encouraging that ultimate end, or even, in general making it possible. The connection between individual rights and human flourishing is neither direct nor isomorphic (pp. 266–68).

How, then, does the justification of rights arise from their ethics? First, they argue that if individualistic perfectionism is true, then six interrelated conditions must be met for a genuine solution to liberalism's problem. The solution must not prejudice the social context in favor of some forms of self-perfection; it must be open-ended; it must be grounded in some common critical element concretely present in all forms of self-perfection; it must provide an agent-relative reason for a person to follow the principle; it should reject moral cannibalism (the ranking of forms of self-perfection independently of the agents that pursue them); and its requirements on human conduct must be realistic or non-utopian. Next, they argue that the protection of the possibility of self-direction meets each of these six conditions and, furthermore, self-direction is the *only* feature of self-perfection that does. Finally, they argue that since the right to liberty requires that individuals not be used or directed without their consent and since it bans all unauthorized force against individuals except when necessary to secure the possibility of self-direction, the right to liberty protects the possibility of self-direction. Maintaining a basic, negative right to liberty solves liberalism's problem.

What has not yet been made clear is why we must view this right as a metanormative principle, rather than a normative ethical principle. After all, if maintaining the right to liberty is necessary to protect the possibility of self-direction, which in turn is necessary to provide an ethical basis to a political/legal order that is structurally unbiased against diverse forms of human flourishing, why must we not think of this right as essentially concerned to regulate human conduct? I believe the answer rests on the fact that, taken as one norm among many, the right of liberty will, in any given number of circumstances, not appear to trump other moral demands. Suppose we accept the need to solve liberalism's problem and their claim that the right of liberty is the only solution to that problem. As a normative principle whose point is to directly regulate conduct, the right to liberty has force, but not maximally overriding force. For we face other problems which other norms may be better suited to fix. Suppose Bernie has a normative right to liberty, but he also has the cure to cancer which millions need and he refuses to share. Metanorms, by contrast, seek to create, interpret and justify a political/legal order "so that conditions might be obtained where moral action can take place" (p. 34).[3] *If* the right to liberty *is* a metanorm (not simply if it is *viewed* as a metanorm), then we will have justified the second tenet of liberalism, the claim that the right to liberty trumps all other moral claims. This follows because a genuine metanorm secures the political/legal conditions necessary for there to be *any* morally good conduct. What we need, then, is not simply the drawing of the distinction, nor even a re-description of liberalism as a political, rather than ethical, theory. We need an argument that the right to liberty is in fact a metanorm. That without such a right guarded by the political/legal order, moral action would not be possible.

From what I can tell that argument is supplied by *Norms of Liberty* in the following way. Individualistic perfectionism holds that morally good action must be uncoerced, related to objective goods or virtues, indexed to an individual's nexus, and be good for an individual, not good in some abstract sense. Thus, their account of the good assumes that coerced action never constitutes a moral good.[4] And so, for moral action to be possible, the political/legal order must, if it is to be legitimate, protect its citizens from coercion. This strategy for demonstrating that the right to liberty is a metanorm obviously requires a prior commitment to their theory of the good. However, some confusion surrounds the distinction because the authors also define a metanorm negatively, as simply a norm "not directly concerned with the self-perfection of particular acting agents" (p. 38). Norms of etiquette, for example, also fit that criterion. Besides being too broad, this way of defining a metanorm clearly misses the target that the distinction is meant to hit, namely, *justifying* the liberal claim that the negative right to liberty trumps all other moral claims. Only by showing that the right to liberty is necessary for the very possibility of moral action will they purchase any justification for the claim that liberty trumps all other moral claims.[5]

Their strategy begins with an elucidation of a "full-blown moral philosophy" and it is on this basis—on the supporting theoretical structure of individualistic perfectionism—that the authors separate politics from morality: politics is ill-suited for soulcraft because of the goodness of diverse forms of human flourishing and the necessity of *self*-direction for all its forms. It is true, as they assert, that one need not adopt their approach to ethics to recognize the metanormative/normative distinction, but the theoretical commitments necessary to *mark* a distinction are thinner than those necessary to show that there is, in fact, a metanormative principle. And as I said, the argument that the right to liberty secures the conditions necessary for the very possibility of moral action depends for its soundness precisely on prior theoretical commitments to individualistic perfectionism. That said, I suppose the authors may respond to these comments by saying, "that's not really a *criticism* of our theory; that simply *is* our theory." Indeed, their intellectual honesty shines through on every page.[6]

Well, suppose my gloss of their central argument is correct. And further suppose that making the negative right to liberty the founding principle of the political/legal order is the only way to solve liberalism's problem; it is the only way to found a political/legal order such that no way of human flourishing is structurally disadvantaged; it is the only way to make all forms of human flourishing possible.[7] One might ask: "Why should I care about solving liberalism's problem? I am not a liberal. A problem faces us, but it is not a problem faced by everyone, it is a problem faced by liberals." Liberalism's problem arises from the *putatively* individualized, agent-relative, profoundly social character of human flourishing.[8] It is the authors' neo-Aristotelian ethical theory that gives rise to the problem. If I reject the ethics that gives rise to the problem you care about, you may not appeal to that problem, and the only means by which to solve it, to argue that I must accept a view of rights as fundamental and metanormative that conflicts with my own ethically based conception of the political sphere. A ladder may be necessary to rid one's gutters of leaves, but one may instead choose to ignore the problem, tear down the gutters, or cut down the trees. The central argument fails because liberalism's problem is a parochial concern.

The non-liberal need not agree that finding a solution to it "is in essence finding a solution to the problem of political legitimation" (p. 283). Though she needs a solution to the problem of political legitimation, that problem is conceptually distinct from liberalism's problem. For example, Plato's ethics advises a perfectionistic, soul-crafting politics because he saw one good, not many, and the solution to political legitimation rested on the Republic's ability to write justice in the hearts of its citizens by conditioning them to function properly, in accord with their natures. As Mill and others have advocated, the argument should be made that the individual is in a far better position to judge whether some conduct is for her own good, but no such arguments will settle fundamental disagreements about goodness, or the conceptual boundaries of morality and politics. A non-liberal may see the metanormative/normative distinction as valuable and even necessary for liberals in their attempt to eliminate tensions within liberal theory, but the central argument advanced by *Norms of Liberty* issues from a prior commitment to contestable liberal tenets. Is it any wonder that a metanorm of liberty is justified by an ethics that sees the good to be highly individualized? By contrast, Kant begins his transcendental argument from the universally recognized fact of experience—things as they appear—and inquires into the noetic conditions that must obtain to make such appearances possible.

My sense is that none of this will come as a surprise to the authors. They make plain that their political liberalism is justified by their ethics, by their philosophical anthropology. Further, they may intend their elucidation of Aristotelian perfectionism to do the heavy lifting, the persuasion of non-liberals. After all, many of the central claims of their ethics are shared by communitarians (see, e.g., p. 9). However, the metanormative/normative distinction fails, by itself, to have the scope and force that we hope for from philosophical distinctions: its application is limited to a problem with parochial appeal, a problem of liberalism, a problem for liberals.

Resolving that problem leaves one less internal tension for the theory and offers a cogent reply to Sandel, but the necessity and adequacy of the distinction as a solution to liberalism's problem does not demonstrate to non-liberals the fundamental and overriding nature of the right to liberty unless they already share an ethics which gives rise to liberalism's problem. How, though, can one fairly pursue the fundamentally important question about the legitimacy of the political/legal order? After reflecting on the argumentative structure of this book and worrying about its unabashed starting place in ethics, one might wonder whether any other sort of foundation would be more satisfying. We might, for example, wait for the spade to turn at our linguistic intuitions. R. M. Hare's universal prescriptivism follows from an analysis of our moral language, thus providing a non-ethical foundation for a specific normative theory. We should be preference-utilitarians, if his argument is sound, because, ultimately, that's what "ought" means. But if we find preference-utilitarianism theoretically and morally unattractive, as some of us do, will we not resist any attempt to render our complaints meaningless? Suppose we are told: "You must be confused when you say utilitarianism *ought not* to be followed, for by prescribing universally you are committing yourself to the very theory you denounce." Well, if that's what "ought" in fact means around here, then non-utilitarians might start offering persuasive definitions of "ought" compatible with non-utilitarian views, or simply coin some new moral (or maybe "shmoral") terms and stop talking about "ought" altogether. It is hard to imagine better foundations than an elucidation of a full-bodied, subtle ethics for the delineation of its conceptual boundaries and its relations to other concepts, like politics. Starting with ordinary language has appeal too. It makes sense to get clear about our linguistic intuitions for terms ubiquitous in philosophic argument: words like self, justification, coercion, etc. But it is hard to see how linguistic analysis, even when we grant its correctness, can settle this sort of philosophic debate. We have the liberty to alter and extend our concepts; we are not prisoners of our own words. There may simply be no better starting place than the elucidation and defense of a coherent, comprehensive moral philosophy. The non-liberal's charge of circularity cannot be completely evaded in such a case, but then, if the circle is complex and interesting and internally consistent, that may be the best a theorist can hope for.

Besides the central argument of the book which invokes the metanormative/normative distinction to counter the communitarian challenge, the authors offer a second argument to defend laissez-faire liberalism. In *Norms of Liberty*'s defense of liberalism, the state is to bracket off the matter of moral perfection: "a perfectionist basis for non-perfectionist politics" as the book's sub-title puts it. The state need not encourage self-direction, let alone self-perfection; it must merely make self-direction possible. Soulcraft is to be left to selves, to persons whose ends are self-perfection. Self-direction, which is uncoerced, reasoned choice, is a fundamentally necessary condition for any and all forms of human flourishing. In a tightly summarized reconstruction of their argument, Rasmussen and Den Uyl conclude that "the political/legal order's purpose is not to engage in soulcraft" (p. 283). Their argument begins uncontentiously: if a political/legal order is to have any legitimacy, it must have some connection to ethical concerns or principles, since legitimacy itself is an ethical concept. However, they say, it would be question-begging against anarchism to assume that there is any connection between the ethical and political/legal orders. Additionally, even if there is some legitimating connection between the two, the nature of that connection must be ascertained and we may not simply assume the two orders are identical (i.e., that whatever is right or good must be promoted or enforced by the political/legal order). Now, at this point in the argument the authors repeat an ubernorm on which they rely at several key points in the book: "Thus," they say, "it is never sufficient in political philosophy merely to show that doing X either ought or ought not to be done. Rather, it must also be shown why doing X ought to be a political/legal concern. It cannot validly be assumed that politics is simply ethics writ large" (p. 283). I suspect most of us find this ubernorm highly intuitive. At least, I certainly do. But I fear its intuitive appeal derives from an assortment of pre-theoretical judgments we have made about the political and moral orders based on received opinions and linguistic intuitions. I am worried that a presumption in favor of liberalism is being unintentionally smuggled in to place the burden of proof on the non-liberal. As Rasmussen and Den Uyl state, there is no basis for assuming, at least at the start, that ethics and politics are identical but, I wish to add, neither is there a basis for assuming that they are not identical. We should have no presumption either way since the question to resolve is precisely the matter of the kind of connection that may or may not exist between the two. For it to follow that "it is never sufficient in political philosophy merely to show that doing X either ought or ought not to be done," we must assume that politics is *not* ethics writ large, which is very different than leaving the question open for philosophical analysis, and we will have begged a very large question against the non-liberal. For, if we grant the ubernorm recommended by our authors, it becomes much easier to say that moral matters should be bracketed off from the political/legal order *unless* an argument can be given for not doing so. In that case, the burden is placed unfairly on the non-liberal to prove that politics is *not* non-perfectionist.

Again, conceptual analysis alone won't satisfy our inquiry into the legitimation of the state and whether statecraft *is* soulcraft. We want to know whether it should be, and that question can only be answered with a complete moral vision, one that includes theories of the self, the good, and a moral epistemology. *Norms of Liberty* sets a high standard for answering that call.

Notes

1. Michael Sandel, *Democracy's Discontent* (Cambridge, Mass.: Harvard University Press, 1996). This discussion is from pp. 19–24.

2. For Rasmussen and Den Uyl, rights are not ethically fundamental but depend ultimately on a conception of the human good for their justification. See, for instance, *Norms of Liberty* p. 338.

3. Note the weakening accomplished in this definition by the words "seek" and "might be obtained." A genuine metanorm would be a principle such that if it were not generally followed, or whenever it is not followed, moral action would not be possible. We need one of these stronger senses of a metanorm to secure the claim that metanorms trump moral claims. Suppose individual cases of promise-breaking weaken, to some extent, the institution itself, such that if promises are not typically kept, no further promises could be made. Even if we accept that Kantian point, it does not follow, without additional premises, that promise-keeping must trump all other moral claims. At most it shows breaking a promise cannot be right, even though it may be good

to do so in some specific case. So, too, if we accept the view that the right to liberty makes moral conduct possible because moral willing must be uncoerced and minimally rational, it nonetheless does not follow from this alone that the protection of liberty must trump all other values.

4. Their reasoning for this claim can be found, for example, in their response to the communitarian objection that simply rejects the metanormative/normative distinction and asserts the legitimacy of the state's use of coercion for soulcraft. The authors say: "There is a difference between conduct adhering to a moral norm that one believes appropriate because it follow that norm, and conduct that proceeds from an understanding of the appropriateness of a moral norm. The latter form of conduct is required for moral excellence. However, understanding the appropriateness of a moral norm requires that the individual exercise both speculative and practical wisdom, but these are essentially self-directed activities. Coercion cannot itself create morally excellent or virtuous persons, because it does not ultimately appeal to individuals' understanding or reason to ground their beliefs in the appropriateness of the moral norm. Conformity does not imply understanding, and coercion bypasses the individual's reason" (*Norms of Liberty*, 94–95).

5. Here I'm not sure whether the authors think liberty trumps all other moral claims merely from the point of view of the political/legal order and its functionaries, or if they mean to include citizens as they pursue their self-perfection. Could it be morally obligatory for me to violate the political right to liberty of another self, someone who was not about to violate any other's liberty? I suspect the authors would answer "no", but that answer follows not so much from the necessity of my respect for another's liberty to make moral conduct possible (that stage is set by the political/legal order), but from their prior commitment to the diversity of human flourishing. If my friend is pursuing a radical environmental ethic that has led to self-cannibalism, my interference with his self-direction can never constitute a moral good, according to individualistic perfectionism. But in cases like this, I wish to say the "objective" and "biocentric" character of their account of the good appears vacuous and has no real power to constrain the possible weightings or accounts of the so-called "objective goods and virtues."

6. For example, they write: "Comprehensive liberalisms are those defenses of liberalism that take place within larger philosophical doctrines that have something to say in general about what is valuable or best for human beings to pursue or embrace. The defense of liberalism

in the comprehensive mode depends in some critical way upon the framework and values of the larger philosophical system. Kant is a comprehensive liberal, and so are we. . . . Our approach is clearly not neutral between theories, nor does it claim that liberalism could be so neutral. We reject "justificatory neutralism." If there is neutralism in our approach at all, it does not come because the theory transcends the good, but rather from an understanding of the nature of the good in practice" (*Norms of Liberty*, 56).

7. One might wonder what sort of possibility is here invoked: natural, metaphysical, logical, etc. It seems to this writer that they have some sense of possibility in mind that depends on the structural impartiality of the political/legal institutions. I cannot "possibly" flourish as an ascetic in a society that bans asceticism. Cf. *Norms of Liberty* p. 304.

8. Of course, liberals have long worried about this problem, but it has arisen from different sources. For example, liberals have argued we need an ethical basis for our politics that is not structurally prejudiced against some moral conceptions because of moral skepticism: nobody knows what is right and wrong, so nobody ought to tell another what to do. Or, Jeffersonian liberalism argues for the negative right of liberty on the grounds that we have conflicting moral intuitions, none of which are self-evident. Mill argues for liberty and the harm principle on utilitarian grounds, and so on. In other words, I am not saying the problem arises *solely* because of one's commitment to individualistic perfectionism. That is simply one path to the problem and my point here is that the problem is not a given, that is, it is not a feature of all political thought simpliciter. It reflects a specific set of concerns which are properly called "liberal."

3

Can the Political Priority of Liberty be Squared with the Ethical Priority of Flourishing?

David Thunder

One of the features of contemporary liberalism that many view as its Achilles' heel is its failure to connect the justification of political norms to the ingredients of a good, successful, or flourishing human life. Liberals often take themselves to be advancing a doctrine of right or an account of public goods that are viewed as instrumental to the good life, and believe they can reserve judgment about the constituents of a successful or flourishing human life to private individuals. But this self-conscious eschewal of debates about human flourishing leaves liberalism in an embarrassing and vulnerable position: when asked the inevitable question, "what has liberalism got to do with the good life?" the liberal can say very little of substance: he must simply assume that certain "primary goods" such as peace and prosperity are the necessary condition for *any* ethical aspirations. But without engaging the deep ethical questions such as the nature of a good life, this assumption seems smug and question-begging. And even if true, it is not sufficient to justify the liberal's commitment to the political primacy of freedom.

As I understand it, the basic project of *Norms of Liberty* is to provide an ethical justification for the political priority of liberty derived principally from a neo-Aristotelian, teleological, worldview. As somebody who is critical of "free-standing" liberalism, I am very pleased to see Douglas Rasmussen and Douglas Den

Uyl offer a defense of liberalism that is rooted not in "free-standing" political norms but in a substantive account of human flourishing. Their willingness to engage ethical problems from the "ground up" so to speak, is not typical among defenders of liberalism. There is a refreshing intellectual honesty in Rasmussen and Den Uyl's willingness to explore the deeper ethical foundations of their liberal commitments, which opens a space for genuine and meaningful dialogue. I hope to take advantage of that space in these brief remarks.

The main target of my critique of *Norms of Liberty* is the priority of liberty, or what Rasmussen and Den Uyl call "liberalism's basic tenet," namely, "[t]hat achieving and maintaining liberty should be the *central* and *primary* concern of the political/legal order" (p. 9). But before I go any further, in order to properly circumscribe the force of my critique, I would like to highlight the aspects of this project that I am in broad agreement with.

Points of Agreement

I join Rasmussen and Den Uyl in firmly rejecting Rawls' and others' aspiration to make political theory "free-standing" from deep and controversial philosophical commitments. I agree with them that any minimally plausible justification of politics must rely upon a philosophical anthropology, whether such reliance is acknowledged or not. Secondly, I am very sympathetic to the basic premise of their project, namely, that neo-Aristotelian ethics is the most promising basis upon which to argue for a free society. I share Rasmussen and Den Uyl's rejection of moral skepticism, relativism, naïve universalism, and excessive individualism as pathologies engendered by modern Enlightenment and post-enlightenment philosophy, and I agree with them that such pathologies are not the inevitable concomitant of liberalism's commitment to individual liberty and rights. I agree with Rasmussen and Den Uyl that the right and the good cannot be treated independently as Kant and (at least the early) Rawls believed. Finally, I agree with Rasmussen and Den Uyl that self-direction, individual contingencies, and practical wisdom play a central role in human flourishing incompatible with the imposition of a single monistic formula for flourishing, and that this role must be respected by any ethically sound political order.

Can the Political Priority of Liberty be Squared with the Ethical Priority of Flourishing?

With these very significant areas of agreement highlighted, I hope the basis and force of my critique will be more evident. The principal target of my critique is the political priority of liberty proposed by Rasmussen and Den Uyl, and my critique can be summed up in one proposition; namely that the political priority of liberty cannot be reconciled with the ethical priority of flourishing. The first question to get straight is the target of my critique: what exactly is the normative weight of liberty in Rasmussen and Den Uyl's political philosophy? Early in the book, they assert their commitment to "liberalism's basic tenet," namely, "[t]hat achieving and maintaining liberty should be the *central* and *primary* concern of the political/legal order" (p. 9). Later, the priority of liberty is asserted in even more absolute terms: "individual rights override all other moral claims . . . when it comes to addressing an important but specific problem—what we have called 'liberalism's problem'" (pp. 92-93). "Liberalism's problem," as understood by Rasmussen and Den Uyl, is the following:

> Since the structure provided by the political/legal order will rule over all equally, how can the universalism of *political/legal* structural principles square with the pluralism and self-direction required by human flourishing? Hence, how is it possible to have an ethical basis for an overall or general social/political context—a context that is open-ended or cosmopolitan—that will not require, as a matter of principle, that one form of flourishing be preferred to another? (p. 271)

The question to consider is whether or not the strict priority of liberty asserted by Rasmussen and Den Uyl in the political domain can be reconciled with the priority of flourishing admitted by Rasmussen and Den Uyl in the domain of relatively unrestricted personal action. The case I will make against assigning strict priority to liberty in the political sphere is an Aristotelian one, and therefore one Rasmussen and Den Uyl should appreciate. What I want to argue is that Aristotle's conception of practical reason and of practical wisdom is unified and directed towards the good in every sphere of life, in sharp contrast to many modern conceptions of practical reason (e.g., Hobbes, Smith, Descartes, Rawls) which allow for rigid partitions within practical reason, between instrumental and moral reasoning, or between the "right" and the "good," between political morality and ethics, and so on. I want to argue that the good agent, on this unified view of reasoning, always aims at doing what is good or conducive to all-round flourishing, both his own and that of his community. By contrast, Rasmussen and Den Uyl, while accepting this picture of practical wisdom at the personal or nonpolitical level, want to exempt political action from it, claiming that politics is quite distinct from the pursuit of perfection or flourishing, that it is constituted by the observance of "metanorms" that provide the conditions for the possibility of flourishing but are not an aspect of flourishing as such. As I will show below, this attempt to rigidly demarcate the political from the ethical is not warranted by the Aristotelian perspective assumed by Rasmussen and Den Uyl's arguments, and can only be justified, if at all, by an extremely demanding Kantian view of autonomy that is not argued for in this book.

Norms and Metanorms

Rasmussen and Den Uyl argue that the solution to "liberalism's problem"—that is, the problem of accommodating diverse forms of flourishing within a single social order—is to distinguish two levels of practical reasoning: one constituted by the norm or norms of flourishing, which every individual must be guided by in order to perfect himself; and another constituted by "metanorms" of social and legal order, which, rather than directly conducing to flourishing, merely secure the conditions under which flourishing can occur. There are thus two types of norms, and a proper appreciation of the limited jurisdiction of the political order depends on a recognition of this distinction:

> Norms are not, in fact, all of one type, differentiated by subject or thinker alone. It may be that some norms regulate the conditions in which moral conduct may take place, while others are more directly prescriptive of moral conduct itself. In light of this possibility, we believe it is not appropriate to say that liberalism is a "normative political philosophy" in the usual sense. It is rather a political philosophy of metanorms. *It seeks not to guide individual conduct in moral activity, but rather to regulate conduct so that conditions might be obtained where moral action can take place.* To contrast liberalism directly with alternative ethical systems or values is, therefore, something of a category mistake. (p. 34)

It is important to note that accepting the priority of liberty need not presuppose Rasmussen and Den Uyl's distinction between norms and metanorms. It may be viewed simply as an application of practical reasoning to the political sphere. However, if the distinction is valid, it does seem to lend some support to the choice of giving content to political norms independently from substantive conceptions of human flourishing, since political reasoning about "metanorms" now looks like a very specialized form of practical reasoning that is somehow set apart from practical reasoning about individual flourishing. Since I regard the procedural independence of political norms from flourishing as unwarranted, it is worth saying a bit about why Rasmussen and Den Uyl's concept of metanorms seems incoherent to me.

Essentially, my worry is that given the inherently social orientation and context of human flourishing, "liberalism's problem," insofar as it concerns the good of one's society, is a problem that confronts individuals *qua* practical reasoners in pursuit of the good. Any solution to "liberalism's problem" is a solution that requires certain actions on the part of individual agents, for example, compliance with law, respect for rights, and so on. The "rules of the game" or the rules that govern the conduct of an entire society, bear directly on the choices and actions of individuals, who must choose either to embrace or reject those rules and live with the consequences. It seems to me that I, as a responsible agent, have no other basis on which to accept or reject political norms than their compatibility with, and conduciveness to, human flourishing, both my own and that of my community. If I allow my conduct to be guided by political norms, I must view such conduct as an instance of my own flourishing, or at least as permitted or required by my flourishing. This is not the same as saying that political norms constitute a comprehensive guide to human flourishing—they provide a very incomplete and general guide to action, a broad constraint within which each individual must flesh out a virtuous plan of life and develop the interior dispositions characteristic of virtuous action. But for all that, political norms, insofar as they are legitimate or morally valid, are a practical guide for individual conduct no less than any other norm. Therefore, while political norms must be distinguished from ordinary ethical norms, I cannot agree with Rasmussen and Den Uyl's assertion that liberalism "seeks not to guide individual conduct in moral activity, but rather to regulate conduct so that conditions might be obtained where moral action can take place." Rather, liberalism, on a good day, does both: it guides moral activity, and creates conditions where further moral action can take place.

The Priority of Liberty

Now, I would like to turn to the main target of my critique: the priority of liberty. I do not believe this normative priority can be justified without recourse to some strong and distinctively modern doctrine of autonomy, for example, Kantian or Rawlsian contractarianism. But more importantly for our purposes, I do not think the arguments offered by Rasmussen and Den Uyl succeed in overcoming the main Aristotelian objections to the priority of liberty. Here is my simplified but hopefully fair-minded reconstruction of Rasmussen and Den Uyl's argument for the political priority of liberty:

1. *Liberalism's Problem*: The fundamental problem of politics is to find a shared social and legal framework within which diverse and potentially conflicting modes of flourishing can co-exist.
2. *The Pluralism of Flourishing*: Although we can identify many generic goods that all forms of flourishing must participate in, e.g. friendship, knowledge, bodily sustenance, etc., there is no universal, all-purpose formula for determining the appropriate weight of each good in a plan of life. There is a legitimate pluralism of forms of flourishing that is a function of individual circumstances and defies any single formula of flourishing to be imposed upon all.
3. *The Political Irrelevance of Substantive Judgments about the Place of Particular Goods in a Good Human Life*: Any political principle that settles the weighting issue by prioritizing some goods over others is illegitimate because it would be guilty of a principled bias in favor of some forms of flourishing and against others. This bias would be morally offensive both (a) because it would be unfair for our shared political system to benefit its members unevenly, and (b) because by disfavoring some forms of flourishing, it would deliberately interfere with or harm the self-directedness of some agents, a central and necessary condition of their flourishing.
4. *The Political Relevance of the Role of Self-Direction in a Good Human Life*: Unlike most generic goods, e.g. friendship and play, self-directedness is a central and constitutive feature of *every form of flourishing*. As Rasmussen and Den Uyl put it, "[r]egardless of the level of achievement or specificity, self-direction is a feature of all acts of human flourishing. Self-direction is what makes human flourishing

a personal activity, rather than simply a behavioral act, on the one hand, or a static, nonrelational state of being, on the other" (p. 87). Therefore, the protection of the possibility for self-direction is a political function that is in the interests of all and is not biased towards some and against other forms of human flourishing.

5. *The Priority of Liberty*: The appropriate way of reconciling diverse forms of flourishing within a single society is to enforce public order in accordance with one simple principle: the priority of liberty. This principle, rather than any substantive judgments about human flourishing, is the exclusive justification for legal coercion. According to the priority of liberty, "[t]he individual, basic, negative right to liberty prohibits all forms of nonconsensual use or direction of persons. That basic right provides the ethical basis for legally proscribing all forms of initiatory physical force and authorizing the use of physical force only for the protection and preservation of the possibility of self-direction [and consequently, the possibility of flourishing] in society" (p. 280).

Steps 2 and 3: The Pluralism of Flourishing and the Political Irrelevance of Substantive Judgments about Flourishing

Now that I have summarized the argument in its essentials, I want to explain why it does not convince me to accept the principle of negative liberty as a normative basis for politics. Let us consider the argument step by step: To begin with, I have no argument with step one, which state's "liberalism's problem" as the problem (roughly) of reconciling diverse forms of flourishing within a single social system. But in my view, too much is made of step 2, the pluralism of flourishing. That there is a plurality of forms of flourishing and that no single formula of flourishing can be imposed upon all is not something I wish to dispute—on the contrary, it seems eminently sensible to me. However, it seems to me that Rasmussen and Den Uyl's denial of the possibility of making sound practical judgments about flourishing across persons, or of making impersonal comparisons across different forms of flourishing, can only be supported by an extreme construal of the pluralism of flourishing. For it is one thing to say that a single pattern of goods can be confidently advanced as *the* formula for human flourishing; and quite another to assert that *some patterns of goods are better than others* irrespective of the persons in whose lives they are instantiated, or that some forms of life and some actions are destructive of human flourishing no matter whose life is concerned.

What I want to argue here is that there are two types of generic judgment about human flourishing that a sensible version of moral pluralism must allow for: first, judgments about the intrinsic superiority of certain forms of flourishing over others; and second, judgments about the defectiveness of certain forms of life and actions or their inherent incompatibility with human flourishing. Both sorts of judgments (a) are informed by a conception of flourishing that goes beyond negative liberty; (b) are impersonal and general in scope (i.e., they apply to all persons) and (c) yet they respect the pluralism of forms of flourishing and the central role of practical reason in discerning the specific ingredients of *my* flourishing as distinct from anyone else's.

To illustrate my point, consider the following judgments: first, there is the judgment that a life spent raising a family and meeting the material, emotional, and spiritual needs of one's children over time, is better than a life devoted to collecting antique cars and maintaining them. Both ways of life have positive features to recommend them and neither life can be readily dismissed as evil or depraved, yet there is something more humanly enriching and rewarding about family life than the life of an antique car society. It is not that the antique-car collector is not flourishing to any degree as a person—there may be various respects in which he is developing his faculties and forming valuable relationships in his antique car society. But the form of flourishing he has chosen does not realize his human faculties and virtues as fully as a life as a husband and father could.

Now, consider the second type of judgment: the judgment that this or that form of life is simply incompatible with human flourishing. A life devoted to gambling with all other goals subordinated to the goal of winning money seems to be one fitting example: such a life is consumed with a narrow project that is inherently individualistic and self-indulgent, and gives its protagonist little opportunity to develop the human virtues to a high degree, whether they be courage, generosity, humility, practical wisdom, justice, or temperance. Another example would be the life of a Don Juan, who goes out in search of love, but refuses to commit to any one person, and leaves a trail of hurt and resentment in his wake. Or consider the example of somebody who becomes addicted to heroin, and is at the beck and call of his cravings for this expensive drug. Even if he can afford to obtain the drug without resorting to stealing, the enslavement of his will that this addiction entails rules out such a life as a contender for genuine human flourishing. The point of adducing these examples is not to secure agreement on every detail, but to suggest that we can and do routinely make valid impersonal judgments about human flourishing that extend beyond negative liberty, and could very well bear on policymaking decisions.

Step 4: The Political Relevance of the Role of Self-Direction in a Good Human Life

Now, let us consider step 4 in the argument for the priority of liberty: the political relevance of the role of self-direction in a flourishing human life. The reason self-direction is considered a valid desideratum to ground political action is that it is universally necessary and central to *all* forms of human flourishing. I will concede for the purposes of argument that self-direction is indeed an essential constituent of all forms of human flourishing (though I would note in passing that this seems to raise a problem for whether infants can flourish qua human beings). The question is, what follows from this? Does the priority of liberty follow necessarily from the centrality of self-direction to flourishing? It does not, for at least four reasons: first, as I have already noted, there are *other* generic or universal features of flourishing lives, including properties they do not and cannot possess, that could be relevant from a policy standpoint. To insist on the priority of liberty is to insist that *other* structural features of flourishing, for example, the property of not being addicted to heroin, are consistently trumped by liberty. But I find no argument in this book for this proposition, and suspect it can only be sustained on a strong Kantian view of moral autonomy, which is not explicitly argued for. Secondly, contrary to what Rasmussen and Den Uyl seem to suggest, there is a very substantial array of possible positions between the unfreedom of a concentration camp and the freedom of a libertarian state. In between these two extremes, there may be certain forms of constraint that still allow a generous degree of free and unconstrained human action, and are compatible with human flourishing in general. For example, many people do not feel their agency or flourishing is significantly threatened by an elaborate regime of laws and tax codes, even when they happen to disagree with many of those laws and with many of the purposes to which their money is put. Thirdly, one possibility that Rasmussen and Den Uyl appear to neglect is a possibility suggested by Thomas Aquinas: namely, that the virtuous citizen may comply with a facially coercive law voluntarily, motivated by respect for political authority and the common good rather than the fear of punishment. If this is a real possibility, then for many people, much of the time, coercive regulation of their actions may be perfectly compatible with personal freedom and flourishing. Fourthly and finally, some people may find the motivation of punishment to be a support, not an enemy, of their freedom: for example, some may *want* to drive responsibly, but find the presence of a public scheme of sanctions helps them overcome their weakness of will and do what they know deep down is in their own and the public interest. What this discussion seems to suggest, in short, is that there is no necessary or in-principle opposition between legal coercion on the one hand, and freedom and human flourishing on the other, and thus that Rasmussen and Den Uyl do not offer a convincing ethical case for the political priority of liberty.

The Relation Between Liberty and Flourishing: A Request for Clarification

So far, I hope to have shown that at critical junctures in the argument for the priority of liberty, Rasmussen and Den Uyl make assumptions, both concerning the pluralism of flourishing and concerning the relation between legal coercion and flourishing, that cannot be sustained. I would like to conclude with one question that is less a challenge to the book's thesis than a request for clarification. *What is the precise relationship between the norm of negative liberty on the one hand, and the achievement of flourishing by humans on the other?* We are told that liberalism is a scheme of liberty designed to secure the conditions for the *possibility* of flourishing, but that liberalism is not concerned with the actual achievement or promotion of flourishing. In fact, it would appear that promoting flourishing is so far from the goal of liberalism that it is not even concerned with fostering conditions that render flourishing a probable outcome: As Rasmussen and Den Uyl put it, "[o]ur argument only shows that the political/legal order should protect the possibility of self-direction, not secure its exercise. . . . To protect the possibility of self-direction is still not the same as creating, inducing, or inciting self-directed actions" (p. 309–310). Thus, it would appear that real outcomes and consequences of government policies are of little or even no concern, from a legal or political or "metanormative" perspective. Whether flourishing actually or even tangentially occurs is politically of no relevance, or so it would appear.

This raises some interesting questions about the purpose of government action: Is it the case that liberalism is only concerned to promote the *bare logical possibility* that human flourishing could occur, or is it a more robust and realistic possibility—even probability—that is at issue? Is it really of no interest to liberalism whether or not its policies ultimately tend to favor human flourishing or merely render it *logically possible*? If the connection between freedom and flourishing is really so tenuous as logical compossibility, then Rasmussen and Den Uyl need to explain why liberalism takes such a restrained interest in the outcomes of its policies. I suspect that in doing so, they may have to rely upon a prior commitment to autonomy that simply trumps considerations of human flourishing in ways that an Aristotelian would find hard to explain.

Conclusion

To sum up my reaction to *Norms of Liberty*, I believe that it offers a refreshing new voice in the debate about the nature and normative grounds of a free society. Though I disagree with the version of liberalism Rasmussen and Den Uyl propose, and ultimately find their derivation of it from neo-Aristotelian ethics unconvincing, this book will stimulate a valuable debate about the prospects for a *rapprochement* between liberal normative theory and neo-Aristotelian ethics. One of the most salient contributions of *Norms of Liberty*, at least in this reader's opinion, is its reminder that we must somehow rise to the challenge of grounding our political principles in a view of the good life without mistaking them for the whole of the good life; while one of its most significant shortcomings is its adoption of an absolute principle of negative liberty rather than a more moderate principle of freedom to be interpreted and applied by practical reason in conjunction with other requirements of human flourishing.

4

Building a Bridge from Both Sides: A Response to *Norms of Liberty*

Charlotte Thomas

In *Norms of Liberty*, Douglas Rasmussen and Douglas Den Uyl offer an ingenious argument for establishing a perfectionist basis for non-perfectionist politics. They begin with a question: "[H]ow is it possible to have an ethical basis for an overall or general social/political context . . . that will not require, as a matter of principle, that one form of flourishing be preferred to another?" (p. 271). This is liberalism's problem, "the unique problem of the political and legal order" that is committed to the flourishing of its citizens, when flourishing is understood as "highly individualized, agent-relative, inclusive, self-directed, and profoundly social." Rasmussen and Den Uyl attribute this problem to liberalism specifically because, "liberalism has been, by and large, the only political tradition whose principles are consistent with an appreciation of this philosophical insight and because a pluralism of the forms of human flourishing points to liberalism as the appropriate solution to the political problem of integrated diversity." They argue "that the key to solving liberalism's problem is the protection of the possibility of self-direction, since self-direction is the common critical element in all the concrete forms of human flourishing" (p. xiv). Grounded by this insight, they make the claim that "the basic, negative, natural right to liberty is, together with its corollary rights of life and property, a metanormative principle, because it protects the possibility of self-direction in a social context." Their argument goes on to show that "concepts as 'social justice' and 'the common good of the political community' are, as normally understood, not metanormative principles and that no ethical principles associated with these concepts, nor any other ethical principles, for that matter, can claim priority over the basic right to liberty as a metanormative principle." All of this leads to a defense of what they call, "'liberalism's basic tenet'—namely, that protecting liberty, as understood in terms of basic negative rights, should be the paramount aim of the political and legal order" (p. xiv).

The significance of Rasmussen and Den Uyl's work is its attempt to remedy the troubling tendency of liberal political theory to end in what appears to be an inescapable approbation of ethical relativism. If one is committed to a political liberalism that limits itself to the protection of citizens' rights to life, liberty, and property, then how can one speak meaningfully about ethics, much less Aristotelian virtue ethics. If, on the other hand, one has a commitment to flourishing as the proper goal of every human life, then how can one continue to embrace a politics founded on negative rights, alone? Their argument employs the distinction between ethical norms and political metanorms to escape this dilemma. If, as they argue, human flourishing is "highly individualized, agent-relative, inclusive, self-directed, and profoundly social," then the liberal political order is going to be the only one to avoid structural impediments to flourishing and to the compossibility of flourishing for its citizens.

Against the authors' claims in at least one instance, the impressive argument of *Norms of Liberty* appears to be grounded on two fundamental commitments, rather than one. Rasmussen and Den Uyl are explicitly committed to the idea that "Self-perfection is the good and the goal of any and every individual human being" (p. 269). This tenet is, in fact, the first claim in the schematic account of the book's argument presented in chapter 11. Self-perfection, or fully realized human flourishing, as the telos of Aristotelian eudaimonistic ethics, is presented clearly as the starting point for each argument and the reference point for each elaboration on its basic structure.

Rasmussen and Den Uyl are also committed to political liberalism. This is an obvious point, of course, for anyone who has read any of Rasmussen and Den Uyl's work; but, the authors make it clear that in *Norms of Liberty*, "our account of liberalism's problem and the importance we give it arises from our conception of human flourishing. It does not come from any antecedent commitment to political liberalism" (p. 268). It is the viability of this claim that I will call into question in this essay. If one begins with Aristotle's account of human flourishing and extends one's argument to consider the political conditions that best suit the human project toward self-perfection, self-direction will not trump all other structural concerns as Rasmussen and Den Uyl claim, although it will moderate them significantly. Rasmussen and Den Uyl's argument begins from two sides of an ancient gorge and works towards the middle; it does not move unidirectionally from Aristotelianism to Liberalism, as they claim. This does not render the project any less impressive, nor does it create a bridge between the two commitments that is any less sturdy.

Foundations of Metanormativity

In chapter 1 of *Norms of Liberty*, entitled "Liberalism in Crisis," Rasmussen and Den Uyl make their commitment to liberalism clear. "We believe," they assert, "the politics of liberalism can be supported with an Aristotelian framework, at least one broadly conceived. We also argue that this framework is the *best* one for supporting liberalism" (pp. 13–14). In terms of their motivation, there is no possible question about the authors' commitment to liberalism or their intention to make an original contribution to liberal political theory. The difficulty originates in the decision they make to leave their political commitments aside in order to establish an ethical justification for them. "Because of the prima facie difference between moral and political propositions . . . the onus of proof is on the person who seeks to move from the ethical to the political/legal. Without such proof, there is no ethical justification for a political order" (p. 85). Rasmussen and Den

Uyl do not want to argue merely that Aristotelian perfectionist ethics and liberal non-perfectionist politics are compatible (a claim that I think is defended fully by their argument) or that an Aristotelian perfectionist ethics can ground a liberal non-perfectionist politics (a claim that follows from their argument, but perhaps not perfectly). Rather, they claim that if one begins with Aristotelian perfectionist ethics and seeks to project a political theory from it, then one will come to the conclusion that liberalism offers the best possible political structure for human flourishing. My skepticism is directed only towards this final, most ambitious statement of their conclusion.

Rasmussen and Den Uyl's solution to "liberalism's problem" comes from an unpacking of the Aristotelian idea of human flourishing and a consideration of the political context necessary (but not sufficient) for it. Specifically, they look to the idea of ethical metanorms, or standards for establishing a context in which individuals may flourish, rather than ethical norms for their answer. "Normative ethics is concerned with one's choosing well or using one's practical reason in a proper manner" (p. 277). A metanorm, on the other hand, "offers guidance in the creation, maintenance, interpretation, evaluation, and justification of the overall or general social context that secures the possibility of individuals pursuing their own forms of human flourishing" (p. 272).

The Aristotelian account of human flourishing at the heart of *Norms of Liberty* finds its center in Aristotelian practical reason, which necessarily involves self-direction. Ethical choices require some measure of autonomy to have integrity as such. Understood in these terms, it becomes clear that a commitment to flourishing implies a commitment to a political context that allows for self-direction, and it is on this basis that Rasmussen and Den Uyl construct their argument for a non-perfectionist political order.

> Self-direction is both central and necessary to the nature of human flourishing, being simultaneously universal and particular. It is the only feature of human flourishing that is common to all acts of human flourishing and peculiar to each, and yet at

> the same time does not imply any particular form of flourishing. It expresses the fundamental core of human flourishing. Self-direction, therefore, meets the requirements for metanormativity. (p. 88)

Since it functions both as a necessary moment in human flourishing and as principle that does not present structural impediments to any possible form of flourishing in a concrete human life, self-direction becomes the metanorm that solves liberalism's problem.

One of the central requirements of metanormativity is that a principle "must not structurally prejudice the overall social context more toward some forms of human flourishing than others" (p. 272). Self-direction meets this requirement because it is free of any concrete commitment to a particular purpose or way of life. Were there to be some element of self-direction that implied that some directions were more appropriate than others it would be self-refuting. That is, "[s]elf-direction cannot exist when certain people direct others to purposes to which they have not consented" (p. 89).

The argument goes on to elaborate this aspect of self-direction by developing the important notion of "compossibility."

> The individual right to liberty allows each person a sphere of freedom—a "moral space" or "moral territory"—whereby self-directed activities can be exercised without being invaded by others. This translates socially into a principle of compossible *and* equal freedom for all. (p. 90)

Freedoms are compossible when they can be exercised without risk of infringing on the freedoms of others. Any principle that might serve as a metanorm for a political order meant to provide an apt context for human flourishing would have to preserve the compossibility of various forms of flourishing. But Rasmussen and Den Uyl are careful to use the criterion of compossibility in a very limited and particular sense.

> It is important to realize that the individual right to liberty is not directly concerned with the promotion of human flourishing

> itself, but only with the condition for its possibility. . . . The concern here is not with how acts will turn out, but rather with setting the appropriate foundation for the taking of any action in the first place. (p. 91)

Rasmussen and Den Uyl's theory does not propound to offer the political context in which individual human beings are most likely to flourish, but instead one that removes structural impediments to the possibility of flourishing for all citizens; in other words, compossible and equal freedom for all.

Rasmussen and Den Uyl make it clear that there should be no "chicken and egg" confusions about their theoretical starting point in this work: "our account of liberalism's problem and the importance we give it arises from our conception of human flourishing. It does not come from any antecedent commitment to political liberalism" (p. 268). They claim to begin from Aristotelian ethics and work toward liberal politics, not to proceed from dual commitments to Aristotelian perfectionist ethics and liberal non-perfectionist politics. Given this ordering of their ideas, perhaps it is fair to raise some Aristotelian questions about their account. Rasmussen and Den Uyl are also clear that their account should be taken on its own merits; that it claims family resemblances to other theories, but should not be made to stand or fall because of them. So, I offer these Aristotelian questions not in order to attempt to topple or prop up Rasmussen and Den Uyl's arguments, but in order better to understand them.

Understanding my critical perspective is particularly important to making sense of this article. If my object were to refute the arguments of *Norms of Liberty* by showing that it is inconsistent with Aristotle, it would be silly indeed; Rasmussen and Den Uyl make it clear that they have no interest in attempting to be true to Aristotle. My purpose is, rather, to look at the conditions Aristotle proposed for human flourishing and, through them, to assess Rasmussen and Den Uyl's account of the special status of self-direction as a metanorm for the political/legal order that follows from a commitment to flourishing. My ultimate claim is not that Rasmussen and Den Uyl are wrong because they are not in agreement with Aristotle, but instead that their elevation of self-direction above all other conditions for the possibility of flourishing only makes sense if they have already embraced some version of liberalism.

In particular, I am interested in how the arguments of *Norms of Liberty* appear in light of Aristotle's accounts in *Nicomachean Ethics* of the importance of (1) habituation and (2) external goods to the possibility of human flourishing. I do my best to present these questions in the spirit of Rasmussen and Den Uyl's work. That is, I will not ask whether or not their version of non-perfectionist ethics will promote the aspects of Aristotelian virtue listed above. Such a line of questioning would violate one of the central conditions of metanormativity, namely that it not promote one version of human flourishing over another. Rather, I will ask whether external goods and habituation are similar to practical wisdom in the sense that they are, on the Aristotelian account, also conditions for the possibility of human flourishing. As such, I will ask whether or not a political order that follows from a commitment to ethical perfectionism, if it is following simply from a commitment to perfectionist ethics and not also from a commitment to non-perfectionist politics, should not speak to these conditions as well as the condition of self-perfection.

II. Habituation and Metanormativity

Habituation is an essential part of Aristotle's account of virtue in *Nicomachean Ethics*. At 1103a, Aristotle puts it this way:

> But we do take on the virtues by first being at work in them, just as also in other things, namely the arts; the things that one who has learned them needs to do, we learn by doing, and people become, say, housebuilders by building houses or harpists by playing the harp. So too, we become just by doing things that are just, temperate by doing things that are temperate, and courageous by doing things that are courageous.[1]

According to this account, virtue, like lyre-playing, is acquired by practice. Just as one must practice playing the lyre in order to be able to play the lyre, one must practice virtue in order to become virtuous. One must go through the motions in order to acquire the art. Those who already have the art of lyre-playing or of virtue must show one how to go through the motions, that is, to practice, so that one may eventually be able to have and understand the art oneself. Aristotle explicitly extends this dynamic to politics. Legislators are to make men act as if they were virtuous in order to help them acquire virtue.

Aristotle also argues that a background of good habits is necessary for the capacity to reason clearly about virtue. This is why good upbringing is important; no one should confuse the actions of a child with virtue, regardless of how shapely they are, but one should understand that acting as if one is virtuous is a necessary step towards actually exercising virtue.

> Now some people think one becomes good by nature, others think it is by habit, and still others think it is by teaching. As for what comes from nature, it is clear that it is not up to us that it is present, but by some divine cause it belongs to those who are fortunate in the true sense; and argument and teaching are perhaps not powerful in all people, but it is necessary for the soul of the listener to have been worked on beforehand by means of habits, with a view to enjoying and hating in a beautiful way, like ground that is going to nourish the seed.[2]

Like a field that must be plowed before it is planted, a soul must be "worked on beforehand by means of habits" so that it will be able to bear fruit. If one is going to flourish, both in the sense Aristotle means above and as it is employed in *Norms of Liberty*, habituation to virtue is a necessary condition. This is not controversial. What is at issue is whether this condition differs in important respects from self-direction, such that the latter becomes the metanormative principle for the political/legal order and the former is deemed an inappropriate object of political concern.

The suggestion of the political/legal order taking responsibility for the habituation to virtue of its citizens is antithetical to Rasmussen and Den Uyl's account. No one can know what goods might constitute flourishing for another individual. More importantly, only those goods that are freely chosen and developed through practical reason will have any relevance to one's individual virtue. Any apparently virtuous activity that is externally imposed, or coerced, loses its integrity because of that imposition.

> Coercion cannot itself create morally excellent or virtuous persons because it does not ultimately appeal to individuals' understanding or reason to ground their beliefs in the appropriateness of the moral norm. Conformity does not imply understanding, and coercion bypasses the individual's reason. (p. 95)

Self-direction trumps habituation in their account because acts which have ethical status must be self-directed, so acts that are externally compelled for the sake of habituation cannot, by definition, have ethical status. This dynamic is not new to Rasmussen and Den Uyl's account of perfectionist ethics, though. Aristotle is clear that not all citizens at all times are acting deliberately, that is, in a way that has ethical status. In fact, most people most of the time are not acting in this way. It is only for those who have become self-conscious and deliberate about their actions that fully ethical activity is possible. For Aristotle, though, actions are not first chosen, they are lived. One deliberates about actions that one has already been engaged in, and one's deliberate, ethical activities cannot always be externally distinguished from those that one pursues through thoughtless habituation.

It is not the case that someone who is coerced to perform an apparently virtuous activity is, on the Aristotelian account, virtuous. It is, instead, that practicing apparently virtuous activity illuminates the possibility of truly virtuous activity. Being forced to play the lyre poorly opens the possibility of choosing to play the lyre well. One might not be able to consider that choice without having had such practice. If the analogy to virtue holds, then certain possibilities for ethical choice may only become apparent through habituation. Going through the motions is a requisite step to being able to choose some activities. That is a problematic possibility for Rasmussen and Den Uyl's account.

In the context of *Norms of Liberty*, the most serious problem with the idea of habituation is the imposition of one individual's understanding of human flourishing on another individual. Such an imposition is problematic because human flourishing requires autonomous choice. No one has the right or the capacity to choose someone else's idea of flourishing. But, according to these accounts of habituation, individuals aren't capable of choosing for themselves certain versions of human flourishing unless they have been habituated to them.

Why is it important to Rasmussen and Den Uyl that one comes to ethical activity through free choice and not through activities that are compelled in the interest of habituation to a particular, culturally determined life of "enjoying and hating in a beautiful way?"[3] Although I share Rasmussen and Den Uyl's sense that coming to ethical activity freely is better, I cannot see that it follows from their commitment to flourishing as the end of a human life. While they are clearly right to argue that coerced activities are not self-directed and, thus, not ethical, it is also true (to Aristotle's view of flourishing and, I believe, to theirs) that one will not act virtuously if one has not first been habituated to "enjoying and hating in a beautiful way." That is, there is no clear reason for self-direction as a necessary condition for flourishing to trump habituation as a necessary condition for flourishing unless (1) habituation can be shown actually not to be a necessary condition for flourishing or (2) self-direction can be shown only to have integrity for those who have not been habituated to a particular view of the good. If one who has been habituated to a particular view of what is enjoyable and what is hateful can then become one who makes deliberate choices about what should be enjoyable and hateful in a shapely human life, then there would be no reason for politics to avoid the habituation of its citizens as a part of its project to provide a context for their flourishing. The reason for the political/legal order not to impose its view of the good on its citizens would have to come from elsewhere.

III. Minimal Externalities and Metanormativity

Another Aristotelian condition for the possibility of cultivating a flourishing life is the possession of external goods. According to Aristotle,

> it appears that there is an additional need of external goods . . . since it is impossible, or not easy, to engage in beautiful actions if one is not equipped for them. For many things are done, as if by instruments, by means of friends and wealth and political power, and those who lack certain things, such as good ancestry, good children, and good looks, disfigure their blessedness; for someone who is completely ugly in appearance, or of bad descent, or solitary and childless is not very apt to be happy, and is still less so perhaps if he were to have utterly corrupt children or friends, or good ones who had died. So as we said, there seems to be an additional need of this sort of prosperity, which is why some people rank good fortune on the same level as happiness, while others give that rank to virtue.[4]

Certain externalities are required for a flourishing life. Good ancestry, good children, and good looks are some of Aristotle's examples, but we could easily substitute externalities more familiar to a contemporary ear, such as a reasonably stable childhood, decent health, and a functional IQ.

For Aristotle, it is clear that flourishing requires some nexus of external goods and that the *polis* should take responsibility for ensuring that citizens are provided with the basic goods that will make it possible to succeed in their project to flourish. Of course, Rasmussen and Den Uyl part ways from Aristotle on this point, as do many other contemporary readers of Aristotle. The question is not whether or not Rasmussen and Den Uyl are in agreement with Aristotle on the issue of the state's proper role in the cultivation, distribution, and protection of the external goods of its citizens. The issue at hand is why the political implications of a commitment to perfectionist ethics in Rasmussen and Den Uyl's project are so different from the political implications that are shown to follow from perfectionist ethics in the Aristotelian account.

This is a tricky and problematic topic, and Rasmussen and Den Uyl deal with it carefully in chapter 12 of *Norms of Liberty*. They present the following objection in order to establish their position through a reply:

> People who suffer extreme poverty lack the minimal material and social resources that are required to have the psychological ability for engaging in practical reasoning and conducting themselves accordingly. Thus, if their self-direction is to be achieved, more is needed than protecting them from having their lives, conduct, and resources used or directed without their consent. Coercion is not the only reason why people are prevented or fail to exercise their capacity for self-direction. Positive action to provide these people with the minimal resources is also required. (p. 303)

Rasmussen and Den Uyl's reply to this objection is careful and helpful. First of all, they call into question the meaning of the word "poor." Are we to define "poor," they ask, in relative terms; that is as those who are (a) "relatively deprived compared to others in the culture or society"; or as (b) "defined by some governmental agency"; or as (c)"failing to meet a certain level or amount of resources as determined by natural law ethics or some other normatively objective standard"; or as (d) "any material, moral, or social conditions wherein individuals fail to exercise their self-direction" (p. 305)?

Definitions (a) and (b) they dismiss summarily. According to definition (a) there could be and are many cases of individuals who are less wealthy than other members of their society and culture, but who have had more success shaping up a flourishing life. Definition (b) doesn't tell us anything about the poor or the proper political response to poverty, because it does not specify the content of the bureaucratic judgment that defines the term. Definition (d) is also unuseful, since it proposes little more than a tautology. That leaves (c), which gears itself to an objective normative standard, as the only definition of poverty worth serious engagement.

It is at this point that Rasmussen and Den Uyl emphasize the focus of their account on establishing a political context for the possibility of self-direction, rather than on establishing the necessary conditions for the possibility of self-perfection.

> Thus, to focus on self-direction is to focus on what is involved for individuals being authors of their own action and conducting themselves according to their own lights, but it is not necessarily to focus on individuals conducting themselves in a righteous or worthwhile or morally excellent manner. (pp. 305–06)

The argument of *Norms of Liberty* presents self-direction, not self-perfection, as the political metanorm that follows from the ethical perspective that takes flourishing as the proper end of a human life. Insofar as no act can be virtuous (and thus have integrity as a constituent part of flourishing) without being self-directed, politics should be designed to avoid structural impediments to self-direction. In this context, it is important to realize that self-direction may or may not lead an individual toward flourishing, and Rasmussen and Den Uyl's political proposal explicitly avoids any attempt to mitigate that possibility.

> Thus, it is one thing to say people are so poor that they will not achieve self-perfection, and it is quite another thing to say that they are so poor that they will not exercise their practical reason or be self-directed. (p. 306)

While Aristotle was interested in constituting a polis that would lead citizens toward self-direction, Rasmussen and Den Uyl are committed to establishing a political context where citizens' self-direction is protected and, thus, their freedom to move according to their own best lights toward or away from self-perfection. This emphasis on negative rights and on a much broader standard renders the poor (and others with diminished externalities) as moral agents capable of self-direction, regardless of their path towards or away from a flourishing life.

Given the crucial distinction between self-direction and self-perfection, what objection would Rasmussen and Den Uyl have to establishing as a metanorm the right to the externalities requisite to self-direction? This standard would establish a much lower threshold and would imply a much less problematic positive right than any version of a right to self-perfection; but it would, of course, leave behind liberalism's commitment to negative rights, alone. While Rasmussen and Den Uyl's commitment to liberalism would make such a metanorm unacceptable, is it truly the case that it would not follow from their commitment to flourishing?

IV. Why Self-Direction Trumps

The problem with allowing for any positive rights is that they run afoul of liberalism's commitment to equal and compossible rights for all. Any redistribution of resources implied by a positive right, even to the most basic externalities, necessitates a violation of another citizen's right to property. There is no question that this requirement is consistent with the tenets of liberalism, indeed, it is one of its pillars; it is less clear, though, that it can be derived from perfectionist ethics.

The account that generates the condition of compossibility from self-direction is schematized in chapter 11. Claim number 3 of the schema holds:

> Although there are generic goods and virtues that define human flourishing for any and every human being, in reality it is both individualized and agent-relative. This means two things: first, that one person's concrete form of flourishing is not the same as someone else's; and second, that it is realized, and thus only real, by individual action. It is not some common good. (p. 269)

Building on the description of flourishing as "individualized and agent-relative," numbers 5 and 6 go on to establish compossibility as an essential criterion for metanormativity.

> Since the pursuit and achievement of one's own concrete form of self-perfection is the moral purpose of each individual, and since there is no guarantee that one individual's concrete form might not be substantially different from another's, there can

> be morally legitimate differences among human beings in the way they pursue their self-perfection. . . .
>
> If P1's good should diverge from P2's good, the ability to universalize "P1 ought to pursue his own good" to "Any and every person ought to pursue his or her own good" is not sufficient either to establish that P1's and P2's goods are the same, or to give a reason for either P1 or P2 to sacrifice the pursuit of his or her good for the other's good. Universalizability is not sufficient to establish common goods. Nor does the nature of human flourishing offer any basis for an agent neutral or impersonal reason to prefer one form of self-protection to any other. (pp. 269–70)

Because flourishing is individualized and agent-relative, we cannot legitimately universalize any generic shape of human flourishing, nor can we universalize a right for any particular individual to have the prerequisites to flourish. But this seems too strong. It does not follow from the claim that human flourishing is highly individualized and agent-relative that it does not also have some intelligible generic shape.

Aristotle's illustration of this in *Nicomachean Ethics* comes at 1106b with the case of the wrestler, Milo, who needs far more food than the average man. When considering the proper amount for Milo to eat, the mean can only be determined in relation to him; that is, it is agent-relative and highly individualized. The individualized, agent-relative character of the mean in relation to Milo, as extreme as it is, does not put it beyond the boundaries of an intelligible nexus of generic human good. In fact, it is the trainer, not Milo, who is said to be best at determining what the mean is for Milo.

I take the example of Milo to illustrate that Rasmussen and Den Uyl's point about the highly individualized and agent-relative character of flourishing does not imply that flourishing cannot have a generic shape as well. If flourishing does take some generic shape, then it would be possible both to honor a positive right to the conditions for the possibility of flourishing in the generic sense and to avoid structural impediments to any and all forms of flourishing.

In chapter 4, the argument from self-direction to the compossibility requirement begins with the claim, "Self-direction cannot exist when certain people direct others to purposes to which they have not consented" (p. 89). This seems straightforward enough, but I wonder whether it is actually as clear as it seems. As I argued above in regards to habituation, unless it can be shown that (1) one cannot become self directed after having been previously coerced and (2) that certain forms of coercion actually open one to certain forms of self-directed lives, then it will not be clear that self-direction is incompatible with all forms of coercion. Likewise in the case of compossibility, if it cannot be shown that (1) certain external goods are not requisite to self-direction and (2) that a government can be committed to the flourishing of its citizens without being committed to the conditions that must obtain in order for that to be possible, then it will not follow that a perfectionist ethic can, without some other concurrent political commitment to liberalism, exclude the positive rights of its citizens to those requisite goods.

In the section of *Norms of Liberty* entitled "Why Individual Rights Trump," Rasmussen and Den Uyl seem to admit that a commitment to liberalism grounds their argument.

> It still needs to be explained why individual rights override all other moral claims. First, it should be made clear, if it is not so already, that rights do not override all other moral claims *tout court*. Instead, they only override other claims when it comes to addressing an important but specific problem—what we have called "liberalism's problem." It is only when addressing this problem that individual rights are primary. (pp. 92–93)

Liberalism's problem, (i.e., the difficulty of establishing an ethical basis for a political context that doesn't structurally impose a hierarchy of various forms of human flourishing) provides the context for the preeminence of individual rights. The priority of individual rights implies the necessary condition of equal and compossible freedom for all citizens. The commitment to compossibility renders "self-direction" the only principle that can satisfy the constitutive criteria of metanormativity. This forms a brilliant bridge between non-perfectionist politics and perfectionist ethics, but it also highlights the necessity of beginning its construction, in part, on liberalism's side of the gap.

V. Conclusion

Norms of Liberty is an incredibly important account of how to bridge the gap between perfectionist ethics and non-perfectionist politics, and I am sympathetic to its central argument. I am less convinced that their argument moves smoothly from flourishing, through self-direction, to liberalism than that it begins with Aristotelianism and Liberalism and finds a brilliant middle term in the metanormative principle of self-direction. I am indeed in debt to Doug Rasmussen and Doug Den Uyl for helping me to clarify my understanding of these seminal ideas and to refine my philosophical and political commitments to liberty and virtue.

Notes

1. Aristotle, *Nicomachean Ethics,* translated by Joe Sachs (Newburyport, Mass.: Focus Publishing, 2002), 1103a31-37.
2. *Nicomachean Ethics,* 1179b21-28.
3. *Nicomachean Ethics,* 1179b28.
4. *Nicomachean Ethics,* 1099a32-b9.

5

Beyond Both the Polis and the Enlightenment: Reflections on *Norms of Liberty* and the Crisis of Contemporary Liberal Theory

Kenneth L. Grasso

In the interest of laying my cards on the table, I want to be clear at the outset that unlike the authors of *Norms of Liberty*, I am not a classical liberal but a proponent of what Michael Novak likes to call the Catholic Whig tradition, of the tradition in Catholic social thought that finds expression in the work of thinkers like Jacques Maritain, John Courtney Murray, and Heinrich Rommen. If I do not share Rasmussen and Den Uyl's classical liberalism, as an adherent to the Catholic Whig tradition, I share their commitments to both what might broadly be termed the neo-Aristotelian tradition in ethics (although I would, of course, embrace that tradition in its neo-Thomistic form); and the ideal of a political order characterized by limited government, the distinction between state and society, a broad sphere of "negative" liberty, and so forth. (Whether, as some have suggested, the latter means that the Catholic Whig tradition is best understood as a form of liberalism depends on how the latter intellectual tradition is defined, on the political and intellectual commitments it is understood to entail.) Beyond these commitments, furthermore, I share their reservations about contemporary liberal theory.

Yet despite my agreement with Rasmussen and Den Uyl on these points, and the fact that (for reasons I hope to make clear) I regard *Norms of Liberty* as an authentically important contribution to contemporary political theory, I nevertheless harbor serious reservations about portions of its argument. Since a systematic treatment of an argument as far-reaching and theoretically sophisticated as theirs is impossible here, all I can do is to briefly call attention to aspects of it that strike me as problematic. Before doing so, however, it is necessary to first briefly explore both their critique of contemporary liberal theory and the nature of the reconstructed version of liberalism they champion.

I

To grasp the agenda—and the importance—of *Norms of Liberty*, I would argue, it is necessary to understand the specters that Rasmussen and Den Uyl believe have haunted contemporary liberalism. It has been haunted, to begin with, by a specter deriving from the work of Plato and Aristotle that launched and has done so much to shape the ongoing conversation about the right ordering of political life that is Western political theory. The specter in question is the specter of the polis. Platonic-Aristotelian political theory not only emerged within the sociopolitical context of the Greek polis, but was informed by an ontology of social life decisively shaped by this form of social life. At the heart of this ontology was an understanding of a political order as a sovereign, all-inclusive, and undifferentiated whole embracing and regulating human life in all its dimensions—political, moral, familial, artistic, economic, cultural, and scientific—and a conception of the relationship of the individual and society characterized by a view of individuals as, in Jean Bethke Elshtain's apt phrase, "instruments to be put to a civic purpose."[1]

What Voegelin calls "the 'mortgage' of the polis" helps explain a number of features of Western political thought.[2] In the present context, one thinks not only of its tendency to envision a rightly ordered polity as a small, intimate, homogeneous society, but more importantly of its tendency to envision the goals of politics as being coextensive with the overall goals of human life; to see in the polity the ultimate milieu of man's perfection; to understand statecraft as soulcraft and to confer upon the state an open-ended mandate to promote human flourishing in all its dimensions; and—if I may borrow a phrase or two from Rasmussen and Den Uyl —to view politics as ethics writ large and insist that the proper relationship between politics and ethics is a direct and isomorphic one. One thinks here, in short, of Western political theory's tendency to equate polity and polis, to attribute to the political order (or, at least, to a rightly ordered political order) important features of the Platonic-Aristotelian—the Greek—polis.

What is important in the present context is that, despite its far-reaching break with the Platonic-Aristotelian heritage, this specter has haunted even the liberal tradition itself. It finds expression in a recurrent tendency to envision liberalism not as a political doctrine (even if one rooted in a broader anthropology and metaphysics) but as a comprehensive system of ethics. The end result of this is what might be called liberal monism, namely, the demand that state power be employed to order all of social life and all social institutions in accordance with liberal values. In such constructions, the Platonic-Aristotelian vision of the polity as an all-encompassing association whose ends are coextensive with the overarching ends of human life and responsible for nothing less than the fostering of human excellence remains. What has changed is simply the understanding of the nature of that excellence; and, if these versions of liberalism allow more scope for individual freedom than did classical thought, this is simply because their understanding of that excellence is thinner.

Ironically, liberal monism puts liberalism on a collision course with itself. More specifically, by authorizing the use of state power to configure the whole of human social life in accordance with liberal values, liberal monism not only effaces the distinctions between state and society and the political and nonpolitical, but rejects the very idea of limited government, the very idea that the state's role in the overall economy of social life is a limited one, that the goals of government are not coextensive with the overarching goals of human life. It thus places liberalism on a collision course with principles with which liberalism has been closely associated (at least in the Anglo-American world), and which are widely held to be constitutive commitments of liberalism as a distinctive tradition in political thought.

The polis, however, has hardly been the only specter to trouble contemporary liberalism. As an even cursory survey of contemporary liberal theory attests, it has also been haunted by the specter of what Rasmussen and Den Uyl term "moral minimalism or skepticism" (p. 15). The former consisting in by "the view that there are only a very few moral truths, dealing exclusively with matters of social cooperation" (p. 13); the latter in the rejection of the very idea of moral truth, in the embrace of moral relativism or subjectivism. Today, not only do their proponents dominate the world of liberal theory, but some form of minimalism or skepticism is widely regarded as providing the essential intellectual foundation of liberal politics.

Minimalism and skepticism, of course, are, to put it mildly, problematic. To begin with, they impoverish liberalism's understanding of both human nature and the moral life. At the same time, they threaten the intangible prerequisites—the cultural foundations—on which a free society depends for its vitality and, ultimately, its very viability; and leave liberalism's commitment to human dignity and freedom precariously suspended over a moral and intellectual abyss by rendering it incapable of mounting a morally principled defense of them.

The sources of this specter might be said to be twofold. On the one hand, there is the "mortgage" of the polis itself: if the goals of politics are conceived of as coextensive with the overarching goals of human life, if the goal of government is nothing less than the inculcation of human excellence, then "liberty and morality are inversely proportional" (p. 16), and minimizing the moral order becomes an obvious (and tempting) way to carve out space for individual freedom.

On the other hand, there are the philosophical commitments in which liberal thinkers have historically sought to ground their political principles, commitments rooted in the Enlightenment and the distinctive understanding of reason that drove it. While its proponents believed that this understanding of reason would place the truths of the moral order on secure foundations, as Alasdair MacIntyre has famously reminded us, the Enlightenment project failed.[3] "Epistemological revolutions, like their political counterparts, sometimes devour their own children,"[4] as

Thomas Spragens points out, and, far from providing a secure foundation for moral knowledge, the Enlightenment's conception of nature and reason led inexorably to the vision of human beings as unencumbered selves, as sovereign wills free to make of themselves and the world whatever they please that dominates contemporary liberal theory.

In any case, taken together, these two specters go a long way in explaining the crisis that has overtaken the liberal tradition, the fact that in recent decades "the vitality of liberalism as a political and theoretical doctrine has continually dissipated." Indeed, if liberalism continues to "hang on" this is largely "because there is no compelling alternative" to it (p. 6).

It is against this backdrop that the audacious intellectual project of our authors unfolds. In the face of the crisis engulfing liberal theory, Rasmussen and Den Uyl seek to articulate a new "deep structure" (p. 223) for liberal thought. Insisting that liberalism's political principles cannot be defended without recourse to a deeper moral vision, they argue that the malaise confronting liberalism is a product, at least in part, of the type of moral philosophies in which liberal thinkers have generally sought to ground their political theory. Eschewing moral philosophies that took shape under the influence of the Enlightenment, they seek to ground these principles in what they describe as a broadly neo-Aristotelian understanding of human nature and the human good. At the heart of their argument is an insistence that the human good is "(1) objective but highly individualized (and thus plural); (2) profoundly social; and (3) self-directed" (p. 79).

By insisting on the objectivity of the human good, Rasmussen and Den Uyl argue, this understanding of human nature and human good avoids the relativism and subjectivism that figure so prominently in contemporary liberal thought. At the same time, they contend that its insistence on the individualized and self-directed character of the human good justifies liberalism's "fundamental tenet," namely, that individual liberty is "the central and primary value of the political/legal order" which "the value to be achieved before and maintained before any other" (pp. 223–24), to a state whose role is restricted to the protection of "the basic, negative, natural right" of individuals "to liberty"

(p. xiv). Liberalism, in other words, is committed to the ideal of "compossible and equal freedom for all" (p. 281).

This, in turn, requires, a framework of law "that is not structurally biased in favor of some forms of flourishing over others" (p. 281); and which allows for "the exercise of self-directed activity" except where such activity diminishes or encroaches upon the exercise of self-directed activity by others. This structural neutrality provides the solution what "liberalism's problem" (p. 78) to the problem of constructing a political/legal order consistent with the pluralistic and self-directed character of human flourishing, of constructing a political/legal order that "will not require, as a matter of principle, that one form of human flourishing be preferred to another" (p. 84).

Against this backdrop, it becomes possible to appreciate the nature of liberalism as a distinctive intellectual tradition. The "central task of political philosophy" (p. 283) consists in the determination of "the nature of the connection between the ethical and the legal/political order" (p. 253). Although liberal thinkers have "not always done so coherently" (p. 78) the "true uniqueness" of liberalism as a distinctive intellectual tradition consists in "its endeavor to distinguish politics from morality" (p. 37), its denial that "the connection" between politics and ethics is "either direct or isomorphic" (p. 283). Properly understood, "the basic defining distinction of liberalism" is "the distinction between the political and nonpolitical" (p. 58). For liberalism, "statecraft is not soulcraft" and politics is not "institutionalized ethics" (p. 17). Thus, "to say that some activity X is morally right or good . . . does not, by itself, imply that doing X ought to be politically/legally required" (p. 85).

Liberalism therefore is "no more an ethics"—although it presupposes one—"than it is a theology" (p. 27); and to contrast it directly with alternative ethical systems (e.g., Aristotelianism, Kantianism, utilitarianism, etc.) is a "category mistake" (p. 34). Rather than a comprehensive system of ethics, a moral philosophy, liberalism must be understood as "a political philosophy of metanorms. It seeks not to guide individual conduct in moral activity, but to regulate conduct so that conditions might be obtained where moral action can take place" (p. 34). Liberalism, in other words, does not seek to specify the substantive norms that should regulate individual conduct but the structural norms necessary for the establishment of a political-legal order in which it is possible to pursue human flourishing in all of its diverse forms.

Now, there can be no question that *Norms of Liberty* represents a major contribution to contemporary liberal theory. It clarifies many of the fundamental issues that today confront liberal thought, offers a brilliant and original reinterpretation of the nature and distinctiveness of liberalism as tradition in political theory, and provides a far-reaching and innovative reconstruction of the ethical foundations of liberal politics. Indeed, this volume represents perhaps one of the most sophisticated and powerful defenses of liberalism available to us.

Nor can there be any question about the persuasiveness of Rasmussen and Den Uyl's criticisms of contemporary liberal theory. Involving as well its liberation from both the mortgage of the polis and its captivity to the intellectual universe of Enlightenment thought, the successful resolution of the crisis besetting liberalism will indeed require a far-reaching reconstruction of the very foundations of liberal thought. Equally persuasive are their contentions this reconstruction must both avail itself of the resources of what might broadly be termed the neo-Aristotelian tradition, and include a systematically developed account of the difference between the political/legal and moral orders. This is not to suggest, however, that either the moral or political theory articulated by *Norms of Liberty* is fully satisfying.

II

Rasmussen and Den Uyl's avowal that they are not particularly "concerned with the neutrality issue here" (p. 56) notwithstanding, no one familiar with developments in liberal theory over the past forty years will be surprised to discover that the idea of neutrality figures prominently in the argument of *Norms of Liberty*. While rejecting either what they term "liberal neutrality"—the idea that a rightly ordered polity must exhibit an "absolute neutrality between forms of flourishing" (p. 323)—or what they label "justificatory neutrality" (p. 268), they embrace the ideal of what might be called "structural" neutrality. A rightly ordered polity, they insist, must display "no a priori and *formal* . . . bias in favor of one form of flourishing over another" (p. 323); it must not *"structurally prejudice* the political/legal order of society more toward some forms of human flourishing than others" (p. 272). For Rasmussen and Den Uyl this structural neutrality is the very linchpin of liberal political morality; indeed, it represents nothing less than "the solution to the problem of political legitimation," the essential precondition of a "morally legitimate political/legal order" (p. 283).

The problem is that it is far from clear that the structural neutrality they seek is achievable. It's true that Rasmussen and Den Uyl's commitment to classical liberalism and a minimalist conception of the state's role perhaps makes the idea of structural neutrality more plausible than would otherwise be the case. (A state that acts vigorously to promote a people's welfare, after all, must have some idea of what that welfare is.) In the final analysis, Rasmussen and Den Uyl never really seriously address the work of the critics of liberal neutrality or show why structural neutrality isn't vulnerable to some of the same objections which have been leveled against the other types of neutrality championed by various liberal theorists.[5] And, even they concede that their version of the liberal order is "not . . . completely open ended" in that "some values" and ways of life are indeed "ruled out" by it (p. 36).

There is, moreover, the whole question of de facto as opposed to de jure bias. Even if it were to be conceded, for the sake of argument, that a structurally neutral political/legal order were possible, it doesn't follow that such an order would not exhibit a de facto bias against certain forms of flourishing. One might in this context raise the whole problem of social ecology. It might well be argued, for example, that it is difficult or even impossible to sustain certain ways of life without an appropriate moral environment, without both an appropriate level of public morality and institutions which acted to inculcate certain virtues so as to assure a certain minimum level of overall societal morality. "Traditional" forms of family life, for instance, might have difficulty sustaining themselves in a social environment saturated with pornography or in one which failed to instill in individuals a capacity for self-restraint, to defer gratification, etc.

Likewise, it might well be argued that certain forms of communal life—institutions and groups that possess a solidaristic as opposed to contractual and instrumental character—are difficult or impossible to sustain absent a supportive framework of law and public policy, without a framework of law and policy designed to assure them access to the material resources they need and to assure that the commitments made to their members are honored. Here again, the traditional family is a case in point.

Now, Rasmussen and Den Uyl are certainly aware of this objection. They respond by suggesting that it is by no means certain their version of the liberal order would exhibit this type of bias, and the claim that it presupposes a "Hobbesian picture of man" (p. 324); and that whether it contains such a bias, this is irrelevant to that order's structural neutrality. A given society, they write,

> may be more or less conducive to any particular form of flourishing. At the metanormative level, we are not interested in this or that form, or even in ensuring that a society remain neutral between the forms of flourishing. We take seriously the idea that the state is not in the business of encouraging any flourishing, the question which means . . . the question of whether or not flourishing is sufficiently promoted is outside the bounds of theoretical concern. Providing there is no a priori attempt to structure rules so that a form of flourishing will result . . . the metanorm of liberty will have no *systemic* bias even if actual practice encourages some forms more than others. (p. 325)

And, even it does favor some forms of flourishing over others, "predominance is not exclusion"—to say that certain forms of flourishing will be more difficult than others isn't to say that they are prohibited.

Yet it is by no means clear that this addresses the underlying problem. To begin with, they never really seriously engage the idea that the form of neutrality they champion might in practice disadvantage certain forms of flourishing or show that such fears are plausible only on the premise of a "Hobbesian picture of man." Nor do they reckon with the implications of such bias for their argument. Does not a system that in "actual practice" gives preference to—privileges—certain forms of flourishing over others, display a systemic bias? In what sense can a system which displays such a de facto bias be said to be "structurally" neutral? Can a purely "formal" neutrality do the work Rasmussen and Den Uyl wish it to do? Can a purely formal neutrality, in other words, solve "liberalism's problem?"

If structural neutrality is the linchpin of Rasmussen and Den Uyl's account of liberal political morality, the foundation of their argument consists in their account of the human good. As we have seen, they argue that if human flourishing is "objective," it is simultaneously both "highly individualized" and "self-directed." Since the individualized character of the human good means that "there are no a priori, universal rules that dictate the proper weighting of the goods and virtues of human flourishing" (p. 87), it follows that there is no "*summum bonum*," but "only many *summa bona*" (p. 190). Embracing "a version of moral pluralism" (p. 81), they insist that each individual has his or her own "unique form of human flourishing" (p. 162), and "that no form of flourishing is objectively or naturally superior to any other" (p. 219). In fact, the human good is so highly individualized that "self-direction" constitutes the "only" element that is "necessary and common to every concrete form of self-perfection" (p. 310).

This understanding of the human good undergirds their commitment not only to structural neutrality, but to the classical liberal understanding of the state's role as consisting simply in the protection of the basic negative right of the individual to liberty. Insofar as this right protects the sole element common to each and every individual's unique form of flourishing, namely, self-direction, only by limiting itself to the protection of this right can the state avoid preferring "as a matter of principle" (p. 271) some forms of flourishing over others. Only by limiting itself to "protecting the conditions for the possibility of the pursuit of self-perfection" (p. 198)—only by limiting itself to protecting the possibility of self-direction—rather than seeking to secure, in Finnis's phrase, "conditions that tend to favour" (p. 197) human flourishing, in other words, can a state avoid a structural bias towards some forms of flourishing at the expense of others.

Rasmussen and Den Uyl's insistence on the radically individualized character of the human good is understandable against the backdrop of their broader political concerns. A more robust conception of the elements common to each and every form of human flourishing would indeed seem to at least open the door to a broader conception of the role of government in the overall economy of human social life and a thicker understanding of the common good of the political community than Rasmussen and Den Uyl are comfortable with. It would seem to at least open the door, in other words, to a vision in which the state would foster the conditions of flourishing rather than merely protecting the possibility of the pursuit of flourishing.

The question remains, however, of whether this account of human flourishing is fully satisfying. Is their claim every individual's form of flourishing really so unique that self-direction" is the "only" element "necessary and common to every concrete form of self-perfection" plausible? Can it be reconciled with their claim that certain actions (e.g., murder, thievery, etc.) are incompatible with human flourishing as such? Does it not imply an agnosticism as regards the human good as it relates to particular individuals? If so, does it not ultimately translate into the type of relativism and skepticism that has plagued contemporary liberalism—and for which it is criticized by Rasmussen and Den Uyl? Is it reconcilable with their commitment to the idea of a common human nature with natural needs and tendencies, a common human nature with a knowable end or good?

What sense does it make, in other words, to assert that human beings possess a natural good if the content of this good varies so fundamentally from individual to individual that the only common element found in each person's unique form of that good is choice? In practice, doesn't this come perilously close to the elevation of "individual choice" to the status of the human good? In practice, doesn't this come perilously close to the sort of moral minimalism that has plagued liberal thought? Given the seemingly infinite number of forms of human flourishing, moreover, how can we be certain that all of these forms are "compossible," that all can coexist together in the same social order? If not, what are the implications of this for liberal political theory?

In the final analysis, one cannot escape the suspicion that *Norms of Liberty*'s insistence on the objectivity of the human good is in tension with its insistence on its radically individualized character. As its argument unfolds, the objectivity of the good gradually seems to dissolve in the seemingly infinite plurality if its individual expressions.

While Rasmussen and Den Uyl seek to take the liberal tradition beyond the horizon of the Enlightenment, furthermore, one wonders if the imprint of the Enlightenment doesn't remain nonetheless in the form of a certain flatness that characterizes their accounts of human nature and the human good. On the one hand, this flatness manifests in a certain closure to what might be termed the spiritual or religious dimension of human existence. Their account of man and the human good seems to proceed on the human and innerworldly level alone, to steadfastly refuse to transcend the horizon of the world of space and time. They simply seem to assume without further argument, for example, that human beings "are the efficient, material, formal, and final causes of our own being" (p. 212). Yet this ignores the fundamental metaphysical questions formulated by Leibnitz: why is there something and not nothing, and why is that something what it is? Surely, there are some fundamental philosophical questions here whose answer cannot simply be taken for granted.

Likewise, there is their failure to come to grips with what Tocqueville once termed man's "taste for the infinite and love of what it is immortal."[6] Indeed, this yearning has played a prominent role in the Aristotelian tradition itself. (One thinks in this context, for instance, of Aristotle's famous account of the *bios theoretikos* in the *Nicomachean Ethics*; and of the role played by the natural desire for the beatific vision in Thomistic anthropology.) One need not be a religious believer to recognize that this longing is a constitutive feature of human nature and has profound implications for our understanding of the human person. Yet it seems not to exist in the intellectual universe of *Norms of Liberty*.

On the other hand, this flatness manifests itself in a certain obliviousness to man's capacity for evil. One need not hold a "Hobbesian" view of human nature to appreciate that history attests to the capacity for individuals and societies for self-destructive behavior, and the proclivity of human beings (both individually and collectively) to injure and exploit one another. And, one need not hold a cynical or unrealistically dark view of human nature to recognize that, contrary to what Rasmussen and Den Uyl seem to suggest at one point, enlightened self-interest is alone a sufficient basis for organizing human social life. ("All that may be necessary," for their version of the liberal order to function, they hypothesize, "is that people conduct themselves . . . with regard to what they understand as their perceived advantage" [p. 282-283n].) One finds it difficult to escape the suspicion that in their intellectual universe evil is simply a matter of ignorance to be corrected to proper education.

If Rasmussen and Den Uyl escape a whole series of pathologies that have plagued moral philosophy since the seventeenth century, it is not entirely clear that their anthropology fully succeeds in escaping the broader intellectual and spiritual atmosphere of the Enlightenment.

III

Over and above these difficulties, there is the whole question of the ontology of social life that undergirds the argument of *Norms of Liberty*. One of the most original and incisive aspects of Rasmussen and Den Uyl's argument is their effort to exorcise the specter of the polis. They demonstrate the degree to which liberal theory has been burdened by the mortgage of the polis. Yet in their zeal to exorcise this specter, they fail to take sufficiently seriously another specter that has haunted liberal thought—the specter of what might be called a thin or minimalist model of human social life.

This specter manifests itself in liberalism's tendency toward a vision of human social relations in wholly voluntarist terms as something external, artificial, adventitious, and contractual, in a tendency, in Sandel's formulation, to view community as "a possible aim of antecedently individualized selves" rather than "an ingredient or constituent" of the identity of individuals[7]; and thus in a denial that human beings possess a natural relational structure. It manifests itself in a tendency to reduce the fundamental questions of political theory to the proper relationship of the individual and the state. It manifests itself in a tendency to view social life through the prism of what Mary Ann Glendon labels the "individual-state-market grid," in a tendency to view social life through a prism that allows it to see only three realities: the individual, the state and the market (the latter understood as realm of instrumental and contractual relations).[8]

The sources of this specter are at least threefold. To begin with, liberalism's tendency toward a minimalist model of social life derives from the tendency of liberal theorists to operate within a metaphysical horizon deriving from the Enlightenment. Just as it pushes liberal thought relentlessly toward a moral skepticism, so, as Francis Canavan remarks, this horizon makes it "hard" for liberalism "to entertain the notion of relations as natural," and drives it relentlessly toward a radically voluntarist conception of social relations as "artificial, external and contractual."[9] It drives it relentlessly, in other words, towards the view that all social relations and institutions are nothing more than the arbitrary products of the subjective desires and preferences of individuals, nothing more than aggregations of individuals united for reasons of mutual utility.

Secondly, it derives the continuing inability of the liberal mind to liberate itself from the mortgage of the polis. Implicit in the idea of the polis is a monistic ontology of social life that focuses on the individual and the state, and which either ignores other social institutions or absorbs them in the overarching unity of the body politic. However much they may differ in certain respects, the idea of the polis and the radically voluntarist understanding of social life sketched above converge to push liberalism toward a vision of social life that focuses single-mindedly on the individual and the state, and marginalizes or devalues what James W. Skillen terms "the nongovernmental, nonmarket relationships and institutions" that compose "civil society."[10] Finally, there is the historical association between "thick" models of society and illiberal values, the fact that the very social and political orders liberalism sought to overturn justified themselves in terms of such models.

It has become increasingly obvious (even to many of liberalism's own theoreticians) that this minimalist vision of human social life is simply untenable. As Glendon points out, it ignores the fact that men and women are not "monads" but "essentially social beings" who "do not 'enter' society, but are constituted in part by society and in turn constitute it."[11] It ignores the fact that a society is not an aggregation of individuals but a community of communities, the fact that man does not live merely as one of a vast aggregate of individuals but as a member of a member of a wide array of diverse social groups and relations. It ignores the fact that human flourishing requires certain types of relational structures, that human beings possess a natural relational structure. It ignores the central role played in human life by institutions and communities bound by ties that are solidaristic rather than instrumental and contractual. When all is said and done, the minimalist model of social life simply fails to do justice to the depth and richness of human sociality.

Now, Rasmussen and Den Uyl go to great lengths to distinguish their understanding of social life from the minimalist model of social life that looms so large in contemporary liberal theory. Affirming the "profoundly social" (p. 215) character of the human person and denying that human beings are "abstract individuals," they insist that "it is a fundamental mistake to conceive of human beings achieving maturity or flourishing apart from others and only later taking it upon themselves to join society or have social concern" (p. 142). At the same time, however, despite their commitment to Aristotelian ethics, they harbor serious reservations about Aristotle's own ontology of social life. This ontology—revolving as it does around the idea of the polis is seriously flawed by virtue of its failure to either distinguish "clearly between state and society" (p. 162n) and "the social and political" (p. 313n) or to appreciate "the open-ended, pluralistic, and cosmopolitan" (p. 271) character of human sociality.

"Though one must flourish in some community or another," they write, "there are . . . different kinds and levels of community life . . . that individuals can participate in simultaneously" (p. 142n).

When Rasmussen and Den Uyl invoke the open-ended, pluralistic, and cosmopolitan nature of human sociality, it should be stressed, they seem to mean more than that human flourishing requires a variety of different types of social relationships (e.g., instrumental and contractual as well as solidaristic relations) or a larger social context than the polis of classical Greece. Rather, they seem to be suggesting that human sociality has the same open-ended and indeterminate character as human flourishing. Just as each individual has his or her unique form of flourishing, so each and every individual's unique form of flourishing requires each own unique set of social relationships. Virtually no generalizations are possible, therefore, about the forms of social life required for human flourishing, the forms of social life issuing from our dynamic orientation toward the fulfillment of our natural ends. When all is said and done, they seem to be saying that the only element common to the social relationships necessary to each individual's flourishing is choice. Society considered as a whole, therefore, has no "telos" (p. 326).

This account of human sociality, however, seems to exhibit problems that parallel those displayed by their accounts of human flourishing. Is it really plausible to say that although humans are profoundly social beings by nature—that social life emerges out of our dynamic orientation towards the realization of our natures—each individual is so unique that it is impossible to generalize about the structure of social relations that should govern human life? How can this be reconciled with their insistence on a knowable human nature with natural needs and tendencies? If the network of social relations that collectively constitutes society issues from our dynamic orientation towards the perfection of our natures, how can it be said that society as such has no telos?

In practice, does their position not amount to the denial that human beings possess a natural relational structure? In practice, how does this understanding of social life differ from the radically voluntarist vision of social life that has figured so prominently in contemporary liberal theory? Does their simultaneous denial of a natural relational structure and implicit identification of choice as the only element common to the social structures required for human flourishing not push us in practice toward a vision of social life in which all social institutions are understood as simply products of individual choice? Does it really take us in any meaningful way beyond the horizon of the individual-state-market grid? Does it not preclude in principle any effort to identify the nature and roles of the various social institutions necessary to human flourishing, or to explore the proper relationships between them and the conditions on which they depend for their vitality (i.e., the whole question of social ecology)?

Here again, one can't quite escape the suspicion that there is a tension between Rasmussen and Den Uyl's affirmation of the profoundly social character of the human person and their simultaneous insistence on the radically individualized structure of social relations necessary to each person's flourishing. Indeed, the social nature of the person ultimately seems to dissolve in the seemingly infinite plurality of its individual expressions. When all is said and done, it is not entirely clear just how fundamentally Rasmussen and Den Uyl's account of social life breaks with the minimalist model that dominates the world of contemporary liberal theory or in just what sense it represents an advance over this model.

An adequate ontology of social life, as Rasmussen and Den Uyl recognize, must steer a course between the Scylla of the polis and Charybdis of the minimalist models of social life associated with contemporary liberal theory. The problem is that it is not entirely clear that their own account of social life succeeds in doing so.[12]

IV

The thinness of *Norms of Liberty*'s account of social life, its tendency to give short-shrift to the social dimension of the human life, in turn, are responsible for certain problems that plague its account of the political order, its account of the state and the broader body politic of which it is a part. To begin with, insofar as its argument tends to move directly from the individualized and self-directed character of the human good to the limits of government, it tends to reduce the basic questions of political theory to the relationship of the individual to the state.

The problem here is that while the basic questions of political theory of course include the question of the relationship of the individual and state, they also necessarily include the whole question of the relationship of the state to other social institutions. Addressing this question, in turn, necessarily involves offering an account of the full range of institutions and groups in which our nature as social beings finds expression and the respective contributions of these institutions to human flourishing.

Indeed, it is difficult to see how an analysis that moves on the level of the individual and state alone can arrive at a satisfactory account of the state itself. It cannot do so because it is only against the backdrop of a comprehensive ontology of social life encompassing an understanding of the full range of institutions that issue from our nature as social beings that the nature, role, and limits of the state as a distinctive social institution can begin to come into view.

It is thus perhaps not surprising that their account of the state and more broadly, "the political community" (which, they rightly insist, is not to be equated with the "polis as traditionally understood") are, to put it gently, cursory. On the one hand, they devote little time to exploring such subjects as the origins and distinctive character of the state as a social institution, its proper organization, or the preconditions on which it depends for its vitality. Insisting that the central task of political philosophy is the determination of the nature of the connection between the political/legal and moral orders, they focus almost exclusively on the question of determining the limits of state action.

Now, it's certainly true that the questions of the proper relationship between the legal and moral orders, and of the proper limits of governmental action, are both vitally important questions, and questions that have seldom received the sort of careful attention they merit. And, Rasmussen and Den Uyl are absolutely correct that far too often the connection between these orders has simply been assumed to be direct or isomorphic, and that far too frequently the state has simply been assumed to have an open-ended mandate to do good things simply because they're good things. Nevertheless, as important as these questions are, they hardly exhaust the subject matter of political theory. Nor is it clear how they can be adequately addressed in isolation from at least some of these other questions.

More specifically, it is difficult to see how they can be adequately addressed except in the context of something with which *Norms of Liberty* fails to provide: a full-fledged theory of the state. How can we begin to address the proper role of government in the overall economy of human social life, how can we know its proper relationship to the various orders—social, religious, economic, ethical, etc.—which the human person inhabits, in short, before we arrive at an adequate account of what the state is? Indeed, attempting to do so would seem to amount to nothing less than putting the proverbial cart before the proverbial horse.

On the other hand, if Rasmussen and Den Uyl's treatment of the state is cursory, they say virtually nothing about the nature of the "political community" as one of the communities to which our nature as social beings gives rise or its distinctive contribution to human flourishing. One need not equate the polity with the Aristotelian polis to appreciate that human beings are naturally political creatures, that the political community plays an essential role in human flourishing, and that the polity is an important source of human identity and focus of human allegiance. Indeed, as Maritain writes, a polity consists of more than a "collection of public commodities and services," a "military force" and a body of laws. It also encompasses a "heritage of . . . historical remembrances," "symbols," "glories," "living traditions and cultural treasures," "political virtues," "customs," and "unconsciously operating hereditary wisdom."[13]

One searches *Norms of Liberty* in vain for any acknowledgement of these facts or its implications for our understanding of the nature of the political community and its common good. To see a polity as essentially no more than a mutual protection association is to embrace what Murray once called "altogether unhistorical" concept of political society.[14] Individuals do not regret that they have but one life to give for a mutual protection society.

In keeping with the perfunctory character of its treatment of both the state and the political community and lack of interest in the whole topic of social ecology, it is not surprising that *Norms of Liberty* affords little attention to the social and cultural preconditions on which the state and polity depend for their vitality (and ultimately their very viability). While alluding to the need for "a culture that values the basic negative right to liberty," they insist on the minimal character of these preconditions. "The most that is required of individuals" for the existence of political/legal order they envision "is "orderly conduct . . . and perhaps not even this, for all that may be necessary is that people conduct themselves according to what the legal system requires with little or no appeal to moral principles and only with regard to what the legal system requires and only with regard to what they understand as their perceived advantage" (p. 282-283n).

Yet surely this account of these preconditions is unrealistic. Political orders that are no more than external orders of command and assent are necessarily unstable and short-lived. On the contrary, a political order—and, in particular, a political order in which the role of government is sharply limited—depends for its vitality on "that spontaneous willingness" on the part of the citizenry "to honor the 'city'" of which they are members that Daniel Bell terms *civitas*.[15] *Civitas* manifests itself in a variety of ways. It manifests itself, to begin with, in law-abidingness, in a willingness to obey the laws even when such obedience runs contrary to the dictates of immediate self-interest. It manifests itself in the willingness to utilize freedom in a responsible manner, and a willingness to abstain from actions which although legal would be damaging to the well-being of others or the community as a whole. It manifests itself in a willingness to subordinate self-interest to the demands of the common good—in a willingness, in other words, to make sacrifices and bear burdens for the goods of others or society as a whole. It manifests itself in a sense of civic amity, of partnership in a common enterprise—and hence in a sense of openness, trust, and goodwill among the various individuals and groups that comprise the polity.

Civitas, in turn, is a function of something more than enlightened self-interest: it presupposes a deep identification with the body politic, a profound sense of loyalty and moral obligation towards it (and thus presupposes an understanding on the part of the citizenry of the body politic of which they are a part as something more than a mutual protection society). If individuals will not lay down their lives for a mutual protection association neither will they do so as a result of a calculus of enlightened self-interest.

My point here isn't to suggest that it is the responsibility of the state to foster *civitas*, or to defend a perfectionist vision of politics. Rather, it is to suggest that the new version of liberalism Rasmussen and Den Uyl seek to elaborate is incomplete without a systematically developed theory of politics which does justice to the nature of the state and political community, their distinctive roles in the overall economy of human social life, their relationships to the full range of institutions and communities in which our nature as social beings find expression, and the conditions on which they depend for their vitality. Only against the backdrop of such a theory is it possible to arrive at a satisfactory account of the relationship of the moral and political/legal orders, and the limits of government.

V

By way of conclusion, I wanted to briefly touch on what I would suggest is an unresolved tension in Rasmussen and Den Uyl's account of the identity—the defining commitments—of liberalism as a distinctive intellectual tradition, a tension that I believe casts light on the crisis of contemporary liberal theory. At some points in Rasmussen and Den Uyl's argument the uniqueness of liberalism consists is its commitment to distinguishing politics and morality, the political and nonpolitical, state and society; its commitment to the idea that the relation distinction between the moral and the political/legal orders is neither a direct nor an isomorphic one. At other points, this uniqueness, this defining commitment, seems to consist in a commitment to the proposition that the political/legal order should be limited to the protection of the basic negative right of the individual to liberty, to the protection of the freedom of each individual to pursue his or her own conception of the good life. This right trumps any other goods or values that the political/legal order might seek to advance.

Now, while these two commitments are not necessarily in conflict with one another, neither, I would argue, does the first of these commitments in and of itself necessarily entail the second. One can, after all, deny that there should exist a direct or isomorphic relation between the moral and political orders without limiting the goal of the former to the protection of the basic negative right of the individual to freedom. Insofar, moreover, as the second of these understandings commits liberalism to a much broader understanding of the scope of freedom than does the first, they open the door to very different understandings of the political implications of liberalism.

Leaving aside the many questions these accounts raise (including whether the purely negative understanding of liberty of the type embodied in Rasmussen and Den Uyl's second account of liberalism's defining commitments is tenable[16]), what I want to suggest is that this tension in their account of liberalism's identity mirrors an unresolved tension within what David Walsh has aptly called "the liberal soul,"[17] two conflicting impulses whose presence help explain the crisis that today engulfs the liberal tradition. On the one hand, liberalism, particularly in the Anglo-American world, has often championed the cause of ethical, ordered liberty, seeking, in Burke's words, "to temper together" the "opposite elements of liberty and restraint in one consistent work."[18] At times, in other words, it has functioned as sober, temperate philosophy that while celebrating liberty insisted that it could endure and be a blessing only if it was combined with goods such as justice, order, morality, and responsibility; a philosophy which while celebrating freedom is sensitive to the social and cultural preconditions without which a free society is impossible.

On the other hand, as Michael Walzer has pointed out, its history reveals that liberalism has been "a self-subverting doctrine" which

> seems continually to undercut itself . . . and to produce in each generation renewed hopes for a more absolute freedom from history and society alike. Much of liberal political theory, from

> Locke to Rawls, is an effort to fix and stabilize the doctrine in order to end the endlessness of liberal liberation. But beyond every version of liberalism there is always a super liberalism, which, as Roberto Unger says of his own doctrine, "pushes liberal premises about state and society, about freedom from dependence and governance of social relations by the will, to the point where they merge into a larger ambition: the building of a social world less alien to a self that can always violate the generative rules of its own mental or social constructs."[19]

If it has at times been a doctrine of ordered, ethical liberty, liberalism has been haunted by the specter of a very different type of freedom, of what Kenneth L. Schmitz terms the idea of "radical freedom."[20] At times, in other words, liberalism has exhibited a restless antinomianism, an impatience with restraint at any kind, a single-minded fixation on the good of individual autonomy finding political expression in a corrosive individualism which, in Canavan's words, privileges "individual freedom over any other human or social good that conflicts with it." Indeed, the yearning for an absolutely untrammeled and undetermined freedom explains, at least in part, why liberals have been so strongly attracted to "agnosticism in religion, skepticism in philosophy, and relativism in morals."[21]

The historical consequences of these two expressions of liberalism have been very different. The first has played a critically important role in laying the groundwork for the free societies of the modern West. It was largely under the aegis of liberalism that limited government, the rule of law, and broad guarantees of individual freedom triumphed in the modern West. The second, however, has proven to be a profoundly destructive force. Its commitment to what the great ordo-liberal Wilhelm Roepke terms "freedom-at-any-price,"[22] its restless antinomianism, has proven inimical to a wide array of goods essential to human flourishing and destructive of the very social and cultural preconditions on which the stability and vitality of a free society depends. Indeed, the acids of its individualism ultimately dissolve the inner architecture of liberty itself, producing in the process a freedom that negates and destroys itself.[23]

When all is said and done, its susceptibility to the siren call of radical freedom puts liberalism on a collision course with itself. The hard fought (and profoundly extraordinarily important) achievements of the liberalism of ethical, ordered liberty are undermined by the yearning for absolute and untrammeled freedom that liberalism seems unable to completely exorcise. And, it is precisely its susceptibility to this call that has made it impossible to fix and stabilize liberal doctrine, which has given the liberal intellectual tradition its self-subverting character.[24]

To understand the crisis of liberalism it is necessary to appreciate the schizophrenia introduced into the liberal tradition itself by these conflicting impulses and the reasons for its susceptibility to the siren call of radical freedom. Rasmussen and Den Uyl are absolutely right that a solution to this crisis will involve moving liberal theory beyond both the social ontology of the polis and the metaphysics of the Enlightenment. This crisis, however, cannot ultimately be addressed without confronting and exorcising the specter of radical freedom, and thereby fixing and stabilizing liberalism as a doctrine of ethical, ordered liberty.

Notes

1. "In Common Together: Unity, Diversity and Civic Virtue," in *The Constitution of the People: Reflections on Citizens and Civil Society*, ed. Robert E. Calvert (Lawrence, Kans.: University Press of Kansas, 1991), 70–71.

2. *Plato and Aristotle*, vol. 3, *Order and History* (Baton Rouge: Louisiana State University Press, 1957), 90.

3. See *After Virtue*, 2nd ed. (Notre Dame: University of Notre Dame Press, 1984), 51–61 and passim.

4. *The Irony of Liberal Reason* (Chicago: University of Chicago Press, 1981), 213–13.

5. For thoughtful critiques of liberal neutrality, see Michael Sandel, *Liberalism and the Limits of Justice*, 2nd ed. (Cambridge: Cambridge University Press, 1998); Alasdair MacIntyre, *Whose Justice? Which Rationality?* (Notre Dame: University of Notre Dame Press, 1988); J. Budziszewski, *True Tolerance: Liberalism and the Necessity of Judgment* (New Brunswick, N.J.: Transaction Publishers, 1992); and Francis Canavan, *The Pluralist Game: Liberalism, Pluralism, and the Moral Conscience* (Lanham, Md.: Rowman & Littlefield Publishers, Inc., 1995).

6. *Democracy in America*, edited by J.P. Mayer, translated by George Lawrence (New York: Harper & Row, 1969), vol. 2, part II, chapter 12, pp. 534–35.

7. Sandel, 64.

8. *Rights Talk: The Impoverishment of Political Discourse* (New York: The Free Press, 1991), 109–44.

9. Canavan, 121, 130.

10. *Recharging the American Experiment: Principled Pluralism for a Genuine Civic Community* (Grand Rapids, Ind.: Baker Books, 1994), 70.

11. Glendon, 74.

12. For an introduction to the very different—and, in my view at least, more successful—effort to steer a middle course between these dangers by the proponents of what is sometimes called normative pluralism, see James W. Skillen and Rockne M. McCarthy, ed., *Political Order and the Plural Structure of Society* (Atlanta: Scholars Press, 1991); and Jeanne Heffernan Schindler, ed., *Christianity and Civil Society: Catholic and Neo-Calvinist Perspectives* (Lanham, Md.: Rowman & Littlefield, 2008). The proponents of normative pluralism combine a vision of human beings as essentially not contingently social creatures with an understanding of society not as a collection of individuals, but as a *communitas communitatum*. Human nature, in this view, gives rise to a wide array of diverse communities and institutions all of which are necessary to human flourishing; and the limits of government derive not merely from the rights of individuals but from the distinctive responsibilities of the various institutions with which the state shares the stage of social life. These institutions are neither creatures of the state nor the purely arbitrary products of the subjective desires of individuals, but original social institutions in their own right which have a right to exist and to make their own unique contributions to human flourishing.

13. *Man and the State* (Washington, D.C.: The Catholic University of America Press 1998; reprint, Chicago: University of Chicago Press, 1951), 11–12.

14. John Courtney Murray, "Leo XIII and the Order of Culture," *Theological Studies* 15 (March 1954): 12.

15. *The Cultural Contradictions of Capitalism* (New York: Basic Books, 1978), 245.

16. Charles Taylor has persuasively argued that it is not. See his essay "What's Wrong with Negative Liberty," in *The Idea of Freedom*, ed. Alan Ryan (Oxford: Oxford University Press, 1979), 175–93.

17. This phrase appears in the title of his *The Growth of the Liberal Soul* (Columbia: University of Missouri Press, 1997).

18. *Reflections on the Revolution in France*, vol. 2, *Select Works of Edmund Burke* (Indianapolis: Liberty Fund, 1999; reprint, Oxford: Clarendon Press, 1874–1878), 362.

19. "The Communitarian Critique of Liberalism," *Political Theory* 18 (February 1990): 15, 14.

20. See "Liberal Liberty and Human Freedom," in *The Chesterton Review* 20, 1–2 (May/August 1994): 223 and passim. This article offers a superb brief overview of this understanding of liberty, its importance to grasping the nature and history of liberalism as an intellectual tradition role, and its intellectual roots. For a more systematic account of its metaphysical roots, see Servais Pinckaers, O.P., *The Sources of Christian Ethics*, trans. Sr. Thomas Noble, O.P. (Washington, D.C.: The Catholic University of America Press, 1995). For some suggestion as the far-reaching impact of this understanding of freedom on modern Western culture, see Jeffrey Hart, "Burke and Radical Freedom," *The Review of Politics* 29 (April 1967) 221–38.

21. Canavan, 76, 84.

22. *The Moral Foundations of Civil Society* (New Brunswick, N.J.: Transaction Publishers, 1996; reprint, London: William Hodges and Company, 1948), 48.

23. For an exploration of the process whereby this freedom negates and destroys itself, see Kenneth L. Grasso, "Saving Modernity from Itself: John Paul II on Human Dignity, 'the Whole Truth about Man,' and the Modern Quest for Freedom," in *In Defense of Human Dignity*, ed. Robert P. Kraynak and Glenn Tinder (Notre Dame: University of Notre Dame Press, 2003), 213–19; and "The Triumph of Will: Rights Mania, the Culture of Death and the Crisis of Enlightenment Liberalism," in *A Moral Enterprise: Politics, Reason, and the Human Good*, ed. Kenneth L. Grasso and Robert P. Hunt (Wilmington, Del.: ISI Books, 2002), 221–44.

24. Liberalism's inability to resist the siren call of radical freedom, as Schmitiz, Pinckaers and others have shown, cannot be understood without appreciating the nominalist horizon against which its thought unfolds. As Pinckaers suggests, however, a full account of liberalism's susceptibility to this call must address the whole question of spiritual atmosphere of modern culture. The appeal of radical freedom, its "origin and dynamism," he writes, cannot be understood apart from "an initial determination to affirm freedom in the face of all else," a determination rooted in "the human will for self-affirmation," and which ultimately requires "the rejection of all dependence whatsoever, and [thus] of any norm . . . not made by itself." It is this initial determination, he argues, that explains modernity's attraction to this freedom, its veritable "worship" of it, "regardless of how negative it results might be and how disruptive its manifestations." (Pinckaers, 338–39.)

6

A Non-"Atomist" Defense of Individual Liberty

Elaine Sternberg

Introduction

The metanormative defense of individual liberty presented in Douglas Rasmussen and Douglas Den Uyl's *Norms of Liberty: A Perfectionist Basis for Non-Perfectionist Politics* differs significantly from most previous attempts to defend negative liberty. One of its most distinctive strengths, is that it is not "atomist." The purpose of this paper is to show that thanks to its physical characterisation of individual liberty, its distinction between norms and metanorms, and its neo-Aristotelian understanding of human flourishing, the metanormative defense is not vulnerable to the antilibertarian challenges posed by social ontology.[1]

As used here, "social ontology" is ontology that asserts the non-reductive existence of systems; it typically denies the existence of the self-sufficient, independent individuals characteristic of "atomism." "Metaphysical" ontology applies to inanimate material particulars and living things as well as to human institutions; it is contrasted with "institutional" ontology, which is usually silent about non-institutional existents. Ontology is "naturalist" or "realist" (versus "idealist") insofar as it acknowledges the existence of a reality whose being and character are not mind-dependent.

Social ontology has historically been associated—both by its advocates and its opponents—with political and ethical views that are characteristically collectivist or communitarian.[2] Although the connection is ordinarily just assumed, it is explicitly asserted in a recent version of social ontology, which is unusually powerful in being both naturalist and metaphysical. Avoiding many of the problems afflicting idealist approaches, the comprehensive social ontology defended in David Weissman's *A Social Ontology*[3] directly challenges the foundations of conventional defenses of individual liberty. Because it claims to provide metaphysical foundation for political communitarianism, it provides a strong basis for assessing the claims of social ontology.

This paper will argue that the metaphysical challenges to individualism posed by social ontology do not touch the defense of individual liberty developed in *Norms of Liberty*. To show this, Weissman's account of social ontology and its arguments against individualism and individual liberty will be outlined, and largely given the benefit of the doubt. The key assumptions and arguments of the metanormative defense will then be set out, and explanation offered as to how and why they would be unaffected even if strong metaphysical social ontology did hold good.

The Claims of *Social Ontology*

Weissman's aim in *A Social Ontology* is to challenge "atomism," the doctrine that ". . . reality is composed—materially, morally, and mentally—of self-sufficient entities, each one having an existence and character that are independent of other things."[4] According to Weissman, atomism is the dominant ontological and social theory, and underlies individualism, liberalism and libertarianism.[5] Among the historical exemplars he cites (and thus challenges) are Aristotle,[6] Descartes, Machiavelli, Hobbes, Locke, Hume, Kant, Nietzsche, Bentham, and Mill; contemporary culprits include Wittgenstein and both Rawls and Nozick. Weissman argues that key individualist notions—particularly those of the self and negative liberty—are incoherent when ontology is properly understood as social. Metaphysical social ontology is said to imply communitarianism, and to justify coercive governmental action to protect the welfare of subordinate systems, especially "the public."

Weissman's main thesis is that individualism mistakenly presupposes an atomist self-sufficiency:

> Political atomism—individualism—misrepresents the material world. It says that reality is composed of separable particulars. . . .[7] Atomism affirms that each of us is morally, intellectually, or materially self-sufficient, and that we engage other people from one or more of these positions of independence.[8]

Against all these views, Weissman argues that atomist self-sufficiency is not possible. At the institutional level, this is a standard communitarian argument.[9] Weissman, however, goes further. On the basis of his metaphysical ontology, he argues that the kind of isolated but fully-formed individuals typically presupposed by social contract theorists not only do not, but could not, exist.[10]

Self-sufficient individuals are ontologically impossible, according to Weissman, because "reality's elements are systems, not autonomous simples. . . ."[11] Depending on causal relations for their identity and integrity,[12] ordinary existents, including physical objects and persons, are neither free-standing nor self-sufficient, even when they are physically separable. As systems, human individuals are, like all other systems, irretrievability enmeshed in reciprocal causal relations. This is enough, Weissman contends, to falsify any claims that humans are self-sufficient, independent or autonomous.[13]

If true, the metaphysical impossibility of atomist individuals would constitute a devastating criticism of any political theory that presupposed their existence, including (arguably) those of Kant(ians) and Rawls(ians). Though Weissman's ontological and political arguments are questionable, the large tasks of criticising them and of addressing the relationship between metaphysics and political philosophy[14] will not be undertaken here. This discussion will instead attempt to show that even if Weissman's social ontology were largely granted the benefit of the doubt, arguments based on it would not touch the metanormative defense of individual liberty propounded in *Norms of Liberty*.

Responsibility and Consent

One of the prime sociopolitical targets of social ontology is the doctrine that legitimate, binding obligations require consent. Weissman identifies the demand for consent as characteristically atomist:

> The individual is said to be a store of rights—freedoms from and freedoms to—that defend him from the demands of others (whether individual people or social systems). His relations to them are only contractual and voluntary . . . .[15]

He rejects this position by applying to human systems his ontological notion of "responsibility to": a part's responsibilities both to the system of which it is a member, and to the system's other parts, are just what the part must do to sustain that system's survival.

In the ontological analysis, Weissman emphasizes the mechanical and conditional qualities of "responsibility to," so as to make it plausible that systems lacking consciousness should nonetheless be considered responsible.[16] And in the political discussion, Weissman acknowledges that human "responsibilities to" a system depend on the member(s)' intention to perpetuate that system.[17] But he is equivocal. Sometimes human (functional/mechanical) responsibilities to abhorred systems are said to arise but not to be morally binding.[18] Elsewhere, however, he maintains that binding moral responsibilities to a system exist independently of what its human members actually do intend[19]: responsibilities arise automatically to systems that are conditions of human well-being: "That we may not know those conditions is incidental: discovering that these are conditions for our well-being, we who value ourselves should, logically and practically, value them."[20] The requisite intention can, according to Weissman, apparently be presumed when the system is itself one on which human flourishing depends. He maintains that the (modern democratic welfare) state is such an essential system, vital for averting the consequences of unmanaged complexity.[21] Other indispensable systems according to Weissman are the families, friendships, schools, and employments presupposed by the "cognitive-affective" posture that he associates with self-identity.

If successful, this claim would undermine a key element of most liberal political philosophies. Obviating the need for consent in respect of crucial systems, it would justify holding their human members morally responsible both to those systems and (in respect of sustaining those systems) to each other.

Freedom *To* and Freedom *From*

That moral "responsibilities to" automatically arise towards vital systems also underlies Weissman's criticism of individual liberty:

> [being] free to do as we like . . . is a fantasy, one we claim to achieve only as we repudiate the substantial responsibilities to others that burden but valorize our actual roles and circumstances. For there could be an unrestricted freedom to do as we please only if there were no higher-order systems that engage us, hence no responsibilities to them and their members.[22]

Because, according to Weissman, people are ineluctably enmeshed in such systems, and are automatically responsible to those that are essential for human well-being, people cannot be free to do as they like.

Weissman's claim that freedom requires the repudiation of responsibility depends on two main premises. The first is that the purportedly repudiated responsibilities actually do exist. Even if it is accepted that human members have mechanical/functional responsibilities to all systems of which they are members, and moral responsibilities towards systems whose perpetuation they actually intend, more is needed to support Weissman's contention that moral responsibilities arise automatically towards systems that are needed for human well-being.

That claim depends, *inter alia*, on the soundness of the underlying ontological analysis, on clarification and justification of the meaning of "well-being," on there being some specific systems that are in fact necessary for human well-being, and on valuing an end's requiring both intending it and also valuing and intending the means to achieving it.[23]

Even if that first problematic premise could be established, the other premise of Weissman's association of freedom with the repudiation of responsibilities is also dubious. That second premise is that freedom is properly characterised by the particular formulations Weissman considers, both of which he identifies with atomism:

> *freedoms to* and *freedoms from*, the one as we have unimpeachable rights to do as we like, up to the point of hurting others, the second as we are, or ought to be, exempt from the intrusions or demands of others.[24]

"Doing as one likes" and "exemption from the will of others" are formulations that Weissman adopts from the philosophers whom he treats as paradigmatic "liberals": John Stuart Mill, John Dewey, and John Rawls. Unfortunately, these and similar characterizations of liberty are often employed; defective in many ways, such formulations render defenses of liberty vulnerable to attack on many grounds.

There is, however, a quite different (libertarian) understanding of sociopolitical liberty that Weissman never considers.[25] In this non-moralized sense of "negative liberty," one is free if and only if one's person and property are not subject to coercion by other persons or human systems.[26] Coercion[27] exists when physical force or the threat thereof is initiated by persons or human systems against persons or their property; it typically involves physically constraining a person or his property without that person's consent. This conception of liberty might, accordingly, be more descriptively labelled "non-coercive" or "defensive" or even "physical" liberty. Libertarianism is the doctrine that any interference with such non-coercive liberty requires justification, and that sufficient justification is seldom if ever available.

Such a conception of negative, non-coercive liberty is not touched by Weissman's criticisms. Unlike the formulations he considers, it presupposes no exemption from all intrusions or demands. It has no need to repudiate any responsibilities or duties. It is also desire-independent. All it requires, is the absence of (physical) coercion.

This is, in fact, the sort of liberty defended by Professors Douglas Rasmussen and Douglas Den Uyl in a series of publications, particularly *Liberty and Nature: An Aristotelian Defense of Liberal Order*, *Liberalism Defended: The Challenge of Post-Modernity*, and the recent *Norms of Liberty: A Perfectionist Basis for Non-Perfectionist Politics*. In *Norms of Liberty*, these staunch libertarians set out a neo-Aristotelian defense of negative liberty as what they call a "metanormative principle"; that defense is referred to here as "the metanormative defense."

Is the metanormative defense of liberty as immune to Weissman's attacks as the non-coercive individual liberty it defends? To assess how the metanormative defense fares against the challenges posed by social ontology, the test will be made as strong as possible: the benefit of the doubt will be given to even the most controversial elements of Weissman's metaphysical analysis.[28] In addition, a key social tenet of social ontology will be granted, that is, that humans depend for both the development and the maintenance of their identities on membership in social systems.

The Metanormative Defense of Liberty

The strength of the *Norms of Liberty* account starts with its understanding of freedom. Liberty is characterized in suitably physical terms, quite unlike the problematic formulations criticized by Weissman. Far from requiring the repudiation of all responsibilities and duties, the liberty defended in *Norms of Liberty* is expressed in terms of obligation: "This negative right to liberty imposes on persons the obligation to refrain from initiating physical force in any or all of its forms against other persons" (p. 282, para 49).[29]

The metanormative defense offered of it is, unlike most previous defenses of individual liberty, explicitly non-atomist. Though the authors discuss metaphysics only briefly, they assert that "reality is not composed of isolated beings that have no relation to other beings . . . reality is a network of related beings" (p. 344).[30] Rasmussen and Den Uyl acknowledge both that human beings are not self-sufficient in the sense of relying on nothing outside themselves for their existence (p. 331), and that "ontological separateness in and of itself provides no ethical support for individual rights" (p. 209).

In addition to presupposing no free-standing existents, the metanormative defense presupposes neither pre-social nor pre-governmental human existence. Rasmussen and Den Uyl affirm that

> We are . . . not abstract individuals. It is a fundamental mistake to conceive of human beings achieving maturity or flourishing apart from others and only later taking it upon themselves to join society or to have social concern. (p. 142)

Accordingly, the metanormative defense does not employ the device of a social contract. It does not depend on the notional choices of individuals who are attenuated, unsocial or veiled in ignorance.

The metanormative defense deals instead with ordinary humans, embodied in the physical world, and enmeshed in all their mundane causal and social relations. It starts from an explicit acknowledgement that relatedness is central to human flourishing:

> Our maturation or flourishing requires a life with others. We do not flourish independent and apart from engagement with others. We have potentialities that are other-oriented, and we cannot find fulfilment without their actualization. (p. 141, para 1)

And it defends liberty as the condition that must be respected if the possibility of flourishing in all its actual variety and complexity is not to be structurally precluded when people live in society. From the outset, therefore, the metanormative defense eschews atomism.

Rasmussen and Den Uyl justify negative liberty rights as the solution to "liberalism's problem":

> Given that there are diverse forms of human flourishing and that our need for sociality is profound and open-ended, we need a political standard that will allow interpersonal life in its widest sense to be possible without, at the same time, *structurally* requiring the sacrifice of the lives and resources of any person or group to others. (p. 246, italics in original)

That standard

> must be universal in the sense of being equally applicable to all individuals. In addition . . . the universality requirement necessitates that we center our principle on that characteristic present in all forms of human flourishing (or its pursuit). (pp. 8–84)

The characteristic must also, they argue, provide an agent-relative reason for compliance with the standard (p. 272). Based on their account of flourishing, Rasmussen and Den Uyl argue that self-directedness is that pervasive characteristic, and that negative, non-coercive liberty is the requisite regulatory, metanormative standard.

They reach this conclusion by analysing the nature of human flourishing. Following Aristotle, they identify human flourishing as self-perfection and the ultimate moral good. According to Rasmussen and Den Uyl, the human good is:

> (1) objective; (2) inclusive; (3) individualized; (4) agent-relative; (5) self-directed; and (6) social. (p. 127) . . . It is not abstract, collectively determined, atomistic, or impersonal. (p. 143)

To show that the metanormative defense based on these characteristics is compatible with social ontology, each of the characteristics will be examined in turn.

First, flourishing is "objective" in two senses. It does not consist merely in a subjective, psychic state; nor is the goodness of its components conferred on them simply because they are the objects of favorable attitudes; "It is a state of being, not a mere feeling or experience" (p. 128).

> Ontologically considered, human flourishing is an activity, an actuality, and an end (or function) that is realized (or performed) through choice. Human flourishing is not the mere possession of needed goods and virtues . . . [as the] that-for-which human conduct is done . . . it is ultimately the standard by which human desires, wishes, and choices are evaluated. (p. 129)

This sort of objectivity should pose no problem for social ontology. Weissman recognizes the existence of both "core interests" and primary goods, and acknowledges health as an "immanent norm."[31] So far, so good.

Next, Rasmussen and Den Uyl characterize human flourishing as "inclusive," by which they mean three things. First, it signifies that a variety of basic goods and virtues are typically necessary for flourishing. According to Rasmussen and Den Uyl, such goods include knowledge, health, friendship, creative achievement, beauty, and pleasure; the virtues include integrity, temperance, courage, and justice (p. 130). Weissman explicitly lists similar conditions for human flourishing.[32] Second, flourishing is inclusive in that the various goods are experienced over the course of a person's life. Flourishing "is not the result of the efforts of a lifetime. . . . Rather, it is a continuous process of living well" (p. 131).

Third, flourishing is inclusive because, as expressions and partial realizations of flourishing, the goods and virtues are not simply means to the end of flourishing, but are experienced as valuable in their own right. This last claim might seem incompatible with Weissman's denial of non-instrumental value to anything but humans themselves.[33] But by "valuable in their own right" Rasmussen and Den Uyl do not mean "independent of relation to humans" (p. 123). They simply mean that the goods and virtues in question are experienced by humans as constituents of, as well as means to, human flourishing. Inclusiveness could therefore be accommodated within Weissman's social ontology.

That flourishing is described as "individualized" might seem more contentious. For Rasmussen and Den Uyl, however, "individualized" does not presuppose individuals who are isolated, self-sufficient, or independent of causal or social relations. Rather, "individualized" simply means two (different) things. First, it indicates that human flourishing is achieved and enjoyed by individual persons, albeit typically in relations with others. Weissman acknowledges that it is individual humans who perceive, think, and act; accordingly, for him, too, flourishing is experienced by individual humans.[35] Second, "individualized" signifies that flourishing is specific to, and must be actualized by, each individual person. It is only through an individual's choices that generic goods and virtues become determinate, real, and valuable (pp. 81, 133). Once again, this seems consistent with Weissman's views, both about how determinables become determinate[35] and how values are constituted.[36]

That flourishing is "agent-relative" (p. 134; see also p. 156) is one of the most distinctive elements of Rasmussen and Den Uyl's account. Unlike most modern philosophers, they deny that ethics is impersonal or agent-neutral. Instead, they maintain, human flourishing "always and necessarily" takes into account what is good for the particular person (p. 134): flourishing is different for different people. There is no single best way of combining the basic goods and virtues that are generally necessary for flourishing. Nor is there any interpersonal way of ranking versions of flourishing (p. 177). Each person must determine what combination best suits him considering his own particular character and specific circumstances, talents, endowments, interests, beliefs, and histories . . . what Rasmussen and Den Uyl call his "nexus" (e.g., pp. 80, 133, 144, 155). This accords with Weissman's own agent-relative analysis of value, and is confirmed by his affirmation that there are "alternative, variable conditions for human flourishing."[37]

That flourishing is "social" is accepted by all the authors under consideration: they agree that flourishing is "achieved with, and among, others" (pp. 142, 166). Unlike Hobbes, they all maintain that human beings need each other even after they have reached maturity. Rasmussen and Den Uyl state explicitly that

> Self-perfection is not atomistic. Human beings are social animals not merely in the Hobbesean sense of needing others,

> because individuals are virtually powerless on their own, but in the fuller sense of human flourishing requiring a life with others. (p. 270, para 8)

In order to thrive, humans normally require other people in their lives; other-regarding goods such as friendship and justice are fundamental constituents of flourishing.[38] Furthermore, human sociality is open-ended, and makes relationships possible with any human, including "persons who as yet share no common values and are strangers to each other" (p. 143). The potential need to accommodate people of diverse values and cultures reinforces the importance of a nonrestrictive political standard.

The feature of flourishing that is most significant for the metanormative defense of liberty is that it is "self-directed": individual agency is needed to discover the particular mix of goods and virtues that constitutes flourishing for any individual, as well as to achieve and integrate that mix (p. 140; p. 275, para 29). Like Aristotle's "practical reason," self-direction is an activity (p. 87), and ensues in action; it is exercised whenever choices are made in concrete situations.[39] As agency, it is something that must be performed by the agents themselves: by its nature, it cannot be imposed by others (p. 87). When properly exercised, it is the virtue of practical wisdom, or what Aristotle called *phronesis* (p. 80).[40]

According to Rasmussen and Den Uyl,

> self-direction is both a necessary condition for, and an operating condition of, the pursuit and achievement of human flourishing. Regardless of the level of achievement or specificity, self-direction is a feature of all acts of human flourishing. Self-direction is what makes human flourishing a personal activity, rather than simply a behavioral act, on the one hand, or a static, nonrelational state of being, on the other. (p. 87; see also p. 276 note 8)

Like the other features of human flourishing, this notion of self-direction seems compatible with social ontology. Weissman admits both individual choice and personal responsibility: it is individual moral agents who are held morally "responsible to" and "responsible for" maintaining systems.[41] He recognizes that individuals deliberate, and explicitly acknowledges self-direction.[42]

This is important, because self-direction is crucial for the metanormative defense of liberty.[43] Self-direction is not simply freedom of will: it involves action in the physical world (p. 280, para 39), and is ordinarily precluded by physical coercion. Even when some attenuated self-direction is possible[44] in responding to a coercive situation, self-perfection—flourishing—normally involves a range of activities and choices that is incompatible with being physically coerced: an agent who is tied up, or whose person or property are otherwise forcibly constrained by the actions of others, is typically prevented from acting in the ways necessary to achieve his self-perfection. Liberty is thus the condition that must be respected for it even to be possible that the multivarious forms of human flourishing be achievable in society. Liberty is the paramount value for the political/ legal order, because it is needed to solve a particular social, political and legal problem that is central to human life which is individualistic but not atomistic.

This is a conclusion that Weissman apparently rejects:

> Freedoms grounded in democratic rights (i.e., the freedoms we have because we live as citizens in democratic states) are not a necessary condition for flourishing in every life, unless we suppose that no one who lived without them—the vast majority of people, past and present—could have flourished.[45]

This rejection is, however, not evidence of an incompatibility between social ontology and the metanormative defense: the claim Weissman rejects is not the one that Rasmussen and Den Uyl make.

First, the freedom that Weissman denies is necessary for flourishing is not the negative liberty defended by Rasmussen and Den Uyl. It is instead a version of positive freedom that encompasses powers and civil rights, and includes such institutional arrangements as majority rule, minority rights, legislative authority, and judicial review.[46] Rasmussen and Den Uyl are as emphatic as Weissman that such institutions are not necessary for everyone's flourishing (pp. 322–23).

Second, they are as aware as Weissman that flourishing can apparently occur even in the absence of negative liberty. Citing Solzhenitsyn (p. 94), they acknowledge that rare individuals can achieve great things even under conditions of dire compulsion. More generally, to the extent that repressive regimes have been less than completely totalitarian, and have left people with control over part of their lives, even ordinary people living under oppressive regimes have had some scope for flourishing.[47] This is, however, more an argument for the diversity of flourishing's forms, than it is for the unimportance of negative liberty.

In any case, Rasmussen and Den Uyl do not defend liberty (as distinct from self-direction) as a necessary condition for every instance of actual flourishing. They defend negative liberty instead as a condition that must be respected if no form of human flourishing in society is to be structurally precluded or privileged: liberty is defended as the solution to liberalism's problem. Since the position that Weissman denies relates to the former thesis rather than the latter, and in respect of a very different meaning of liberty, the metanormative defense is not touched by Weissman's objection.

Significantly, Rasmussen and Den Uyl do not maintain either that negative liberty is a sufficient condition of flourishing. The mere presence of liberty neither guaranties that flourishing will be achieved, nor offers any guidance as to how it can or should be. Such guidance is provided by moral norms, whereas the liberty defended by *Norms of Liberty* is a *meta*norm. It specifies a necessary condition for the possibility of people's seeking their diverse forms of flourishing while living in society:

> A metanorm offers guidance in the creation, maintenance, interpretation, evaluation, and justification of the overall or general social context that secures the possibility of people pursuing their own forms of human flourishing. (p. 273, para 19)

Though Weissman never uses the term "metanorm," he sometimes employs "regulative principle" in a similar way.[48]

The failure to identify the metanormative character of liberalism is, according to Rasmussen and Den Uyl, what accounts for liberalism's apparent reliance on a separation of the right and the good, and its historical association with "relativism, minimalism, emotivism, skepticism, atomism, universalism, and materialism" (p. 43). That failure underlies what they call "the dilemma of liberalism—a tendency to either impoverish morality or trivialize rights" (p. 47):

> If . . . one's central moral obligations tend to be defined in terms of what is owed to others, and if one should also be left free to pursue personal interests as one sees fit to the maximum degree possible, then squaring these two would seem to require a minimal amount of restrictive interpersonal duties. (pp. 32–33)

Rejecting the first premise, and respecting the difference between norms and metanorms, *Norms of Liberty* demonstrates the compatibility of substantive ethics and individual liberty . . . and falsifies Weissman's claim that individual freedom necessarily requires the repudiation of legitimate responsibilities.

Far from being atomistic, or vulnerable to the challenges posed by social ontology, the metanormative defense of individual liberty might actually gain support from it. Recall that in *A Social Ontology*, Weissman claimed that people have a binding moral responsibility to sustain those systems necessary for human well-being. *Norms of Liberty* argues that negative liberty rights are necessary if the diverse forms of human well-being are to be pursued when people live in society. To the extent, therefore, that Weissman's argument succeeds, it might even—*contra* Weissman—support rather than undermine individual liberty properly understood.

Conclusion

The metanormative defense of liberty provided by Rasmussen and Den Uyl in *Norms of Liberty* is distinctive in virtue of its neo-Aristotelian understanding of human flourishing, its objective definition of liberty, its avoidance of self-ownership assumptions and social contract arguments, and its recognition of the difference between norms and metanorms. Unlike defenses of liberty that rely on atomist assumptions, and employ problematic characterisations of liberty, the metanormative defense is impervious to the challenges of social ontology, and might even derive metaphysical support from it.

The metanormative defense thus demonstrates that the historical association of social ontology with political views that are typically communitarian or collectivist is not necessary . . . however often the connection has been assumed to hold by both its advocates and its opponents. Just as there is no need to reject the possibility of (absolute) truth to defend an open society, there is no need to deny the truths captured by a social ontology[49] to defend individual liberty. A full bodied defense of liberty is compatible with a metaphysics that encompasses the reality of systems.

Notes

1. This paper is part of a project that was started as a Visiting Scholar at the Social Philosophy and Policy Center ('SPPC') of Bowling Green University in 2003–2004, and continued as Visiting Fellow of the Center for Ethics and Public Affairs ('CEPA') of Tulane University's Murphy Institute. I am grateful to the SPPC, the CEPA and the Institute of Economic Affairs for their support, and to Fred Miller and Eric Mack for constructive criticism. A paper ("Individualist Implications of Social Ontology") containing early versions of some of the material presented here, along with a more detailed examination of the metaphysical ontology, was delivered to the Philosophy Department of St. John's University, NYC in February 2004, and to the SPPC and Philosophy Department of Bowling Green University in April 2004; early versions of this paper were presented to CEPA/Society and the Professions, Washington and Lee University in April 2006, and at the American Political Science Association in September 2006.

2. Consider, for example, J. A. Hobson's 1898 attempt to base socialism on a social ontology, and the contemporary (reductionist) criticism of that attempt by Auberon Herbert in "Salvation by Force" and "Lost in the Region of Phrases". Auberon Herbert, *The Right and Wrong of Compulsion by the State and Other Essays*, ed. Eric Mack, (Indianapolis: Liberty Classics, 1978), pp. 227–58. I am grateful to Eric Mack for this observation.

3. David Weissman (New Haven, Conn.: Yale University Press, 2000. For Weissman, the "social" in "social ontology" has no necessary connection with biological beings or their interpersonal relationships; it applies as well to inanimate existents. As such, it might be better described as "systematic" or—if that has too many connotations—as "systemic."

4. Weissman, 2; see also 163.

5. Weissman, 222, 16. "Atomism['s] . . . effects—including the public, the rule of law, free markets, secular values, personal freedom, and the minimal state—are conspicuous and desirable. . . . Atomism empowers individuals by endowing them with personal and political rights. It also makes them morally and legally responsible for their conduct and regulates their conflicts" (Weissman, 250). See also pp. 2, 167, 226, 234, 255, 310. Weissman uses "freedom" and "liberty" interchangeably, as does *Norms of Liberty* and this paper.

6. While acknowledging his debt to Aristotle, Weissman considers that Aristotle's metaphysics renders even the essentially social Aristotelian ethics and politics atomistic, in virtue of his "reading Aristotle's politics in terms of his ontology . . ." (Weissman, 358, n.31, see also 94–97) Because of Aristotle's explicitly atomist metaphysics, Weissman denies that the polis is a system (220), even though it would otherwise have qualified as such (because it is stabilized by the reciprocal causal relations of its members), and even though much looser associations are described as systems in *A Social Ontology* (e.g., pp. 148–49), To the extent that Rasmussen and Den Uyl presuppose a neo-Aristotelian metaphysics, Weissman would presumably also dismiss them as atomists, regardless of the content of their political philosophy.

7. Weissman, 224; see also pp. 2, 212.

8. Weissman, 246.

9. See, for example, Charles Taylor, *Philosophy and the Human Sciences* (Cambridge: Cambridge University Press, 1985), especially chapter 7, "Atomism". Taylor holds explicitly that the dependence of human development on society makes traditional rights claims incoherent (193, 198), and claims that "A human being alone is an impossibility, not just *de facto*, but as it were *de jure*." (Introduction, 8). But he does not offer any general ontological theory. Moreover, unlike Weissman, Taylor rejects "naturalism," which he considers to be essentially reductionist (3).

10. Social contract theorists mentioned include Hobbes, Locke, Rousseau, and Rawls; Weissman, 146, 225, 109.

11. Weissman, 25.

12. To support this view, he invites us to

> Consider . . . the integrity of things that suffer no apparent change of shape or size when moved. . . . Does this establish that a primary substance is self-sufficient. . . . No, it proves only that whatever conditions support or establish a thing's character and apparent singularity . . . tolerate this change of relative position. This point is easily tested: rather than move a thing slowly, we move it, with nearly instant acceleration, at half the speed of light. Now it doesn't remain the same (it vaporizes) . . . A structure's integrity is, therefore, derivative: its integrity—its separability—is a function of the structure's relations to the pervading conditions that operate within and upon the materials that compose it. Self-sufficiency is an idealization that applies to nothing but the universe itself . . . (Weissman, 9).

13. Weissman, 13, 35; 209, 249. "Relations to other systems reduce each system's autonomy: human freedom is limited by our roles within systems and by other systems that supply a context for those in which we participate." Weissman, 18. See also Weissman 15, 35, 41, 226, but compare 219.

14. A metaphysics that denies the existence or knowability of a mind-independent external world leaves persons radically ungrounded or incoherent; it affords little scope for political philosophy. To the extent, however, that a political philosophy does not explicitly depend on a defective metaphysics, it deserves to be considered on its own terms. Although, for example, Hobbes and Locke may well have been atomist ontologists, in that they recognized the existence of self-sufficient, independent, material particulars, neither's political philosophy assumed humans to be independent of all causal connections. Equally, neither held that people in the state of nature lived in isolation or were unaffected by relationships; had they done so, there would have been no need for the remedies of civil society. But insofar as a political philosophy (e.g., Hobbes's) does not acknowledge a fundamental and continuing need for sociality, it remains "atomist" in a way that the metanormative defense is not.

15. Weissman, 244. For an argument that consent is the key to political obligation, see A. John Simmons, "Consent Theory for Libertarians", in *Natural Rights Liberalism from Locke to Nozick: Essays in Honor of Robert Nozick*, ed. Ellen Frankel Paul, Fred D. Miller and Jeffrey Paul (Cambridge: Cambridge University Press, 2005).

16. "Assuming the system's survival as the point of reference, we say that each part is responsible to the others for such behaviors as would sustain the system. . . . These responsibilities are less than obli-

gations or duties. They fall to individual[s] . . . because of the mechanical prejudice—the inertial identity—that favors a system's survival" (Weissman, 118).

17. "Responsibility *to* in us humans has an intention, a locus and a development. Its intention is the perpetuation of the system or systems in which we participate" (Weissman, 119).

18. ". . . responsibility *to* is not always a positive duty. Indeed, responsibility *to* is amoral, given that members may find themselves responsible to odious systems. Sometimes these duties are consciously fulfilled or rejected. More often—even among human societies—they are honored, unconsciously, because of the reciprocal causal relations that mechanically bind a system's parts. Careless or distracted members fail to override reciprocities they should abjure" (Weissman, 51–52; italics in original).

19. Taylor makes a similarly unjustified shift from conditional to unconditional obligation ("Atomism", 206–07). This move is particularly problematic for Weissman, insofar as he does not define "well-being". He explicitly states that the conditions of human flourishing are variable (Weissman, 255), and that the only immanent norm he recognizes is health (Weissman, 264).

20. Weissman, 307. He also asks "does personhood imply the obligation to support other persons by participating in reciprocities that nourish them as well as ourselves?" (Weissman, 141), and affirms that it does in chapter 4.

21. "public self-regulation is a principal condition for the well-being of individuals and the social systems they create. . ." (Weissman, 171); "we say [of] *government*. . . that its functions are critical for the welfare of other systems" (Weissman, 167; italics in original; see also 172, 176). Among the necessary roles of government Weissman includes "planning for control, planning to reduce conflict and encourage initiative, planning to endow people with the power for initiative, planning to exploit resources, and planning to formulate and rank shared values" (Weissman, 189).

Weissman's claim about the state is unconvincing, and reflects an apparent lack of awareness of how the valued public functions he attributes to it could be achieved without it. He dismisses with a rhetorical question the possibility that the state might not be required: "Which is the more egregious fantasy: that governments cannot regulate honestly and effectively; or that competitors such as businesses will regulate themselves in ways that make them coherent internally, and safe for the rest of us?" (Weissman, 177; see also 140–41, 164, 196, 225). His claim that the state is both vital and necessarily valued is particularly problematic in light of his agent-relative notion of value.

22. Weissman, 226. See also Weissman, 225, and Weissman, *Lost Souls: The Philosophic Origins of a Cultural Dilemma* (Albany: State University of New York Press, 2003), 128. The association of liberty with the evasion of moral responsibilities might also reflect a failure to understand that libertarianism is primarily a political doctrine. In declaring liberty to be the prime political value, libertarianism is asserting that enforcing and promoting moral values is not a legitimate function of coercive government; it is not denying that moral values are vital for guiding human lives. Equally, claims that rights to (negative) liberty "trump" moral values typically imply only that the moral values may not be forcibly imposed, not that they are dispensable. It may also be that the skepticism and relativism sometimes associated with (inappropriate and unsuccessful) defenses of negative liberty have contributed to an undermining of traditional responsibilities.

23. As argued in Sternberg, "Individualist Implications of Social Ontology," Weissman's metaphysical analysis shows at most that human existence is impossible when detached from *every* (social and other) system. It does not preclude sequential detachment from any particular system(s), so long as connection to some (other, suitable) system(s) remain(s). Metaphysical analysis alone could also not suffice to establish which (if any) systems might actually be necessary for human well-being. So the ontological argument would seem to support an unconditional "responsibility to" only in the innocuous mechanical/functional sense, and moral "responsibility to" a system only to the extent that its perpetuation were actually intended by the member.

24. Weissman, 310; italics in original. See also p. 13.

25. The closest Weissman comes is single quotation from Robert Nozick, used simply to illustrate atomism (Weissman, 2n1). Though *Anarchy, State, and Utopia* does contain explicitly atomist elements, Nozick never claimed that it provided a moral foundation for the view of rights it presented. Its arguments are, moreover, not accepted by many libertarians.

26. One's movements may well be restricted if one is trapped in a cave by the incoming tide, but one's liberty is not limited by natural forces, only by the acts of persons (or systems of them); merely being within a causal nexus does not restrict liberty. For discussions of why characterizing negative liberty other than as the absence of human coercion is problematic see Murray Rothbard, *The Ethics of Liberty* (Atlantic Highlands, NJ: Humanities Press, 1982) part IV, chapters 27 and

28, 215–28, and Charles Taylor, "What's Wrong with Negative Liberty" in *Philosophy and the Human Sciences*, 211–29. For an extended, meticulous analysis of a concept of negative liberty defined in terms of physical unpreventedness, see Matthew Kramer, *The Quality of Freedom* (Oxford: Oxford University Press, 2003).

27. Because humans are embodied in the physical world, all interactions (ultimately) involve the operation of physical forces. But interactions are not coercive in the sense employed here unless they are backed up by fairly direct, typically aggressive, physical constraint. Coercion is not involved in every use of physical force involving another's person or property: in handing you your pen I am applying physical force *to* your property, but not *against* it. Nor are all coercive uses of force violent. As a reminder of this necessary condition, the pleonastic description "physical coercion" is sometimes used. Coercion may be legitimate if undertaken in self-defense, just rectification or punishment. For discussions of coercion, see Alan Wertheimer, *Coercion*, (Princeton: Princeton University Press, 1987) and Michael J. Gorr, *Coercion, Freedom, and Exploitation* (NY: P. Lang, 1989).

28. Though not to the implications that he draws from them. Views that are explicitly rejected or contested by Weissman may nevertheless be compatible with the metaphysical analysis presented in *A Social Ontology*. For the sake of the challenge, "social ontology" will consist of the following claims: (a) everything is either a property, a system or an aggregate of systems; (b) systems are created and sustained by the reciprocal causal relations of their interdependent parts; (c) emergent properties, including systems, are causally efficacious and are not reducible to their parts; and (d) the parts of systems are (mechanically) responsible both *for* and *to* the systems of which they are the parts.

29. Although Rasmussen and Den Uyl often characterize liberty in terms of consent, they also explain that "The single more basic and threatening encroachment on self-direction is the use of physical force" (p. 280, para 41).

30. They do, however, share the Aristotelian presupposition of discrete material particulars, and go on to affirm that "The natures of most beings are what they are apart from others" (p. 344). The extent to which Weissman's social ontology can admit natures or essences is problematic. According to Aristotle, essence is precisely that which remains unchanging in a particular, and is intrinsic to it. Since Weissman maintains that nothing is unchanging or intrinsic in the requisite ways (Weissman, 7), he is forced to reject that Aristotelian notion. But there does not appear to be anything in Weissman's ontological analysis that

would preclude a reinterpreted (perhaps functional) account of essence, even though he does not provide any; the analysis explicitly admits "immanent norms", "natural norms" and "natural ideals" (Weissman, 256–61).

31. Weissman, 265; 235–37; 257. But cf. note 30 above. Although Weissman rejects final causes, he does recognize "two kinds of benign teleology" (70); the ontological analysis might be capable of accommodating something closer to the teleology presupposed by the metanormative defense even if he would not. See also note 36 below.

32. "Conditions for human flourishing include health, work appropriate to one's talents, fellowship, civil order, and the absence of arbitrary authority and war. Additional, desirable conditions include the development of physical and intellectual skills, the cultivation of sensibility, and a network of sustaining social relations." (Weissman, 255)

33. ". . . values are only instrumental or self-affirmed" (Weissman, 295).

34. "Having thought is an act or power of human bodies." (Weissman, 146) "Some things—the feel of one's body—are available principally or only to introspection. Equally personal and private are the memories, feelings of anticipation, satisfaction or guilt, plans, and the *sotto voce* commentaries that pour through us" (Weissman, 160; italics in original). "Our separability and self-sufficiency—with respect to consciousness, thought, will, feeling, action , and responsibility—promote the individualist, atomist doctrine that society is an aggregate of autonomous agents" (Weissman, 10). He explicitly states that the existence of "corporate effects does not imply that systems, like their members, have attitudes . . ." (Weissman, 275).

35. For him, every existent "exhibits these three factors: a determinable property, a determining condition, and a determinate expression (a specific value) for the determinable. . . .Determinables always achieve determinacy in the actual world. . ." (Weissman, 25). "No determinable property is self-determining; no property determines its own specific value" (Weissman, 30). But cf. note 47 below.

36. "We *choose* the objects of ultimate value. . . .We, by self-election, are good-in-themselves [sic]. This is a considered choice, one that is justified by experience and interest, as we value human beings and human flourishing for the good reason that we are humans who want to flourish. . . . If we nominate other things to this community of ends, it is usually because they are human associations or products . . . or because their well-being is a condition of our own" (Weissman, 307; italics in original; see also p. 237).

37. Weissman's notion of value is agent-relative in three senses: values are experienced by individuals rather than collectives; what represents value to any individual reflects that individual's preferences (though they may well have been influenced by the systems in which he developed); the values of any individual are of value to that individual. See Weissman, chapter 4, especially 255.

38. Consider Fred Miller's response to the Nozickian challenge: "Why should the value to X of having a meaningful life give rise to any sort of obligation on the part of *anyone else* not to frustrate this value?" (Fred D. Miller, Jr., *Nature, Justice, and Rights in Aristotle's Politics* (Oxford: Clarendon Press, 1995), 375, italics in original). Miller maintains that "justice is necessary for the individual good, but not merely instrumentally; for justice is a necessary feature of co-operative activity which is a constituent of the good life. Therefore, a practically rational agent pursuing the good life ought to choose to enter into a just system of co-operation" (Miller, 376).

39. For a fuller justification of this interpretation of practical reason, see Fred Miller, Jr., "Aristotle on Rationality in Action", *Review of Metaphysics*, XXXVII, no. 3 (March 1984): 499–520; also Fred D. Miller, Jr., *Nature, Justice, and Rights in Aristotle's Politics*, especially 9–11.

40. "Practical wisdom is not merely cleverness or means-end reasoning. Instead, it is the ability of the individual at the time of action to discern in particular and contingent circumstances what is morally required." (p. 146) "this is above all the work of the man of practical wisdom, to deliberate well . . . The man who is without qualification good at deliberating is the man who is capable of aiming in accordance with calculation at the best for man of things attainable by action." Aristotle, *Nicomachean Ethics*, 1141b10–14 (book VI, chapter 7).

41. E.g., "Each [member] . . . is responsible for choosing to participate in the system (if this was a choice) . . ." (Weissman, 275). But note that for Weissman, institutional systems can also be moral and morally responsible (Weissman, 276).

42. Autonomy is "supplied by self-valorizing, self-directing attitudes. . . . Shall we be self-directing or safely programmed? One requires that we trust our self-affirming attitudes; the other commits us to the accumulated, homogenized values of other people. . . .leaving our choices to other people doesn't solve the problem of having justifiable values" (Weissman, 295).

43. Since protecting the possibility of self-direction in a social context solves liberalism's problem . . . and since using persons without their consent is incompatible with the possibility of self-direction, a

principle that required that individuals not be used or directed without their consent—a principle that banned the initiation of physical force by some persons against others in all its forms and authorized such force only for the protection and preservation of the possibility of self-direction—would be a metanormative principle. The individual, basic, negative right to liberty prohibits all forms of nonconsensual use or direction of persons (p. 280, paras 42, 43). See also *Liberalism Defended*, 56–57.

44. Consider Jack Benny's famous pause while considering "Your money or your life!" (see p. 89, note 15).

45. Weissman, 255.

46. Weissman, 14.

47. Cf. "freedom survives in the spaces left determinable when causes fix values incompletely." (Weissman, 60) "The spaces that tolerate self-determination are critical . . . because they justify the insistent impression that we humans are both determined and free" (Weissman, 61).

48. "systems . . . are mutually independent (but interacting), reciprocally engaged, overlapping, or nested. Systems having these relations are richly entwined. Power—war—may eliminate some of the conflicts among them. But there is a better solution: tolerate difference, then formulate and apply the regulative, procedural principles that promote sustainable freedom-in-difference. . . ." (Weissman, 181).

49. Although most of the political claims Weissman makes in *A Social Ontology* are not justified by his ontological arguments, this discrepancy enhances rather than diminishes the value of the ontology: the strictly ontological analysis seems capable (with appropriate correction and clarification of terms) of supporting views that are much sounder than those its author identifies. Given the range and power of a naturalist, social ontology, with its salutary emphasis on the importance of metaphysics, its recognition of the richness of being and the reality of systems, and its potential for accommodating essence and saving the appeara

7

Aristotle and Aristotelianism in *Norms of Liberty*

Susan D. Collins

Norms of Liberty: A Perfectionist Basis for a Non-Perfectionist Politics confronts directly one of the significant dilemmas of our time, which the authors call "liberalism's problem": the possibility of a legal-political order that can obtain the conditions for moral action and individual flourishing while also protecting individual liberty (p. xiv). The book is impressive in the first place because it so clearly articulates and addresses a problem that has both bedeviled and been obscured by much contemporary liberal theory. In response to practical and theoretical challenges to liberalism in the last thirty years, the rise of a new Aristotelianism, among other developments, has highlighted the inadequacies of a political theory that does not confront the question of the conditions, if not the nature, of moral action and individual flourishing. In fact, I would put the dilemma to which this challenge has given rise more strongly than the statement from the book's preface does, though, in doing so, I capture an important dimension of the authors' thought: Does liberalism, the political order that enshrines individual liberty, lack the robustness to protect, not to say encourage, the conditions for moral action and individual flourishing; in fact, does it actually undermine these conditions?

The latter concern is implicit in Rasmussen and Den Uyl's critique of certain forms of liberalism, particularly Rawlsianism, that reduce ethics and individual flourishing to versions of social cooperation: "what is impartial and universal comes to take precedence over [partial and particular] goods," with the consequence that "particularized ethical content is increasingly sacrificed to abstract and universalized norms" (p. 26). Indeed, in such cases, the individual, thought to be central to liberalism, becomes "ethically more irrelevant" (p. 26). In confronting this problem, the authors do not seek to infuse liberal theory or political principles, especially liberty and rights, with ethical spirit or life. "It shall be our contention," they write, "that liberalism is quite correct to ignore the individual and be universalistic in its outlook" (p. 27). But, they insist, "it is correct in doing so only if it relinquishes all pretenses to being an ethics. Liberalism is no more an ethics than it is a theology" (p. 27).

In taking their fellow liberal thinkers to task on this issue, Rasmussen and Den Uyl are able to highlight the consequences for individual liberty of a lack of clarity concerning the influence of liberalism on moral action and individual flourishing. The great problem arises when liberal thought confuses the purpose of liberal politics as seeking not the conditions for the possibility of individual flourishing but the conditions of that flourishing itself (p. 28). The result is that ethics becomes socialized and the state or society becomes the moral arbiter of individual action. One of the many strengths of the book is its critique of authors, old and new, who make this error, and Rasmussen and Den Uyl rightly assess the significance of this error for both the question of the individual good and the protection of individual liberty.

The authors thus offer a compelling calling to account in order to assess better the present dangers. In light of their assessment of these dangers and of the possibility of individual flourishing and liberty, the authors look elsewhere for what they call the "deep structure" that supports flourishing within the context of political liberalism's distinctive commitment to liberty. They look, obviously, to Aristotle, or, more precisely, to an Aristotle made young and beautiful, and relevant to the problems of our time. The innovative neo-Aristotelian approach of the book proposes to craft a limited and so truly liberal politics that protects the possibility of a robust ethics of flourishing while also preserving diversity.

As *neo*-Aristotelians, then, the authors do not pretend to uncover or simply to be led by Aristotle's own thought. Nevertheless, in the interests of full clarity, Aristotle's own treatment of the question of the good or flourishing can be brought to bear on many of their assertions—their Aristotle made young may have something to learn from his older, perhaps less beautiful, ancestor. I take up three examples in support of this suggestion: (1) the individualized character of human flourishing, (2) the nature of self-direction, and (3) the political conditions of flourishing. I consider in the context of these examples the light that Aristotle sheds on the current dilemma of liberalism and, in conclusion, raise the question of whether, nevertheless, the authors' prescriptions represent the best possible practical solution to it.

In their neo-Aristotelian version of perfectionist ethics, the authors argue that flourishing is not only objective and inclusive (it includes all ends that are final), it is also individualized and diverse: "dependent on *who* as well as *what* one is" (p. 132, emphasis in text). Their argument rests importantly on the claim that individuals are not mere "placeholders or loci" for the instantiation of some ultimate good—that what is good for each is contingent upon the "circumstances, talents, endowments, interests, beliefs and histories that descriptively characterize each individual" (p. 133). Accordingly, the neo-Aristotelian account of flourishing is both objective and plural: "There are many *summa bona*, because each individual's flourishing is the *summum bonum* for him- or herself and because there is no single *summum bonum* without unique form or apart from the lives of individual human beings" (p. 134).

Now, in one sense, Aristotle appears to agree with the claim that individual happiness is tied to the fulfillment or satisfaction of the needs, desires, and capacities of particular individuals in particular circumstances. In his discussion of justice in the *Nicomachean Ethics*, he even counsels individuals, who "pray for and pursue" the good things simply, not to do so but to "choose the things that are good for them."[1] Unlike Rasmussen and Den Uyl, however, Aristotle clearly does not equate these particular instances of individual goods with human flourishing at its peak or, in short, with the highest human good. He does not remain at the level of individual or particular ends in the matter, arguing that the hierarchy of ends itself raises the question of whether there is some good, the best, in the realm of action that we wish for and on account of which we choose other things. He suggests that the significance of this question for human beings, who wish the good for themselves, is of "great weight" and that, moreover, every human being born into a political community receives an authoritative answer to this question—an answer which, as authoritative, invites investigation.[2] When Aristotle sorts through alternative views of the good, he thus does so to see whether there is a fulfillment or completion that is best or most complete and which is, therefore, the standard, if not a possibility, for all. He also seeks to consider whether the authoritative political answer is the true good for a human being.

Aristotle's treatment of the good sheds light on the authors' own argument about flourishing in at least two ways. First, despite their claim that the good is individualized, they have difficulty completely eschewing a ranking of goods, having recourse instead to what they call "generic" goods that imply a ranking: for example, "knowledge, friendship, justice, creative work, leisure, pleasure, health, aesthetic appreciation, honor, self-esteem, and moral virtue" (p. 171). The authors claim that this list is open-ended and subject to revision, but especially given what becomes their emphasis on self-direction and practical reason, some if not all of these goods are necessary to a good life—for all individuals—and are even constitutive of it. Moreover, given the authors' own well-placed concern that ethics not become socialized—that the state or society not be viewed as the moral arbiter of our actions—there is a compelling reason to take up the investigation of the good in the manner of Aristotle, that is, as a "political investigation."[3]

Perhaps the authors could object that both of these issues can be resolved in their version of human flourishing by recalling its central constituent: self-direction or choice. Yet, here too, Aristotle's consideration of the matter is a helpful challenge, for self-direction or choice is a much vexed question in his treatment of the good, and a consideration of Aristotle's view would cast some doubt on whether self-direction must or can be what the authors claim for it: "the central necessary constituent or ingredient of human flourishing" (p. 140).

According to Rasmussen and Den Uyl, self-direction springs from the capacity for intellectual "insight" or "apprehension" (p. 138), and, in the context of this claim, the authors also recall the three conditions of virtuous action that Aristotle lays down in the *Nicomachean Ethics*: "(1) The agent must act in full consciousness of what he is doing. (2) He must 'will' the action, and will it for its own sake. (3) The act must proceed from a fixed and unchangeable disposition (*Nicomachean Ethics*, 1105a31–32)" (p. 139, authors' translation). The authors conclude in this context that "only by initiating and maintaining the effort to gain the knowledge, to cultivate the proper habits of character, to exercise correct choices, and to perform the right actions can someone achieve moral excellence" (p. 139).

Yet, as the authors' own summary of Aristotle's view of moral excellence already indicates, his treatment of choice counsels sobriety about the conditions and possibility of self-direction. In particular, Aristotle's emphasis on the role of habituation in moral education—a consideration largely absent from the authors' account of flourishing—raises troubling questions about the freedom of human action and therefore about self-direction understood as a form of free choice, as opposed to a "fixed and unchangeable character" formed by habituation. It is true that the authors touch upon the question of whether children, for example, could be said to be self-directed, but they offer no sustained consideration of the character of moral education and its connection with habituation, which, Aristotle notes, involves a form of force or coercion.[4]

For Aristotle, in brief, to know and to choose on the basis of a fixed and unchangeable disposition proceeds from the habituation of the irrational part of the soul that is the seat of the desires and longings—and not, for example, from a faculty of the will, even one developed through the proper education. The education at which habituation aims is provided and supported by law, which in the best case represents "right reason" (*orthos logos*) but is still a form of compulsion.[5] In the best case, such an education produces virtuous human beings—those capable of making the right choice for the right reasons on the basis of the character or disposition to which they've been habituated. From the point of view of the political community, these are human beings who are, in particular, "obedient to law."[6] Whether action that is obedient to law can be also called self-directed is a serious question in its own right and for moral and political theory.

The issue at stake is not whether the authors get Aristotle right. Indeed, they acknowledge that their version of self-direction may not be Aristotle's "ultimate position" and insist only that it is the ultimate position of "the neo-Aristotelian conception we are advancing" (p. 139). The issue at stake is whether the neo-Aristotelian conception of self-direction is fully consistent with the requirements of moral education, the nature of human action, and the necessities governing political life. In opposing confused strands of liberal theory that do not draw a hard enough distinction between politics and ethics, and that thereby undermine individual liberty, the authors so closely identify flourishing with the liberty of self-direction that it becomes hard to see the status or role of compulsion and coercion in moral education, human action, and politics.

To take up a final example that brings out the problem of compulsion most simply: the work is generally optimistic about the "compossibility" of individual forms of flourishing, especially in a liberal order that, taking the Rasmussen and Den Uyl prescriptions to heart, strives to protect the possibility of individual flourishing. The authors themselves admit to their optimism, albeit a qualified one, at the end of the work "because reality allows, for the most part, ample opportunity for most people to find fulfillment, at least to some extent, *if* they will but exercise the effort to use their minds and develop the appropriate virtues, and *if* there are political/legal orders whose structural conditions protect liberty" (p. 345, emphasis in text). But just how possible is the full flourishing of every member or even most members of a political association? I mean to ask not whether the authors overlook the inherent conflict of goods or forms of flourishing, that is, the conflict grounded in the opposition or tension between different ways of life, which the authors believe can be ameliorated under the right "metanorms," especially the basic negative right to liberty (p. 281). Rather, my question is whether the authors' emphasis on individual liberty and flourishing takes account of the prerequisites of every political association and, consequently, of the necessities connected with these prerequisites that are, for those burdened by them, an obstacle to flourishing.

Aristotle's tough-mindedness regarding politics is evidenced in part in his account of the political association as a compound whole, a topic central to Book 3 of his *Politics*. Although, as the opening of his *Politics* underscores, the political community promises our completion or flourishing, it also, as becomes clear in Book 3, entails particular kinds of necessary functions and actions: someone needs to sweep the streets, take out the garbage, dig the ditches, clean up the convention center, not to mention, defend the borders, police and protect us, guard malefactors, and so forth. The necessary and necessitous nature of these kinds of tasks—and Aristotle would include commercial activities as well as many others—has the effect that those who do them, even those of potentially good or high natures, are barred from and eventually made incapable of flourishing. Their natures are deformed by their function, a function that is necessary for the very existence of a political association. More precisely, those who are free to flourish depend on these functions—that they are done by others—and there is no guarantee that those who do them are such by nature as to be simply suited for them (see especially *Politics* 3, chapters. 4–5, 9, 12–13).

Indeed, by the authors' own account, most individuals are by nature suited to self-directed flourishing. Yet, it is not possible for any political community—even a liberal community—to overcome the harsh facts illuminated by Aristotle's investigation of the compound nature of the political association and the subordination of some natures to the prerequisites of the flourishing of others. If we do not acknowledge these facts, are we not in danger, as Aristotle would suggest, of perpetuating a kind of fraud?

As harsh as this question is, it can provoke serious reflection on the relation between the requirements of political life and the issues central to *Norms of Liberty*: the conditions of individual flourishing and the protection of liberty. It is true that an assessment of these harsh facts introduces a note of caution about the full flourishing of every individual. But it also suggests ways in which, for example, a limited politics can protect individuals from forms of authority, especially political and social forms, that would confine them to functions or to economic and social stations that do not accord with their talents, endowments, and interests—to their particular natures—simply on the basis of, say, birth or gender. Moreover, a consideration of Aristotle's treatment of the feature of individual liberty fundamental to the Rasmussen and Den Uyl version of flourishing—choice or self-direction—can illuminate not only the role but the power of political community in shaping its members' understanding of their good, and so underscore the need for a kind of education that investigates the authoritative opinions with a view to an independent understanding of the good.

Yet, in this connection, *Norms of Liberty* presents an appropriate challenge and perhaps the best practical solution to a liberalism that has become either unsure of itself or unaware of the dangers that threaten the individual liberty it most values. For to insist on the separation of ethics and politics and, at the same time, to argue for the centrality of self-direction and practical reason for a human flourishing worthy of the name may well protect and encourage the conditions for the possibility of flourishing and do so in the best way possible given the apparent failure of contemporary liberal theory to confront squarely its own shortcomings in the defense of liberty.

Notes

1. *Nicomachean Ethics*, 1129b4-6.
2. *Nicomachean Ethics*, 1094a18-b11.
3. *Nicomachean Ethics*, 1094b10-11.
4. See, for example, *Nicomachean Ethics*, 1102b29-1103a1, 1104b9-19, 1105b9-17, 1179b31-1180a24.
5. *Nicomachean Ethics*, 1102a7-10, 1103a1-10, 1103b31-34.
6. *Nicomachean Ethics*, 1102a7-10.

8

Moral Truth, Moral Disagreement, and the Agent-Relative Conception of Moral Value

Denis F. Sullivan

Norms of Liberty is a book about ethics and a book about politics, the ethical position presented as the basis for the political position. In the Western philosophical tradition, and, I presume, in every philosophical tradition, one of the major purposes of ethical thought is to provide guidance that would help us lead good human lives. One of the themes of this book is that, while ethics can and should provide guidance, this guidance should be left vague and that consequently individuals should be left free to shape their own lives. And, while there is certainly much more to their argument, just this point would seem to provide some basis for the conclusion that the proper function of the state is not to make citizens good but to protect the freedom they need to make themselves good.

The focus of this paper, however, is very narrow in scope. I will deal only with the ethical position the authors defend, and only a piece of that, namely, their rejection of universalizability as a requirement for moral judgments, or, in other words, their rejection of the persistent tendency to turn all our moral lore into moral law.[1] But I hope this paper will be of some significance because I will argue that this position, because of the light it sheds on the nature of our general moral beliefs, is of use in rebutting an assumption that has provided much of the ground for the common contemporary skepticism about the very possibility of moral truth.

Before starting, I should note that while I will be defending a position that the authors defend, I will be doing so in a different way, by looking at the use of descriptions in justifying moral judgments. Furthermore, while the authors defend their position as part of a neo-Aristotelian package, I will be defending it as a stand-alone position. But this should say only so much more for the strength of the position they take.

One of the common themes in contemporary philosophical thought is that moral propositions cannot be true, at least not in any robust sense. Thus in the prescriptive or emotive theory[2] the claim is made that in saying an action is good all we are doing is recommending that action or, to be more precise, recommending that actions of that kind be performed. This theory does not quite eliminate truth from moral claims. For, on this theory, in saying that an action is good I am saying something that could be true of that action, namely, that that action is recommended by me. (This could also turn out to be false of that action if in saying the action in question was good I was not sincere.) But while this theory does admit truth into moral discourse, it admits it in such a limited way that it eliminates any distinction between what is valued and what is valuable, between what seems to be good and what is good, and this is a distinction that no one who thinks seriously about ethics would want to do without.

The prescriptive theory of ethics should not be viewed as just a technical, philosophical stand, for it has its reflection in the speech of people who are not professional philosophers. In ethics courses, for example, one often hears students mark a distinction between questions of fact and questions of value, and then go on to say that when it comes to questions of value, as opposed to questions of fact, it is just a matter of opinion. And by this they do not seem to mean that in saying, for example, that an action is good, we are expressing what we believe, for this is what we do when we utter a sentence about the current state of the weather. Rather, what they seem to mean is that if someone says that an action is good, and she is sincerely expressing what she believes, there is no possibility of error. But what can eliminate the possibility of error in this way except the claim that in saying an action is good all I am doing is recommending it?

John Mackie has famously, or infamously, defended a very different position. He admits that if I say an action is good (or bad) I am attributing a property that an action has, if it has it, independently of what I happen to say or believe. But he goes on to argue that all we say in this way about action is false.[3] The problem here is that, as Mackie concedes, in everyday life, nobody can seriously believe this.

Still another position maintains that, while ethical statements cannot be called true in the same sense as the statements we make about the mass of a particle or the current state of the weather are true, they can be called true in a weaker sense. This is the position sketched by Quine[4] and elaborately defended in a more sophisticated way by Crispin Wright.[5] Roughly, the idea here is that the best we can do in ethics is to construct an ethical theory so that all its propositions are consistent with one another. Then we can call the sentences of this theory true in the sense that they are consistent with one another. The obvious problem here, as Quine admits, is that one could construct internally consistent moral theories, which are inconsistent with one another, and with no grounds for choosing any one of these theories over the others. This makes the truth we arrive at not really worth being called truth.

I certainly would not claim that the account of the philosophical positions I have just given is complete or even fair to those who defend them. But I am only interested in showing that the position they adopt, which involves the denial that what we say about actions being good and bad can be true in the common, robust sense, is a difficult one to defend. And this raises the question of why they have felt compelled to adopt such positions in the first place.

I would suggest that one of the primary factors leading to the suspicion or even conviction that we should not think of truth, in its standard robust sense, as being a property of moral propositions has to do with irresolvable disagreements. Thus Quine contrasts the strong method we have for resolving disagreements in science with the lack of such a method in ethics.[6] In science we can, in principle at least, resolve any theoretical disagreement by appealing to observations. The parties who initially disagreed would agree on what is observed and this agreement will provide the basis for resolving their initial disagreement. But, according to Quine, no such extra-theoretical source of agreement exists in relation to our moral theories for these theories themselves determine how we morally judge what we observe. Because of this contrast, Quine concludes that while science has "some title to a correspondence theory of truth," ethics has none.[7]

Quine's position could be challenged both for its assumption of an epistemic conception of truth (what is true must be provably so) and for its even sterner assumption that the only way we can justify what we say about how things really are is ultimately by an appeal to observations. But what gives Quine's position its force is a broader assumption shared by many both within and without the field of philosophy. This is the assumption that while one might find consistency in the moral beliefs of an individual or a limited set of individuals, the further one extends the range of people involved in moral discussion the more one runs into irresolvable disagreements. Now, if this is the case, there are no rational grounds for choosing one set of consistent but locally defined moral beliefs over any other such set of beliefs because to say that these locally defined sets of beliefs are separated by irresolvable disagreements would be to say that there are no criteria for such a choice. On the other hand, just to accept what people in general believe about good and bad is also not a credible option, for such an ethical "theory" would be marked by extensive, inexpugnable inconsistencies. A third option is to take everything everyone believes about good and bad, purge it of all irresolvable disagreements, and propose the residue as one's ethical theory. The problem with this suggestion is that, given the assumption we are considering, the moral theory arrived at in this way would be so slight that no one would be willing to accept it. So the conclusion would seem to be that it is a mistake to take what we say about good and bad, right and wrong, as an account of the way things are.

No one would deny that there exist now, as there has in every period of human history, significant moral disagreements that we have not yet been able to find ways to resolve. This, however, should not provide grounds for skepticism about truth in ethics, for similar disagreements are to be found even in the narrowly defined confines of science. Furthermore, it would not be surprising if there were more such disagreements in ethics than in science because our moral beliefs are much more intimately related to the way we live than are the beliefs we find in science. Consequently, it should be expected that pathology should play a greater role in the persistence of disagreements in ethics than in science. In other words, more often in ethics than in science one should expect to find people attempting to defend the indefensible.

The question, then, is not whether there are irresolvable disagreements in ethics or even whether there are more irresolvable disagreements in ethics than in science. Rather the question is: are irresolvable disagreements such a common and persistent feature of moral discourse that they raise questions about the existence of moral truth? I will argue that the agent-relative conception of ethics, defended by the authors of *Norms of Liberty* provides us with the grounds to answer this question.

There are moral disagreements about particular acts, for example Truman's decision to drop the bomb, and disagreements about general moral beliefs, that is, beliefs about the moral value of kinds of action. Clearly, the more fundamental issue has to do with general moral beliefs. For to the extent that there is agreement in general moral belief, the difficulty in resolving moral disagreements about particular acts would be a function of the difficulty in determining all the relevant facts of the case. So in this paper I will deal primarily with general moral beliefs. I will discuss first our beliefs about what is good and then turn to a special issue in connection with our beliefs about what is bad.

As Aristotle remarked long ago, it is a mistake to try to find in ethics the kind of precision one looks for in science.[8] A mistake of this sort is still with us. I will argue it is the implicit assumption that our moral beliefs should be thought of as having something like the precision we find in science that has led a number of philosophers, and many people outside the profession, to believe that irresolvable disagreement is such a common feature of moral discourse. But what an agent-relative approach to morality shows is that, for the most part, our general moral beliefs, that is, our beliefs about the moral value of certain kinds of actions have to be thought of as vague and when this element of vagueness is appreciated the illusion of relatively massive irresolvable moral disagreement disappears.

Let me start with an account of the concept of vagueness introduced by C. S. Peirce.[9] Peirce describes an assertion such as "Socrates is wise" as determinate with respect to its object in that it names the object of which the predicate in the assertion is held to be true; it has, in other words, a singular reference. If, on the other hand, an assertion does not identify a single object of which the predicate is to be true, it is general. (I am modifying Peirce's terminology.) If an assertion is, in this sense, objectively general, it would be either precise or vague. If it is precise, it leaves the interpreter free to pick, from a set of objects, an object of which the predicate is said to be true. "Man is mortal." "What man?" "Any man you please." If, on the other hand, an assertion is vague, such as "Some man in this room is a spy," "it reserves for some other sign or experience the function of completing the determination."[10] Note that an assertion can be vague and still have significant, that is, useful content to the extent that it narrows down the set of objects with regard to which a predicate may be true. Thus the assertions "some man in this city . . ." or "some man in this state . . ." would have far less useful content than "some man in this room is a spy."

This concept of vagueness has a fairly straightforward application to sentences expressing moral belief. Thus one might say "Giving alms to the poor is good" or "Inflicting pain on a human being is bad." But these sentences are not meant to be precise in Peirce's sense. The first does not mean "Any act you please, if it can be truly described as giving alms to the poor then it is good." And the second does not mean "Any act you please, if it can be truly described as inflicting pain on a human being then it is bad." Rather the first means "Generally, but not necessarily always, an act which can be truly described as giving alms to the poor is good." And the second means "Generally, but not necessarily always, an act which can be described as inflicting pain on a human being is bad." Thus both these sentences, like the sentence "Someone in this room is a spy," do tell us something useful in that they serve to narrow down the range of objects to which a predicate applies and so the claim that our moral beliefs are, for the most part, vague would be consistent with an insistence that they can provide real direction.

So far, following Peirce, I have been discussing the way in which vagueness can enter into moral beliefs in connection with the predicate. In the proposition "Giving alms to the poor is good" the predicate "good" is only vaguely attached to the subject "giving alms to the poor." It might seem that one could avoid this vagueness by recasting the subject as "reasonable acts of giving alms to the poor." Here, in response to the question "What reasonable acts of giving alms to the poor are good?" the answer would be "Any such acts you please." But it should be obvious that this ploy would take us nowhere because all we would be doing would be transferring the vagueness which was originally associated with the predicate to the subject. For the answer to the question "Which acts of giving alms to the poor are reasonable?" would certainly not be "Any such acts you please."

Now it might be thought that a sentence like "Giving alms to the poor is good" could be made precise by specifying the conditions under which such acts would be good. What an agent-relative approach to morality shows is that this cannot be done, and consequently, all our general beliefs about what is good and at least most of our general beliefs about what is bad must be vague. The argument for this point proceeds from an analysis of what is involved in making a particular moral judgment.

By a particular moral judgment I mean a judgment we make about an action. Now, actions are dated, unrepeatable particulars. This morning I buttered my toast. That action is gone and done with forever. We sometimes miss this obvious point because we speak of some individual performing the same action on a number of occasions or of a number of different people separately performing the same action. But what we mean when we say, for example, that an individual performed the same action a number of times is that this individual performed a number of actions and, with regard to each of these actions, the same description, for example, "he buttered his toast," was true.

We judge the moral worth of an action, as a dated, unrepeatable event, on the basis of some description which we hold to be true of it. It might seem, then, if we find that same description to be true of another action, we should judge that other action in the same way. What an agent-relative morality does is supply us with grounds for denying this conclusion and in so doing it provides us with grounds for holding that most of our general moral beliefs should be understood to be vague.

Let me begin by distinguishing between two conclusions, both of which I believe are implied by an agent-relative conception of morality, but only one of which is clearly endorsed by the authors of *Norms of Liberty*. The first conclusion, which they clearly endorse, is that a description can show that an action, as a dated unrepeatable particular, is good even if that description were never to be true of any other action.[11] They see this conclusion as significant in that it shows that it is distortion to think of morality as consisting of a set of universal laws that individuals are to apply to their various actions, a distortion that obscures the extent to which individuals should be allowed to shape their own moral lives. But I will argue that their position on agent-relative morality supports an even stronger conclusion: any description, no matter how complete, that shows that one action is good, could be true of another action and still not be sufficient to show that this other action is also good. This second conclusion puts even more emphasis on the individualistic nature of what is involved in leading a good life.

The authors point out that, in a given situation, what might be good for one agent might not be good for another because of a difference in background, ability, interest, and so on (pp. 132–38). But this point depends on how the situation is described. Certainly a chair that might be a good place for one person to sit might not be a good place for another because of a difference in the size and weight of the individuals. But there is nothing to prevent us from describing the situation in such a way as to take into account the size and weight of these individuals. Furthermore, we might extend the description of the situation to take in abilities, interests and so on, of the individual agent. So it would seem if we loaded up enough details in the description that showed an action to be good then this description would be such that if it happened to be true of another action it would show that other action would also be good.

I believe the authors of *Norms of Liberty* would respond to this point by saying that a description so loaded with detail would rarely apply to any other situation. In a paper they quote approvingly Sir David Ross's statement that "the only safe way to apply Kant's test of universalizability is to envisage the act in its whole concrete particularity."[12] Ross's phrase "to envisage the act in its whole concrete particularity" would, if taken literally, mean saying everything that was true of the act except, one would have to assume, for the time and place of its occurrence. And if we were to come up with such a description the possibility it would ever be true of another act would be, to say the least, negligible. And thus universalizability in any strict sense should not be seen as playing a significant role in moral thought.

Furthermore, with respect to Ross's suggestion that we "envisage the act in its whole concrete particularity," I would say that this is impossible. If we take an act, as he seems to be doing, as a dated, unrepeatable particular, there are an infinite number of things that could be said that would be true of this act. If, for example, one of the descriptions that was true of this act was "she moved her hand," then the description "she changed the position of her hand in relation to Jupiter's moon Io" would also be true of this act. And similar things could be said with regard to any astronomical body or any other body one could name. Thus the idea that we could ever arrive at a complete description of an act is an illusion.

Perhaps, it might be suggested, a more realistic goal would be to come up with a complete description of all the morally relevant aspects of the act. Here we would bump into the problem of supplying criteria for determining what is morally relevant and what it not. I doubt we can come up with such criteria; I can easily imagine that how a particular food tastes to an individual might be morally relevant. But, putting this point aside, what makes a particular act, that is an act performed on a particular occasion, a good act is not just the characteristics it has, but also the characteristics it doesn't have. Thus a particular act might be good not only because it could be truly described as "donating to a charitable organization" but also because it could not be truly described as "putting the agent in position in which she could not fulfill a vital familial obligation." So if we are to come up with a description of a particular action which was good and which was complete in the sense that, if this description were true of any other action, that action would also be good, this description would have to include more that just a specification of all the conditions which lead us to say the action was good; it would also have to include, in a series of negation, a specification of all the conditions which were not true of that action that, had any of them been true, it would have changed the evaluation. But this is virtually as impossible as "envisaging the act in its whole concrete particularity."

In one of his papers, Henry Veatch quotes Frankena's formulation of the principle of universalizability in ethics: "moral and value predicates are such that if they belong to an action or object, they also belong to any other action or object which has those same properties."[13] Veatch then goes one to say that "one can hardly fault such a principle of universalizability in itself," although he criticizes the use that Frankena makes of it.[14]

I am suggesting that we go further than Veatch and abandon this principle as useless.

All the descriptions, then, that we might use to call an action good must admit exceptions; there can always be occasions on which such a description is true of an action and that action is not good. Consequently, all our general moral beliefs about what kinds of actions are good should be taken to be vague.[15] They tell us that certain kinds of actions are often, but not necessarily always good. And I would say that this is also true of most of our general beliefs about what kinds of actions are bad. I would be reluctant, however, to say this is the case with regard to all of our beliefs about kinds of actions that we believe to be bad.

I would be reluctant to say that this is true of all the beliefs we employ in judging which actions are bad because of an ancient and enduring tradition which is often formulated in a somewhat misleading way by saying that certain actions are intrinsically evil.[16] I call this formulation misleading because the position is not really just about actions, but rather about actions and the descriptions that are held to be true of them. What this positions maintains is that there are certain descriptions, for example, "intentionally killing an innocent," that are such that if one of those descriptions is true of an action, that action is wrong, *no matter what other descriptions might also be true of it*. The point here is that once we are satisfied that such a description is true of an action, we need not consider any other details about that action. The action is wrong and should not have been or should not be done.

The arguments I have been using so far would not be relevant to such intrinsically evil acts. Thus if one believes that "stealing" is a description of an intrinsically evil act, when one says "stealing is wrong" one is not saying that generally, but not always, if one can truly describe an action as stealing, it is wrong. Rather, one is saying any action which can be truly described as stealing is wrong. And if one judges that a particular act is stealing, then no consideration of the other details of that act can change the judgment that it is wrong.

There is a medieval principle: *Bonum ex integra causa, malum ex quocumque defectu*. If one takes this as a moral principle and interprets it to mean "an act is good, if it is good in all respects; it is bad, if it is bad in any respect," then it is entirely implausible. Many of the acts we would call good, and certainly all those actions we would call heroically good, involve things that we would call bad, such as pain, suffering, the loss of wealth and even the loss of human life. But this principle, as a moral principle, can be seen as legitimate if it is taken as indicating an asymmetry between what is involved in judging that an action is morally good and judging that an action is morally bad. To say that an action is morally good is to say that it is good, all things considered. But if one accepts the idea that there are descriptions that specify actions as intrinsically evil, and if one finds that one of these descriptions is true of an action, then all things need not and should not be considered. That action is bad.

The belief that certain kinds of actions are, in this sense, intrinsically evil plays a significant role in the lives of most people by setting absolute boundaries to what, even in terrible situations, they might consider doing. But such beliefs are certainly not central because, among other things, we do not live a good life by *not doing things*. Consequently it would not seem that any intractable disagreements we might have about such beliefs would not be sufficient to raise questions about the very possibility of moral truth. And there is a way in which vagueness also might play a role even in connection with such beliefs. On the assumption that stealing is a description of an intrinsically evil act, all acts of stealing would be wrong. So the predicate "wrong" would not be vaguely attached to the subject "stealing." But vagueness could still enter into this proposition on the part of the subject in the sense that it could be unclear whether or not a particular act was in fact stealing. The point here is that some of the actions we might initially call stealing might, on closer examination, turn out not to be stealing at all. Here again we find the conclusion to which an agent-relative morality leads: it is the complex of details of the actual act that determine the evaluation.

What an agent-relative approach shows, then, is that, with respect to our general moral beliefs, moral disagreements are not nearly as common as they are often thought to be. It shows this by demonstrating that most, if not all, of our general moral beliefs have got to be taken to be vague. Thus any citation of instances which supposedly show that what we generally believe to be good turns out to be bad, or what we generally take to be bad turns out to be good, need not be seen as a disagreement with these beliefs. And even in connection with that narrowly defined class of beliefs that purportedly identify intrinsically evil acts, a recognition of vagueness can go some way toward resolving moral disagreement.

I should emphasize that the point I am making has to do with an actual act, something someone has actually done. I say this to distinguish it from the kind of classroom or armchair discussion in which one says: "Consider a case in which . . ." and then one goes on to imagine an act and the situation in which it is performed. With regard to a real act, an act that has, on a particular occasion, been performed, it is not unreasonable to think that we can often come to an agreement as to whether the act is, say, an act of theft, on the basis of discovering what descriptions are true of this act. But this possibility does not exist in connections with imagined scenarios because with regard to such scenarios only what is stipulated to be the case constitutes the facts of the case.

This leads to one further point. What I have been arguing so far is that an agent-relative approach shows that irresolvable disagreements with regard to our general moral beliefs are not nearly as common as they are often thought to be. But there are also disagreements about particular acts, acts as dated, unrepeatable events. With regard to such disagreements, I would suggest that we are often too quick to judge the actions of others on the basis of an incomplete knowledge of what is going on. "What she did in leaving her husband and children was wrong." It could be that if we knew more about her action, if we had a more complete description of what she did, it would become clear that what she did was not wrong at all. This point becomes even more prominent in judging actions of people living in cultures very different from our own. This certainly doesn't mean we should never judge the actions of other people, even of people living in a very different culture. But we should be more careful than we often are in making such judgments because of the difficulty in determining, especially for people in other cultures, just what morally relevant descriptions are true of the actions we judge. I would suggest that our tendency to rush to such judgments is another factor in creating the illusion that there is much more irresolvable moral disagreement than, in fact, there really is.

The basic thesis of this paper is primarily negative. The conclusion I have tried to defend is that what an agent-relative (perhaps it might be better called an act-relative) approach to morality shows is that, contrary to what is commonly assumed, irresolvable moral disagreement is not so common that it should raise doubts about the very existence of moral truth. I would like to conclude with a brief suggestion of how we might be able to formulate a more positive argument for moral truth. This argument is derived from the work of Thomas Aquinas.[17]

Aquinas maintains that all true moral beliefs are either common, and by this he means accepted by all, or logically derivable from such common beliefs. Consequently, if there were a disagreement about the truth of a moral proposition, that disagreement would have to be, in principle, resolvable. For, if there is a disagreement about a moral belief, and that belief is true, it would be possible to eventually show the person who rejects this belief that it follows from some other belief that she finds she cannot reject and so the disagreement would be resolved. On the other hand, if it becomes clear that the disputed belief does not follow from any other belief that all the parties to the disagreement accept, and admittedly it is obscure as to how this would become clear, then the disputed belief would be shown to be false. So here again, the disagreement would be resolved. In other words, for Aquinas, if one can show that a moral disagreement is truly irresolvable, that disagreement is resolved. So that to the extent we become convinced that a disagreement cannot be resolved, to that extent we should be convinced that it is resolved.

Of course, if irresolvable disagreements are common features of moral discourse, then the position of Aquinas would not work, for when one had resolved, in the way suggested by the work of Aquinas, all irresolvable disagreements, then, as was noted earlier, what would be left would be an ethical position so slight that no one would be willing to accept it. But if the argument of this paper works, such an objection can be set aside.

What the argument of Aquinas presupposes, however, is that we should accept what he calls our common moral beliefs as evidence in the same way that we now accept the observations appealed to in science. But even if there are common beliefs which play the role Aquinas assigns to them, why should we accept them in this way as evidence for truth? To answer this question would be beyond the scope of this paper. But I would suggest that material for an adequate answer to this question might be found in Donald Davidson's argument that, given what is required to learn a language, our general beliefs, including our general beliefs about what is good and what is bad, have to be true.[18]

Notes

1. "The essence of moral conduct is not action in accord with some universal rule. . . . *What lies at the heart of ethics for us is not the universalizable but the meliorizable*" (*Norms of Liberty*, 193).

2. The position I am referring to is described by Alasdair MacIntyre as emotivism. See Alasdair MacIntyre, *After Virtue: A Study in Moral Theory* (Notre Dame: University of Notre Dame Press, 1981), 6–21. I would be reluctant to use this term because, as originally introduced by A. J. Ayer, it designated the claim that moral sentences, taken precisely as moral sentences, say literally nothing at all.

3. John Mackie, *Ethics: Inventing Right and Wrong* (Penguin Books, 1977).

4. Willard V. O. Quine, "On the Nature of Moral Values" in *Theory and Things* (Cambridge, Mass.: Harvard University Press, 1981), 55–66.

5. Crispin Wright, *Truth and Objectivity* (Cambridge, Mass.: Harvard University Press, 1992). See also "Truth in Ethics" in *Truth in Ethics*, Ed. B. Hooker (Oxford: Blackwell, 1966), 1–18.

6. Quine, 63.

7. Quine, 63.

8. Aristotle, *Nicomachean Ethics*, 1094b 11–23.

9. *The Collected Papers of Charles Sanders Peirce*, Vol. VII, eds. Charles Hartshorne and Paul Weiss (Cambridge, Mass.: The Belknap Press of Harvard University, 1934), 505.

10. Peirce, 505.

11. The authors say that considerations can justify a moral judgment even if these considerations *may not* serve to justify such a judgment for any other person (p. 134). And elsewhere they write that "there is no justification for regarding considerations that only apply to one person as morally irrelevant" (p. 21).

12. David Ross, *Kant's Ethical Theory* (Westport Ct.: Greenwood Press, 1978), 34. The authors use this quote as an epigraph for their paper "In Search of Universal Political Principles."

13. W. K. Frankena, *Ethics*, 2nd ed. (Englewood Cliffs, N.J.: Prentice-Hall, 1973), 82, quoted in H. B. Veatch, "On the Use and Abuse of the Principle of Universalizability," *Proceedings of the American Catholic Philosophical Association*, Vol. LI (1977), 162–70.

14. Veatch, 165.

15. From a logical point of view it could be said that what I am calling a vague proposition is really an existentially quantified proposition. In other words the proposition "Giving alms to the poor is good"

should understood as "Some (at least one) acts of giving alms to the poor are good." But this would obscure the point, which is that the positions which express our moral beliefs at the very least narrow down that range of actions that could be called good and thus create a presumption that a certain kind of action would be good.

16. I have discussed this issue in "Intrinsically Evil Acts: Clarifying a Confused Debate" *Proceedings of the American Catholic Philosophical Association*, Vol. LXXII (1998), 329–40.

17. I have discussed this position in "Disagreement and Objectivity in Ethics: Aquinas on the Common Precepts of the Natural Law," *Proceedings of the American Catholic Philosophical Association*, Vol. 74 (2001), 231–44. What follows involves a slight modification of the position I took in this earlier paper.

18. Donald Davidson, "The Objectivity of Values" in *Problems of Rationality* (Oxford: Clarendon Press, 2004), 39–57.

9

Reflections on *Norms of Liberty*: What Makes Liberty Worthy of the Name?

Timothy Fuller

This is an admirable work in several dimensions. First, it is among the most comprehensive surveys of modern liberalism of which I am aware. Virtually every major contributor to thought on liberalism, for and against, from the seventeenth century forward, is discussed in illuminating and intelligent ways. Second, the authors have a well developed point of view about the liberal tradition, about what it is and what it is not, and about how they think it can best be articulated and defended. There is no doubt that it is a significant contribution to the political philosophy of the liberal tradition. Here is a work which both synthesizes a wide range of the literature, offers original views of the subject, and provokes renewed discussion of just what the character of liberal thought is.

Among its distinctive features are:

1. A demonstration of the continuity between Aristotelian thought on ethics and politics and modern liberal thought. This is important because it denies, in effect, the oft-asserted radical dichotomy between "ancients" and "moderns," offering a way to reconceive this relationship as complementary rather than antagonistic.
2. A demonstration that the fundamental aim of liberal thought is to achieve well-functioning civil order and

civility—stability consistent with the reality of individuality and self-interest—but not to prescribe a substantive ethics or "system of values." This point might not initially be seen as unusual or novel. But what distinguishes the argument here is the authors' insistence, contra various contemporary critics of the liberal tradition, that this is not a defect but a strength of liberal thought. They note the frequent criticism of liberalism that it is inadequate ethically and morally, or that it fails to address ethical and moral issues, or that it dwells entirely on increasingly trivial expansions of "rights." Their response is to say that liberalism properly understood does not intend to resolve moral/ethical questions, but does provide a framework in which the opportunity for individuals and groups to resolve such questions is enhanced, and they add to this by arguing further for the validity of an Aristotelian approach to resolving moral/ethical questions which they endorse as fully compatible with a basically liberal framework. They envision free assent to Aristotelian ideas of virtue. In short, a morally serious person might well pursue moral excellence in the deep sense of the ancient and medieval thinkers within the liberal framework—the liberal framework is not an excuse for dismissing or rejecting such an option. It is, of course, the case that some proponents of the liberal tradition do think these are incompatible, that allegiance to one demands rejection of the other. It must be kept in mind that the personal commitment of the authors to an Aristotelian approach to moral excellence must remain for them a personal commitment for which they are willing to offer arguments.

3. What they hope to offer is a realistic appraisal of political and social life. They argue that moral excellence cannot be imposed by government, while government can provide the framework within which serious moral inquiry can be undertaken. The polity is necessary to the moral life but not determinative of the moral life. The authors say:

> The moral propositions of a teleocentric perspective are concerned with their relationship to personal flourishing. There may

> be generic elements that resemble the Kantian conditions of universality, but of equal or superior importance to us—given our agent-centered perspective—are the elements of a moral judgment that include the particular, the partial, the interested, and the personal. These latter elements are as critical to the morality of an action as any universal features that might be applicable. (p. 60–61)

And they go on to distinguish "between different types of ethical principles—the normative and the metanormative—and this means that the moral and political can be distinguished more readily and that the temptation to confuse the one with the other is lessened" (p. 61).

Human flourishing is not accomplished in politics and by rules, although these are necessary features of a polity. What is required are (1) agent-chosen paths to flourishing and (2) a cooperative mechanism for civil purposes. We need both of these and both exist simultaneously in our experience in some form. The authors see this as combining Aristotelian ideas with Lockean negative natural rights. Human beings are both social and individual. Since there are Aristotelian elements in Locke's political philosophy, is this more than just reading Locke in whole rather than in part? If it is the latter, as I think it is, it is a welcome corrective to interpretations of Locke as implicitly rejecting the idea of moral excellence or reducing it to "bourgeois virtues." The authors, nevertheless, might be more attentive to the mystery of the human situation in which the aspiration for moral excellence is in tension with a polity that can defeat as well as promote it.

Later the authors say this: "If self-direction were not involved, human flourishing would not *be* human flourishing. Self-direction is the central necessary constituent or ingredient of human flourishing. It is that feature of human flourishing without which no other feature could be a constituent. That is to say, it is both a necessary condition for, and an operating condition of, the pursuit and achievement of human flourishing" (p. 140). Yet also "It is a fundamental mistake to conceive of human beings achieving maturity or flourishing apart from others and only later taking it upon themselves to join society or to have social concern" (p. 142).

Yet they do recognize that they must address the possibility of universal characteristics of flourishing even if these must be realized in individual human beings in their relations with other individual human beings. Flourishing is achieved in practice, not merely in the abstract. This is a good Aristotelian point. To be moral is constituted in one's actual conduct; intellectual assent to moral propositions, though of course important, is insufficient. But Aristotle also thought in terms of the compact life of the *polis* where citizens shared a way of life in common. This gave a certain boundary and direction to the exploration of how one ought to live without having to depend on a system of abstract principles. Even so, however, Aristotle saw that there inevitably will be diversity in the manner in which agents flourish, in the way they each appropriate the way of life they share in common. Harmony, not unison. Since modern liberal societies are highly differentiated and not compact, the conditions are different and the guide to the use of liberty cannot, it seems, be the same. One must wonder, therefore, if invoking Aristotelian ideas requires a distinctly "modern" or principled Aristotle, one that serves the background conditions of modern liberal polities. How Aristotelian is their Aristotle? What is the ground for preferring their Aristotelianism to some other outlook?

The authors also address natural law theory in both old and new forms, and they describe their "individualistic perfectionism" as a natural law theory, albeit not a supernaturalist theory. They accept the idea that human flourishing is objective and not merely a matter of opinion. They are modern "NL theorists" in emphasizing strongly the role of the agent in balancing the various goods to be sought in a manner suitable to each individual's situation. They deny that every agent-determined weighting of goods to be sought is equally valid with every other. But the question of how to judge the relative merits of the various weightings of goods necessarily arises. This question is dramatized by the fact that the authors also deny that individuals are merely the locations in which the basic goods are instantiated in the world, insisting that the reality of the goods is to be found only in the individuals and not independently of them. Whether they are right in arguing that John Finnis and Robert George are properly to be criticized on this score is a matter requiring further reflection. Rasmussen and Den Uyl say "Strictly speaking, we should not say that a human being is a locus of human flourishing or that flourishing occurs in an individual. Rather, we should say that a human being is a flourisher or that an individual is flourishing. Though we may abstractly speak of a *summum bonum*, there are in reality only many *summa bona*" (p. 190). This is a tricky point in the argument both on its own grounds and with respect to the issue of judging better and worse flourishings in agents. Are agents appropriating something that has independent significance, thereby giving it local habitation and a name? Are agents continually inventing or constructing something? Are Rasmussen and Den Uyl nominalists? What is this anti-foundationalist natural law theory? Is it anything more than a description of some background considerations that inevitably enter into moral deliberation? Can it offer direction to moral deliberation?

Even if we accept their argument that goods are only instantiated in individuals, we still could ask in what sense individuals participate in goods or the good. Is there not a linkage that is unexplained here? This issue eventually brings one back to the question of the transcendent or the supernatural structure of reality. To do what they want to do would seem to necessitate serious consideration of a larger structure of reality in which human beings participate even though they are individual agents. At this point theorists such as John Finnis and Robert George retain connections to the Aristotelian/Christian tradition of natural law thinking, but are at the same time believers in the real agency of individuals. The new natural law theorists do not fail to notice the immense variety of ways people choose to live, but they do say, Finnis for instance, that one should always intend to pursue the full range of basic goods even while, practically speaking, balancing them in different ways in differing circumstances. Thus there is not one right way of balancing, but there can be an improper imbalance if the balancing ignores or denies some basic goods in pursuing others. The emphasis thus is on the prudence or practical reasoning necessary to proceed successfully with balancing and rebalancing. To pursue knowledge as better than ignorance is not to say that there is a specific knowledge that must be the model for all knowing, but it is to suggest that it would be absurd to argue that ignorance is better than knowledge (such a proposition itself being knowledge, and so on). Does this not have a kind of universality such that it is not illiberal to take issue with individuals who would deny it? On the grounds that they are denying what is required for flourishing? That they are engaged in an absurdity? And how do we avoid the question of the relative merits of different sorts of knowledge once we agree that knowledge is self-evidently good. What the authors have shown is that there is great variety. Whether they have shown that the fact of great variety precludes agreement on the best sort of human life remains a matter for argument. At the same time, those making such an argument are afforded a place in a liberal regime of the sort they defend. But, to use Charles Taylor's formulation, while our authors can countenance "common goods" can they accept "convergent goods"?

Finally, natural law theorists traditionally do not deny that flourishing must be different in different individuals. Aquinas held that we have a common final end but not as a mere species. It appears that the authors do not accept the idea of an end, but there is nothing definitive in the arguments they bring against it. I think they are right, however, to say that a liberal regime constitutes itself in wary skepticism about how to settle this issue. Yet the liberal regime cannot exclude this issue, or those who would seek to settle it, because it appears to be one of the natural alternatives for reflective thought to consider. In this respect, there remains tension between the requirements of a liberal regime and the quest for wisdom. While we may not expect the authors to resolve the tension, it does seem that they presuppose its insolubility.

In the end, the authors state that they defend liberalism by "linking modern politics with a premodern moral tradition . . . this combination may itself be a kind of post-modernism" (p. 338). But their postmodernism combines premodern ideas adapted through acceptance of fundamental assumptions of modern individualist liberalism, a combination of background conditions for achieving individual flourishing or moral perfection, with substantial reserve about specifying the form or forms that such perfection could or should take. Finally, some questions I would ask them to elaborate include: How do you identify moral failing apart from failing in lawfulness, civility, or sociability? How do you view patriotism or republican virtue? If there is no approach to answering these questions without violating civility or sociability, then the norms of liberty seem destined to remain pretty thin.

10

Human Flourishing and Voluntarist Self-Direction

James Stacey Taylor

In *Norms of Liberty*, Douglas B. Rasmussen and Douglas J. Den Uyl develop a neo-Aristotelian view of human flourishing that appeals to human nature. In developing this account of human flourishing Rasmussen and Den Uyl assume two things: that "human nature is teleological, that is, that human beings have a *telos* or natural function," and that "this natural function has moral import," such that "knowing what our natural function is tells us something about the character of human flourishing and that moral evaluation of human conduct is in terms of flourishing" (p. 117). These are controversial claims. The first, that human beings have a natural function, is subject to the straightforward challenge that humans do not have a distinctive function in the way neo-Aristotelians believe.[1] The second, that knowing what our natural function is tells us something about how we ought to behave, is subject to the charge that it commits the naturalistic fallacy, moving illegitimately from claims about what is to claims about what ought to be.[2] Rather than addressing these issues, however, I will in this paper turn to developing further Rasmussen and Den Uyl's account of human flourishing as essentially involving self-direction.[3] In particular, I will develop further their implicit argument against existentialist or voluntarist accounts of self-direction. As I will note in the conclusion, this will lend additional support to their neo-Aristotelian approach to ethics, insofar as it will show that liberty will only have value to an agent if it is bounded by the nature of her self.

Against Existentialist Self-Direction

In *Norms of Liberty* Rasmussen and Den Uyl adopt a neo-Aristotelian view of human flourishing, which is based on the assumption that human nature is teleological. If this is so, then human self-direction will be for the sake of the human good. And, as Rasmussen and Den Uyl note, "if self-direction is for the sake of the human good, then agency or self-direction is not radically free, as existentialists or voluntarists would apparently have it" (p. 118). Rasmussen and Den Uyl do not elaborate on this claim—which is unfortunate, since if they are correct here an important aspect of the so-called existentialist approach to philosophy will have been undermined. It seems, however, that their argument is this: (1) Human flourishing is the end of human life. (2) Human self-direction is thus naturally aimed at securing this end. (3) Hence (from 2 and 3), the aim of human self-direction is restricted. (4) Hence (from 3), not everything is choiceworthy for humans. (5) Hence (from 4), it is not the case that humans can choose *ex nihilo*. (6) Therefore, the existential claim that such radical choice is possible is false.

The Existentialist Response

If this is an accurate reconstruction of Rasmussen and Den Uyl's argument against the possibility of existentialist radical choice, however, it suffers from two serious problems. First, and most obviously, it rests on the assumption that human nature is teleological. Second, it rests on the assumption that humans cannot conform to their teleology by making radical choices; that their choices must, instead, be restricted to a certain set of individual ends. I will not defend here Rasmussen and Den Uyl's argument against the first objection. As they themselves note, a complete defense of this assumption is a task "for a much larger project"

(p. 117). However, a complete defense of the second assumption—that humans cannot conform to their teleology by making radical choices—is possible here, and it is to this I now turn.

In criticizing this argument of Rasmussen and Den Uyl, the existentialist might well charge that, even if we accept that human nature is teleological, this in itself does not obviously preclude an existentialist view of human nature. This is because, such an existentialist might argue, adult humans are to be distinguished from non-human animals by their ability to design their own wills. That is, unlike, for example, a dog, whose conative and volitional nature is fixed for it, humans are in the unique position of being able to decide their volitional natures for themselves. Given this, such an existentialist might continue, human flourishing would involve a person intentionally embracing this aspect of her nature and constructing her will for herself. Since this is so, such an existentialist might conclude, to truly flourish as a human one must make radical choices. Rather than not being radically free, then, as Rasmussen and Den Uyl would have it, authentic human self-direction is only exemplified in the making of radically free choices.

As it stands this existential criticism requires refinement. In particular, the existentialist needs to clarify whether humans will flourish only in making radically free choices, or whether they could flourish by making choices that are bounded by their self-imposed volitional natures *provided that* these natures are indeed self-imposed rather than imposed upon them by the contingencies of their circumstances, and then adopted as their own in bad faith. However, it is clear what the main thrust of this existentialist response is: That Rasmussen and Den Uyl err in assuming that a teleological account of human flourishing commits them to rejecting the possibility of radical choice.

The Incoherence of Radical Choice

On the face of it, this existentialist criticism is plausible. However, it is possible to respond to it on behalf of Rasmussen and Den Uyl by showing that the existentialist idea of the flourishing human being who constructs his own authentic will through engaging in radical choice is incoherent. To see this, it should first be noted that for a person's choices to be normative for him he must have some reason for making them. This claim need not commit us to the view that a person's choices are normative for him only if he has some particular reason in mind when he makes them. A person who acts spontaneously but who can *ex post facto* offer non-*ad hoc* justifications for his actions will still be acting for reasons. A person who chooses a will for himself through making a radically free choice will lack any reason for preferring one course of action over another; none of his choices will be normative for him. This is because in constructing his will de novo through making a radically free choice he will have had to have been entirely unbounded with respect to what will he could choose. He would thus have no reason to choose one will over another. The will that he does choose, then, will be one that he has no reason to adopt as his own. But, since this is so, even though this will might itself subsequently appear to give him reasons for action it will always be open to him to question why he should care about such normativity. This is because he had no reason for choosing the will that appears to provide such normativity to him. He thus has no reason for accepting the apparent normativity drawn from that will, over that which he could draw (albeit equally apparently) from another. A radically free agent, then, might be radically free, but he would lack all self-direction, for he would have no *self* to direct.

With this in hand, let us return now to the existentialist response to Rasmussen and Den Uyl's argument. Recall that this response was based on the claim that Rasmussen and Den Uyl fail to recognize that human flourishing might require the making of radically free choices, and so, even if we accept that human nature if teleological, this does not preclude an existentialist approach to understanding human nature, as they hold. The crucial part of this response to Rasmussen and Den Uyl is the claim that human nature might require the making of radically free choices. However, given the arguments above concerning the lack of normativity that existentialists would enjoy with respect to their post-radical choice choices, the existentialist view of human flourishing cannot be accepted. This is because to have an account of what it is for an X to flourish one must have an account of what it is to be an X. In emphasizing the possibility of making radical choices, choices that are unbound by any considerations whatsoever, however, the existentialist has erased the possibility of humans having any definitive nature, for were they to have this their choices would not be radically free. As such, then, through emphasizing radical choice the existentialists preclude themselves from offering an account of human nature that could ground an account of what it is for a human to flourish. Thus, since this is so, they preclude themselves from claiming against Rasmussen and Den Uyl that human nature might require the possibility of making radically free choices.

Two Existentialist Replies

Yet although this way of fleshing out Rasmussen and Den Uyl's rejection of existentialist or voluntarist accounts of self-direction might be plausible, their existentialist critics have two possible lines of response to it. First, they might simply claim that the possibility of making radical choices simply is constitutive of human nature, and no more determinate account need be given. Second, they might respond that the above line of argument is too strong, and proves too much—and so for this reason should be rejected.

Let us consider these two possible responses in order. At least initially, the first seems plausible. After all, it might be the case that human nature simply consists of the ability to make radically free choices, and thus humans will flourish were they simply to make such choices. There certainly seems to be no *a priori* bar to this. But this first response to the above defense of Rasmussen' and Den Uyl's position moves too quickly, for it overlooks what is required for something to have a nature such that it could be said to flourish or not. To begin, the concept of flourishing admits of degrees, and so for something to have a nature that could flourish it should be able to flourish to a greater or a lesser degree. But the claim that human nature just is the ability to make radically free choices does not admit of this, for one is either making such choices or one is not. There is no possibility that one might make a partially radically free choice. Furthermore, something's flourishing should be good for it. However, it is not clear how making a radically free choice would in itself be good for humans. Indeed, we typically think that the making of choices by humans is of primarily instrumental value for us, as furthering some further goal that we have—a view of the value of choice that cuts directly against that proposed by the existentialist. As such, then, without considerable argument to the contrary we seem not only to have no reason to accept the possible existentialist claim that human nature just is to make radically free choices, but we have reason to reject it.

The second existentialist response is more interesting: That the above line of argument in defense of Rasmussen and Den Uyl's position is too strong, and proves too much. This is because if it is true that a person's merely picking to adopt a particular preference structure for no reason precludes it from giving him any reason to act one way rather than another in the future, then when a person is ambivalent about endorsing a particular motivational structure and so has to just pick whether to endorse it precludes it from subsequently giving him reasons to act. However, the existentialist might continue, we typically don't think that ambivalence leads to a person's subsequently not having reasons for action when he acts on the preferences that he arbitrarily endorsed. Thus, it seems that we should not assume that when a person constructs a will for himself through radical choice this will undermine the possibility of his having reasons for his future actions.

This is a plausible response—but there are disanalogies between ambivalence and radical choice that serve to undermine it. When a person is ambivalent between endorsing or rejecting aspects of his preference structure that he has he will be in a situation whereby his motivational set gives him equally good reasons to accept it and reject it, and so he just has to pick whether to do so or not. However, this does not mean that this aspect of his motivational set would not give him reasons to act subsequent to its (arbitrary) endorsement. This is because prior to his recognizing that he was ambivalent towards it, it did give him reasons to act, reasons that were not dependent upon his own will. In picking to endorse aspects of his preference structure, then, he was picking to continue to be bound by the reasons that it gave him. Unlike the reasons that a will that is the construct of a radical choice would purport to impose upon a person, the reasons that would be imposed upon him by aspects of his preference structure that he picked to retain after being ambivalent towards it would not be entirely dependent upon his will, for they would have applied to him *prior* to his picking them. Although a person who picks to endorse aspects of his preference structure to resolve ambivalence would partially constitute himself in so doing, he would not be constructing himself *de novo*, and the reasons given by the preference structure that he picked would be supported by other aspects of his preference structure that he did not pick. Thus, it is not his endorsement alone that makes the reasons that flow from the aspect of his preference structure that he picks to endorse normative for him, as is the case with will constituted through radical choice. Rather, it is his endorsement of it together with its history of independently supplying him with reasons for action.

Conclusion

From the above arguments it is clear that Rasmussen and Den Uyl are correct to reject the existentialist, or voluntarist, conception of self-direction which essentially involves radical choice. This rejection of this conception of self-direction is not unimportant to their project, for it shows that liberty is only of value if it is bounded by the nature of the self that is engaged in the self-direction in question. And this claim is at the heart of their neo-Aristotelian approach to ethics.[4]

Notes

1. For discussion see Jerome C. Wakefield, "Aristotle as Sociobiologist: The 'Function of a Human Being' Argument, Black Box Essentialism, and the Concept of Mental Disorder," *Philosophy, Psychiatry, & Psychology* 7 (2000), 17-44.

2. For a discussion of this point see *Norms of Liberty*, pp. 117-18.

3. See *Norms of Liberty*, pp. 117, 123-24.

4. I thank the Social Philosophy and Policy Center at Bowling Green State University for the invaluable support that they afforded me while I completed this paper as a Visiting Scholar.

11

Flourishing Through Trade

William Kline

John Stuart Mill in *On Liberty* tells us that the "principle of free trade and the principle of liberty rest on different grounds and that the principle of individual liberty is not involved in the doctrine of Free Trade."[1] Mill is wrong. There is at least one moral consideration that unites, and grounds, the arguments for individual liberty and free trade: Human Flourishing. In their book, *Norms of Liberty*, Douglas Rasmussen and Douglas Den Uyl provide an account of how human flourishing grounds the principle of liberty in the political/legal framework of society. This paper extends their argument into economics as well, by showing that the principle of liberty protects trading for the same reason the right to liberty protects any other human activity: to protect the possibility of flourishing.

Mill does not argue for the distinction he makes between free trade and liberty. Perhaps, like many, he simply finds it obvious. The social and political realms are important in a way that the economic simply is not. Drawing on Mill's own arguments in *On Liberty*, we can see the importance of the pursuit of truth and experimentations in living not simply as increasing general utility but as also being integral to personal development. Mill is ostensibly not running an argument about flourishing. His concern is general utility, but his focus is on individual development and there is something about the individual exposed to many arguments and living styles, who then chooses his path in life, that makes that person's life worth living. People should not be pigs eating whatever swill is placed in front of them; even if unhappy they ought to emulate Socrates by choosing their own path. Liberty would matter in economics, the same way it does in the social and political sphere, only if there were moral considerations internal to the market, endogenous in market institutions, which affected individuals in a manner similar to their choices of beliefs and lifestyles. Mill clearly does not think this is the case, and he is not alone.

The economic model of perfect competition stipulates that agents cannot take pleasure in the utility of others, that they intend only their own gain through market activity, and that there is basically nothing more to trading than an agent getting what they want.[2] "The effect of the perfectly competitive market is to ensure, at the interpersonal level, the same freedom enjoyed by Robinson Crusoe in her [*sic*] solitude, while making possible the enormously expanded range of benefits afforded by exchange and the division of labour. . . ."[3] Those who uphold the model of perfect competition as a good approximation of what the market is, or should be, hold to the notion that trading is a subjective, instrumental, unsocial activity for satisfying selfish desires.

Unfortunately, many market critics also hold up the model of perfect competition as the essence of trading. Market critics who focus their attention on this model make the same point as Gauthier, but with a bit more verve and a difference in emphasis: Robinson Crusoe remains free in the perfectly competitive economy precisely because market activity continues to enforce his solitude. Robinson Crusoe remains alone in the market, locked into himself, because trading is thought to be a subjective, instrumental, unsocial activity for satisfying selfish desires.

This is an unfortunate view of trading. It is unfortunate because trading is a human activity. Like language, there are perhaps other animals that engage in trade, but none anywhere near as extensively as humans. To damn trading is to damn a large part of our lives. *A priori* definitions of trade that confine it to the narrow pursuit of instrumental desire satisfaction deserve our scrutiny. They especially do so when experience teaches us that the activity in question can be so much more than the theory allows. An analogy with sex is relevant here.

There is no doubt that sex can be a subjective, instrumental, unsocial activity for satisfying selfish desires. Yet, anyone who says that all sex is, and can ever be, is an activity for the purpose of a final grunt and groan ignores the broader meanings, purposes, and roles sex can and does have in our lives. The same goes for trading. Trading is not simply about a final grunt of physical exchange, although it can be. Experience shows us that trading can be an integral part of a flourishing life. This paper goes one step further and argues that experience also shows us that trading itself can be a flourishing *way of life*. Trading does not only help one to flourish, under the proper circumstances it can be how one flourishes as well. To make this argument we will use the definition of human flourishing Douglas Rasmussen and Douglas Den Uyl provide in their book *Norms of Liberty*. We shall see how trading, as an activity, satisfies each of the requirements for human flourishing and thus is justifiably included as not only a part of a flourishing life, but as a flourishing way of life itself.

According to Rasmussen and Den Uyl, the characteristics of human flourishing are that it is: "(1) objective; (2) inclusive; (3) individualized; (4) agent-relative; (5) self-directed; and (6) social" (p. 127). The activity of trading satisfies all of these requirements of human flourishing. An individual can flourish through trading because trading, as an activity, is a good which is objective, inclusive, individualized, agent-relative, self-directed, and social. This claim requires showing how trade satisfies each of these elements of a flourishing life.

Human flourishing is objective. The objectivity of human flourishing stems from the kinds of beings we are. Part of this objectivity is found in a biocentric context that recognizes the physical and animal nature of human beings. Flourishing includes those things we need for self-preservation and survival, but it is also something more. Flourishing is a way of living, a way which is integral to our shared nature as human beings (p. 128). For Rasmussen and Den Uyl, the most important aspect of this nature is self-direction and choice. We are, in the end, beings that must choose for ourselves and this is why flourishing does not simply, if at all, consist in getting what we want. Flourishing is activity guided by our own choices that serves our good as human beings.

Satisfying our biocentric needs in a way that permits flourishing requires trading with other individuals. We simply do not have the time or knowledge to produce everything for ourselves and then also have the time to satisfy those elements of our nature that are not bound to pure survival. The broader the scope of trade, the more extensive the division of labor, and the better we can satisfy our basic needs for survival.

Trading, though, is more than getting what we need to survive. Adam Smith makes the observation that in addition to the beneficial effects of trade, we have a natural propensity to truck and barter.[4] In this light, trading is not simply something that we happen to do to get the things we need and want. We trade because of what we are. Trading is an objective good because it serves our biocentric need for physical survival in a manner that is fundamentally human.

Human flourishing is inclusive. There are many activities that both lead to, and are constitutive of, human flourishing. "Such goods as knowledge, health, friendship, creative achievement, beauty, and pleasure; and such virtues as integrity, temperance, courage, and justice. These are valuable not as mere means to human flourishing, but as expressions of it, and thus as partial realizations of it as well. As such, these goods and virtues are final ends and valuable in their own right" (p. 130). Trading deserves a place on this list as well. Like other goods and character traits, trading is an activity that is a means to human flourishing. Often overlooked, though, is that it is also expressive of, and integral to, our human nature. Trading is a means and an end in a flourishing life. Unfortunately, the latter is often denied because of the obvious existence of the former. However, Rasmussen and Den Uyl correctly point out that with respect to human flourishing, rather than Kantian autonomy, final ends need not be only final ends. The fact that trading is pursued for the sake of other things need not preclude that fact that trading is also something valuable in its own right.

Whether it is finding the best sale in town, haggling in the bazaar, or negotiating real estate deals, there is an art to trading that can be enjoyed for its own sake.[5] Purchasing can be done in a manner that is both a means to an end and an end in itself. There are those who are good shoppers and, while it makes their lives better, they are also proud of simply being good buyers. The same holds true for selling and negotiating. It is not just that people enjoy these activities. Trading is an expression and realization of our faculties of reason and speech. Using these faculties well is something valuable in itself. Even if not the most final end, trading can be an end in a flourishing life.

Human flourishing is individualized. Because there are many possible ends that could constitute a flourishing life, and there is no preset algorithm for how to choose among these, there is no single form of human flourishing. Flourishing "is dependent on *who* as well as *what* one is" (p. 132). Our individual personalities and circumstances morally matter. While there may be generic goods and virtues valuable to humans *per se*, how we weigh those goods and virtues is "rooted in factors that are unique to each person, for it is not the universal as such that is valuable" (p. 133).

This is precisely the insight of marginal utility theory in economics.[6] Goods and services are not valued as a type, they are only valued according to their least valuable use for an individual. The marginal utility of a good is the value of one additional unit of the good. Given that the most urgent desires are satisfied first, each additional unit will go to satisfying a lesser desire. The larger the supply, the lower the value that any single unit of the good will have. There is no value of bread or diamonds as such. A loaf of bread on a desert island would be vastly more valuable to an individual than that same loaf in a supermarket. In the former case the least value that loaf has is to sustain life and in the latter case there are so many loaves that they may be used to feed the birds.

Marginal utility, though, is not solely a function of supply. The marginal utility of a good to an agent depends upon the decision maker's individual personality and knowledge. If the agent does not like bread, does not know the actual supply, or has found a hitherto unknown use for bread, this affects her valuation. It is this local, individualized knowledge that informs practical economic calculation and that Hayek identifies as beyond the scope of any one single mind.[7] Flourishing through trade is individualized and diverse not contingently, but as a matter of our human nature with regards to valuation and knowledge.

Human flourishing is agent-relative. Individual personality, circumstances, and knowledge determine how an agent values specific goods and services, but it is how those things relate to the evaluating agent that determines what she must do to flourish. An individual may evaluate the monetary value of a loaf of bread at one, or even a hundred dollars, but it is the relation of the good to the evaluating agent that determines whether she should sell or eat it. "Abstractly stated, human flourishing, F, for a person, P, is agent-relative if and only if its distinctive presence in a world W1 is a basis for P ranking W1 over world W2, even though F may not be the basis for any other persons ranking W1 over W2" (p. 134). My flourishing is not your flourishing. How I balance the values that constitute my flourishing may be very different from the values you must balance, and how you balance them, to flourish. For something to be of value to an agent's flourishing it need not be valuable to everyone or, indeed, anyone else.

Buyers and sellers in the market realize the agent-relativity of value. Trading requires both parties consent to the exchange. Achieving consent requires that agent A offer to agent B for good x something, y, that agent B values more than x. Let us take W1 as the world of the successful trade where, after trading, A possesses x and B possesses y. Let us take as W2 the world before the trade where A possesses y, and B possesses x. In this case, A and B both rank W1 over W2 but for entirely different reasons. A ranks W1 over W2 because of her possession of x, and B values W1 over W2 because of his possession of y. The values traded are agent-relative, but often unnoticed is the fact that the value of the process itself is also agent-relative.

A minister can trade for the goods and services that will help her flourish just as a purchasing agent can for a chain of bookstores. The difference between them lies in the agent-relative value of trading itself. For the minister, the value of trading for her may be minimal. Not that it is value-less, but it is weighed less than charity and the duties of ministry in terms of the minister's flourishing life. For the purchasing agent, trading can justifiably be weighed highly as being central to both her work and her notion of self. The value of trading itself, as an activity, is agent-relative. While everyone must trade, how they value that activity can vary just as much as any other flourishing activity such as education and exercise. Trading is a voluntary method for individuals to exchange agent-relative values and is itself, as an activity, an agent-relative value. Both of these are important to the possibility of a flourishing life. How important, of course, depends on the agent.

The fact that trading is agent-relative is not enough, though, to establish that it constitutes a way of flourishing. Rasmussen and Den Uyl correctly point out that agent-relative values are not coextensive with desire satisfaction. Nor are agent-relative values merely instrumental values. Finally, agent-relativity is not egoism. Unfortunately, trade is seen in economics as a purely instrumental method of satisfying self-interested desires. If economics is correct, trading cannot constitute a flourishing way of life.

Trading, though, can be about more than satisfying subjective desires. The argument that trading is only instrumental in desire satisfaction, mistakenly focuses solely on the utility of the goods and services traded, instead of on the activity of trading itself. The objects that agents receive, and the desires they satisfy, may or may not help them to flourish. The question though, is not about *what* is received so much as *what is done* in order to obtain the good or service. Agents can also obtain things by force. In such cases at least one agent in the transaction is having their values totally disregarded. Alternatively, agents can obtain goods and services by voluntary consent. In order to achieve voluntary consent, agents willingly accept the values they will receive. When using force I do not need to consider your values beyond fear of harm. Using trade, the only way I can get what I want is to take account of what you want. Using force is solipsistic in nature, trading is communicative both of what I want and of what I think you want. More is involved in the process of trading than simply satisfying one's desires. This may be precisely why some individuals do resort to force. There are many ways to get what one wants, but to choose trading requires respecting the rights, values, and potential flourishing of others. One must not only *choose what* to trade, one must *choose to* trade in the first place, and this prior choice can be about more than maximizing desire satisfaction.

In the matter of choice we must address the question of motivation. In economics, the motive of self-interest reigns supreme. Adam Smith notes that

> it is not from the benevolence of the butcher, the brewer, or the baker, that we expect our dinner, but from their regard to their own interest. We address ourselves, not to their humanity but to their self-love, and never talk to them of our own necessities but of their advantage.[8]

From Smith's insight to the theory of perfect competition, self-interest is the guiding assumption in economic theory. Rasmussen and Den Uyl, though, are clear that "agent-relativity should not be confused with egoism" (p. 138). If trading is merely egoism made manifest in the economic sphere, then trading could be part of a flourishing life but it would be too narrow to constitute a flourishing way of life.

The model, however, is not the thing. Milton Friedman argues that the purpose of economic modeling is predictive power, not realism in its assumptions.[9] The concept of perfect competition complies with this dictum, at least its latter half. The model of perfect competition assumes agents do not care about the preferences of others. This occurs in the requirements that "each person's utility is determined by and only by the size and composition of his bundle" and that preferences be non-tuistic so "that persons be conceived as not taking an interest in the interests of those with whom they exchange."[10] These assumptions are then incorporated into a model that then prohibits these types of concern. *Homo Economicus*, the mathematical automaton that he is, cannot do what is not in the equation. This, however, is more an artifact of mathematical tractability than of reality.

There is no reason to assume that an agent cannot take pleasure in what others have or that the actual motive for trading could not be, in some part, for the benefit of those with whom we trade. If other regarding actions are possible at all, then they are possible in trading.

Rasmussen and Den Uyl correctly point out such examples of other regarding behavior as parents sacrificing for their children and friends helping one another. In the market this sacrifice and assistance takes the form of trading for goods and services that benefit the child or friend. To say that trade always must be selfish theoretically prohibits the very real act of buying something for someone else's benefit. Too many birthday parties speak contrary to the model. Charities like Habitat for Humanity engage in market activities explicitly and intentionally for the benefit of others. This is not to say that gift bearers and charity workers have no self-interested motives of their own. Our standard, though, is not one of selflessness. All that is necessary is that an element of the transaction contain other regarding sentiments. Except for the sake of mathematically tractable predictive models, there is no reason to exclude these sentiments from real trades even if these actions could be *represented* as totally selfish actions. There can be just as many motives for trading as there can be for any other human activity. Trading can be, and is, motivated by more than egoistic concerns.

On another note, we should not throw out the baby with the bath water. There are egoistic concerns that do contribute to an agent's flourishing. This is implicit in *Norms of Liberty*, but it needs to be made explicit. Flourishing should not be confused with complete altruism. It is not the case that because an action is other regarding that it then contributes to an agent's flourishing. There are other-regarding actions that are foolish, ineffective, and self-destructive. It is perhaps the rare individual who could give up all egoistic concerns and still flourish. The beauty of trading is that it satisfies both egoistic and non-egoistic concerns, and this flexibility is one of the features that makes flourishing through trading possible.

Human flourishing is self-directed. It is a necessary condition of flourishing such that if an act is not self-directed it cannot constitute flourishing (pp. 139–40). Agents must make their own choices and initiate the effort required to gain and keep those goods and virtues requisite for their flourishing. Trading requires self-directed choice in both the decision to trade and the decision of what to trade. Deciding to trade, rather than use force, requires accepting a set of moral principles, at least in action if not always in the heart. It also requires weighing how important trading is in relation to other values an agent holds. Many people decided not to trade with South Africa during apartheid precisely because trading was not as important as other moral values held by the abstaining agents. While trading has ties to our objective natures and individual selves, we can still decide not to trade. When we do decide to trade, final consent requires the processing of information and this processing must be initiated and maintained by the agent. Trading is not some sort of reflex. Trading *is* the self-directed exchange of agent-relative values.

Self-direction, though, is not an unmitigated good. Protecting the possibility for self-direction only upholds the possibility that an agent may flourish. Self-direction also allows for the possibility of agents choosing their own destruction. This leads to a potential counter argument against the moral justification of free trade. If the purpose of liberty is to secure the possibility of flourishing, allowing people to trade for those items we know will result in their own devastation seems ludicrous. Pornography, gambling, cigarettes, alcohol, and other drugs are items that usually top the lists for prohibition in the name of flourishing. If this argument is correct, it seems that human flourishing actually requires a prohibition on trade in those goods and services that supposedly prevent flourishing.

This debate involves both considerations over the feasibility of prohibition and whether any of these vices could be a part of a flourishing life. That is, whether all or any of these are in fact vices. Let us assume, though, both that they are vices, in that they do detract from human flourishing, and that it is possible to effectively prohibit them. Even granting these assumptions, it still does not follow that trade in vices ought to be prohibited in the name of flourishing.

Flourishing requires self-direction in the face of real choices. "Only by initiating and maintaining the effort to gain the knowledge, to cultivate the proper habits of character, to exercise correct choices, and to perform the right actions can someone achieve moral excellence" (p. 139). There is no virtue by default. Remove all the temptations and you still have not guaranteed flourishing, and you may even destroy the virtue you are trying to promote. There is no temperance in a world without alcohol or similar drugs. Removing alcohol does not make a world of virtuous people, only a world of sober ones. Such prohibitions do not advance flourishing one iota, but they may maximize general utility. Legally prohibiting people from bad choices through the threat of punishment may change how people act, and the consequences of their actions, but these are utilitarian considerations. As noted earlier, flourishing should not be confused with preference satisfaction and, for similar reasons, should not be confused with general utility. People may be happy in a brave new world, but they are not flourishing. Liberty as a metanorm is not about maximizing the greatest good for the greatest number, even though it may have that effect. It is about securing the possibility for people to flourish, for people to live as humans and not as well watered plants. Liberty allows people to live as humans by letting them make their own decisions concerning virtue and vice. By removing the choice of vice, effective prohibition overrides self-direction and, to that extent, removes the possibility of flourishing.

One obvious concern over allowing people to choose vice is that any plausible political or moral theory prohibits murder, rape, and robbery. Political institutions threaten individuals with force in an effort to prevent such crimes and this threat is carried out against those who perpetrate them. Liberty does not allow self-direction with regards to these matters. The question now is whether founding liberty in the potential for flourishing is, at heart, contradictory by preventing the very self-directed choices between morality and immorality that make flourishing possible.

In answering this question it will not do to point out that the political structure merely raises the costs of certain actions and that criminals still have a choice in the face of these potential costs. The same could be said about any type of legal prohibition where people, on this line of thought, remain free because they still have a choice. They still have a choice because the state only raises the costs of the prohibited activity and people are still self-determined in that they can weigh such costs and make their decisions based on them. This, though, is really a question of metaphysical free will: How high must a cost be before we are not free? That is not the question we are addressing here. The question here concerns the justifiability of raising those costs through political means and interfering with self-determination in the first place. In this question is the seed of an answer.

The answer lies in the notion of self-direction. Unjust harms to others violates the self-directedness of the victims. By their very nature, these actions violate flourishing. If the political structure is to protect the possibility of flourishing it must prevent those actions that directly negate it. So far the argument looks the same as the prohibitionists' with one important exception: the focus on political action is whether the activity violates the self-directed choices of others. The focus is not on whether the choosing agent herself flourishes or not.

Indeed, arguments for banning pornography and gambling often advance the claim that nonparticipating others, women who have nothing to do with pornography and non-gambling spouses, are unjustly harmed by these activities. This acknowledgement is all the argument this chapter requires. It is a matter of theoretical and empirical debate whether an activity has negative externalities that unjustly impinge on the self-directed choices of others. If an activity does then its prohibition or regulation will not be a restriction of trade. It will be a justified protection of the self-directedness that makes trading possible. This is not a neat line, it will not be answered *a priori*, and it will not satisfy those looking for the silver bullet argument against government regulations. However, debating about the nature of self-direction and its violation *is the argument*, and this paper makes no attempt to downplay the importance and difficulty of that argument. The argument here is that those activities which unjustly violate the self-directed choices of others ought to be banned while those that do not, even if immoral on some accounts, ought to be left to individual decision making because that is what makes flourishing possible.[11]

Human flourishing is social. The focus on self-direction in arguments concerning liberty and prohibition often leads to the claim that the emphasis on self-directed choices assumes an atomistic, asocial, view of human agents. This is mistaken. Even though human flourishing requires self-direction it is not atomistic or asocial. Human flourishing also *requires* a life with others (p.141). This is not simply a life among others, but a life that meaningfully interacts with others. Friendship, family, and community are important for human flourishing. Our sociality, though, should neither in theory nor in practice be confined to those we already know. Human sociality "is open to relationships with *any* human" (p. 142). The question is whether trading is sufficiently social for human flourishing.

To begin with, trading allows strangers to form new bonds. "Markets maximize social interaction without individuals first being required to agree upon fundamental social values or to share a conception of the good or of the constitutive elements of the good life."[12] Trading opens the door to new relationships. What kind of relationships these are depends on the social nature of trading and whether trading itself constitutes any type of meaningful interaction, or is simply an impersonal arm's length transaction. If it is just the latter then trading should have no part between intimates and the relations it establishes with strangers are superficial at best. In neither case would trading constitute, or even give rise to, the types of relationships required for human flourishing.

Just as with self-directedness, there is a flexibility with regards to the social nature of trading. Trading can be either an arm's length transaction or something more. Trading with vending machines is quite impersonal. Alternatively, goods carried by early explorers were used to develop ties as a first step towards more meaningful relations.[13] States often use trade as both a precursor to, and in furtherance of, other peaceful diplomatic interests. Using trade in this manner can certainly be abused, but it can be abused precisely because there is something about trade that often gives it more meaning than simply an exchange of goods or services. If this were not the case, if no further sentiments and beliefs were engaged, it would be impossible to gain anyone's trust, friendship, or cooperation simply through the act of trading. It is, however, possible to gain trust, cooperation, and friendship through trade because at the heart of trading there is something that speaks to our social nature.

Trading is how we economically talk to one another. "If we should enquire into the principle in the human mind on which this disposition of trucking is founded, it is clearly on the natural inclination every one has to persuade. The offering of a schilling, which to us appears to have so plain and simple a meaning, is in reality offering an argument to persuade one to do so and so as it is for his interest."[14] If talking can influence and maintain relationships then trading can as well, and in the same manner. Trading is communicating. At the very least, sellers and buyers must consider each other's interests and then communicate their estimations to each other. The offer to sell, or the offer to buy, contains within it a distilled argument of what each thinks it will take to persuade the other to trade.

It could be argued that even if this captures the sociality of one-on-one trading, it does not capture the reality of most trades. Trading in a modern market economy is done through the impersonal price system. Where prices are already determined all we need to do is pay the cashier. This constitutes the bulk of transactions in a modern market economy and it does not seem to be all that social. This argument, though, overlooks the fact that there is more to trading than simply determining price.

Simply because prices are determined in advance does not disprove the social nature of trading. With supposedly impersonal transactions it should not be overlooked that trading is a signal as well as an activity. It is a signal that this buyer or seller will not violate certain basic rights. I am safe to pass any shop in the mall, or mill about within, without fear that the salesperson will strike me and take my money. Similarly, when I buy things over time the shopkeeper comes to see my desire to respect her rights. A salesperson can get to know me through my purchases. The fact that the prices are determined in advance still leaves open a wide array of social signals and interactions constitutive of trading that are glaringly important to any sales force. Trading is not love or friendship, but it is social.

Rasmussen and Den Uyl argue that liberty as a metanormative principle is grounded in securing the possibility of flourishing where flourishing is understood as "(1) objective; (2) inclusive; (3) individualized; (4) agent-relative; (5) self-directed; and (6) social" (p. 127). We have shown that the activity of trading satisfies each and every one of these requirements. Trading is an objective, inclusive, individualized, agent-relative, self-directed, social good. It is part of our human nature to trade and one of many final ends that depends for its value upon our individual circumstances. Engaging in trade requires self-motivation and choice. Finally, trading quite often is not something you do alone. This is why it is possible to flourish through trading. This is not to say that one should only engage in trade, but that a life of trading does hold out the possibility of human flourishing. Mill is wrong to assert that the principles of liberty and free trade rest on different grounds. Rasmussen and Den Uyl's account of flourishing and the metanormativity of liberty provides this connection. The principle of liberty protects trading for the same reason the right to liberty protects any other human activity: to protect the possibility of human flourishing.

Notes

1. *On Liberty*, in *Mill On Liberty and Other Essays*, edited by John Gray (Oxford: Oxford University Press, 1991), 105.

2. See David Gauthier, *Morals by Agreement* (Oxford: Clarendon Press, 1986), 85–91. There are more assumptions than these that go into the model of perfect competition, but these are the ones relevant for the present discussion.

3. Gauthier, 90.

4. See Adam Smith, *An Inquiry into the Nature and Causes of the Wealth of Nations*, edited by R. H. Campbell and A. S. Skinner (Indianapolis: Liberty Fund, 1981), I.ii.1 and I.ii.5 for further reference to a natural propensity to truck, barter and exchange. "Whether this propensity be one of those original principles in human nature, of which no further account can be given; or whether, as seems more probable, it be the

necessary consequence of the faculties of reason and speech, it belongs not to our present subject to enquire."

5. "If you ask me exactly what the deals I'm about to describe all add up to in the end, I'm not sure I have a very good answer. Except that I've had a very good time making them" (Donald Trump, *TRUMP: The Art of the Deal* (New York: Warner Books, 1987), 63).

6. The use of utility here does not preclude the concept of flourishing. "Utility means, in this context simply: causal relevance for the removal of felt uneasiness. Acting man believes that the services a thing can render are apt to improve his own well-being, and calls this the utility of the thing concerned" (Ludwig von Mises, *Human Action*, 3rd Revised Edition (Chicago: Contemporary Books, 1963), 120). See also pp. 121–27: People may make marginal utility assessments of both the good and the bad.

7. Friedrich A. Hayek, "The Use of Knowledge in Society" in *Individualism and Economic Order* (Chicago: University of Chicago Press, 1948), 77.

8. Smith, *Wealth of Nations*, I, ii, 2.

9. Milton Friedman, "The Methodology of Positive Economics," in *Essays in Positive Economics* (The University of Chicago Press, 1953), p. 41.

10. Gauthier, p. 87.

11. Notice, the argument of this paper is different than Mill's claim "That the only purpose for which power can be rightfully exercised over any member of a civilized community, against his will, is to prevent harm to others" (Mill, *On Liberty*, 14), unless the set of harmful acts and the set of acts that violate the self-direction of others are coterminous. I doubt they are, but examining this point would take us outside the scope of this project. Mill's argument comes closest to our own in *Principles of Political Economy* (e.g., at pp. 858–59), but he stills holds that there are many exceptions in economics (871), while almost none in the sphere of personal liberty (859).

12. Jules Coleman, *Risks and Wrongs* (Cambridge, England: Cambridge University Press, 1992), 5.

13. See, for instance, Terry L. Anderson and P. J. Hill, *The Not So Wild, Wild West: Property Rights on the Frontier* (Stanford, Calif.: Stanford University Press, 2004), 83.

14. Smith, *Lectures on Jurisprudence* (Indianapolis: Liberty Fund, 1982), 352.

12

Self-Directedness and the Human Good in *Norms of Liberty*

Peter E. Vedder

The aim of *Norms of Liberty* is to establish the true ethical foundations of the liberal political/legal order. The authors see the need for a principled defense of liberalism and clarity about its fundamental principles as liberalism today finds itself in a state of profound practical crisis and theoretical confusion. The liberal regime is not understood to possess moral and political legitimacy by its contemporary opponents and is neither honored nor even esteemed by its contemporary lukewarm defenders. Post-liberal "communitarian" and contemporary natural-law critics of liberalism, for example, speak of the degrading and even immoral character of liberalism, claiming that the liberal regime "subverts moral life" and fosters "injustice and inhumanity" (p. 11). According to these same critics, liberalism is theoretically indefensible because it is based on "false," "illegitimate," and "pernicious" principles of the Enlightenment. The principles of liberalism destroy human community and its doctrine of the "autonomous rights-bearing" individual leads to moral "subjectivism, and skepticism" (p. 7). Liberalism implies moral subjectivism because the individual is posited as the "sole determinant of value" and it invites moral skepticism because knowledge of the human good is said to be unavailable to man as man (p. 7).

Douglas Rasmussen and Douglas Den Uyl demonstrate that the crisis of liberalism can be traced to its roots. Classical liberalism is vulnerable to the charge of moral subjectivism and skepticism because it self-consciously identifies claims made about the human good with personal preferences or tastes. The inquiries of the "Philosophers" concerning the "*Summum bonum*," declares Locke, were vain and useless. They might have as "reasonably disputed whether the best Relish were to be found in Apples, Plumbs, or Nuts."[1] Skepticism concerning the possibility of knowledge of the human good, however, underlies the "fundamental tenets" of liberalism. Liberalism holds that "political power is not due anyone by natural right," that the "people ought to have the freedom or liberty to pursue their own conception of the good life," and that the purpose of the "political/legal order should be limited to protecting individuals in their pursuit of their own conception of the good life" (p. 11). It is, however, precisely because the human good is not and cannot be a matter of knowledge that "values are reduced to preferences and substantive moral commitments are trivialized" (p. 12). More fundamentally, liberalism's skepticism about the human good undermines its moral legitimacy. By remaining "neutral to rival conceptions of the good and right," liberalism has no basis from which to claim that its own values are best (p. 12).

The practical and theoretical crisis of liberalism is further aggravated by contemporary liberals' understanding of liberalism as a complete moral doctrine or ethics rather than as a political solution to a fundamental political and human problem (p. 93). This contemporary liberal ethics reduces morality to obligations of "toleration or cooperation" and to a very "narrow, instrumental, and minimalistic understanding of values and ethical life" (p. 12). Contemporary liberals' defense of the moral goodness of liberalism simply invite the contemptuous attacks of the communitarian and natural-law critics of liberalism. "Moral minimalism," however, also has its roots in the classical liberal tradition. The authors point to Hobbes' reduction of moral virtue to the virtues of justice and charity (pp. 28–29). Hobbes' moral philosophy lays the foundation for the liberal "socialization of ethics" (p. 28).

Liberalism's minimalistic conception of values and socialization of ethics is questioned today by liberalism's communitarian and natural-law critics on the basis of a "neo-Aristotelian" ethics of moral virtue. According to these critics, liberalism implicitly or even explicitly denies claims central to an ethics of human virtue. Liberalism, for example, denies that human beings are by nature social. It denies the non-instrumental nature and, hence, ethical value of practical reason or prudence. Its rights-centered and legalistic conception of human obligation renders it blind to the moral significance of the particular and contingent in the determination of moral conduct. And its skepticism concerning knowledge of human happiness fractures the ontological bond that exists between human liberty and the human good (p. 9).

The authors of *Norms of Liberty* emphatically agree with all of these neo-Aristotelian criticisms of liberalism. Their powerful strategy of demonstration attempts to prove that the ethical commitments of the communitarian and natural-law critics of liberalism are not only compatible with but, in fact, presuppose the existence of the liberal political/legal order. The neo-Aristotelian claims defended by the communitarian and natural-law critics of liberalism require accepting "liberalism's basic tenet," which affirms that achieving and maintaining liberty is the central and primary concern of the political/legal order (p. 9; see also p. 225). The lived reality of these neo-Aristotelian moral propositions presupposes the existence of the political order dedicated to liberalism's most basic teaching because the exercise of moral virtue presupposes the possibility of moral agency. The possibility of moral agency, in turn, presupposes the existence of the political liberty uniquely maintained by the liberal political/legal order.

The authors' own defense of liberalism, however, leads their argument into a "structural paradox" (p. 12). Liberalism must import its theoretical and practical foundations from the non-liberal pre-modern philosophical tradition. The reason for this paradoxical necessity is that liberalism does not consistently maintain one of its own defining principles, i.e., the distinction between the political and the non-political (p. 58). Liberalism violates this liberal principle by understanding itself to be an "equinormative" or "complete" moral philosophy (p. 34; see also p. 93). To be a defensible political philosophy, however, liberalism must relinquish "all pretenses to being an ethics" at all

(p. 27). Liberalism's tendency to universalize and legalize moral norms has had the effect of undermining the "moral propriety of the individualism" that liberalism claims to "cherish and foster" (p. 27).

Rasmussen and Den Uyl's defense of the moral propriety of individualism makes full use of the liberal distinction between the political and the non-political. Liberalism can be defended if it respects the "division of ethics" into a "language of liberty for the political order" and a language of "personal morality" for the non-political order. This distinction corresponds to the authors' distinction between "norms" and "metanorms." Metanorms are moral principles that do not directly guide or determine moral conduct; rather their purpose is to establish the appropriate context within which moral conduct may take place (p. 34). The authors identify metanorms with rights, specifically the right to liberty.

Liberalism properly understood rejects the management of moral conduct as a legitimate function of politics. The purpose of politics is not to define moral conduct but to protect the possibility of the self-directed activity of each and every member of the political community. Contemporary critics and defenders of liberalism share a common assumption that politics ought to be a "vehicle for promoting and securing the moral" (p. 16). Both fail to grasp the "essential uniqueness" of liberalism, that is, its intentional "divestment of substantive morality from politics" (p. 17, also p. 324). Once the distinction between norms and metanorms is accepted, then and only then, can the "value of liberty" be understood to be "directly proportional" to the moral substantiveness of ethics (p. 17). The defect of traditional and contemporary liberal moral theory consists in its identification of rights respecting conduct with the "whole of morality" (p. 47). This feature of liberalism leads inevitably to the "dilemma of liberalism," that is, its own tendency to "either impoverish morality or trivialize rights" (p. 47).

The solution to the problem of the self-defeating foundations and dilemma of liberalism is the neo-Aristotelian conception of human virtue and its relation to the human good. This conception proves to be a synthesis of the teleological eudaimonism of Aristotle and the moral individualism of Ayn Rand. Rasmussen and Den Uyl ground the right to liberty not in the prior right to self-preservation as in Hobbes, but in a conception of human flourishing or self-perfection (p. 95). Human flourishing, in turn, is grounded in a teleological understanding of human nature (p. 124).

The authors' novel understanding of the human good is the basis of their claim that liberalism is the "best regime." The human good, according to the authors, is something real or "objective" and, at the same time, something highly individualized, chosen, and "agent-relative" (p. 93). The human good is the actualization and manifestation of the human potentialities and capacities along with the basic or generic goods and virtues of human nature. The good life is the "self-sufficient life," that is, a life whose management and direction is under the control of the individual (p. 147). The self-sufficient individual, however, is not a god living beyond need and community but a human being actively engaged in the actualization of his or her unique potentials and capacities in the activities and thinking of a "mature" adult living in a social context (p. 142; 167). Such a life presupposes not only the acquisition of all of the moral and intellectual virtues but their actual exercise guided by practical wisdom in the contingent and particular affairs of daily life. The good for man is not merely a personal preference or taste but the very perfection of the nature of each individual human being (p. 152).

The perfection of human nature is not the perfection of an "abstraction" but the perfection of real human beings. The human capacities, goods, and excellences that "constitute human flourishing only become real, determinate, and valuable when they are given particular form by the choices" of individuals (p. 80). The choices of individuals, however, do not take place in a moral vacuum. Each individual always already exists within a particular "nexus," or highly individualized set of circumstances, talents, endowments, interest, beliefs, and histories that determine the "appropriate valuation or weighting" of the capacities, goods, and virtues for that individual (p. 80; 150). The human good is real only in so far as it is "individually realized" (p. 80; see also p. 137). It would seem to follow from this account of the human good that "there are many forms of human flourishing, but there is no *single* best form of human flourishing" (p. 81). There is, then, no one *summum bonum* but "many *summa bona*" (p. 81; also p. 190). For this reason the ethics of human flourishing is a form of "moral pluralism" (p. 81; also p. 134).

The human good, precisely because it is something *objective* and *chosen*, must be understood to be something *inclusive*, for the human *telos* comprehends without reducing to mere means all of the other human ends, pursuits, virtues, and goods. It must be *individualized* because it is brought into being by the deliberative choices and actions of individuals, *agent-relative* because the unique form of flourishing of each individual is the real good for that individual, *self-directed* because the human good becomes determinate and real only in so far as it is chosen and sought, and *social* because the individual's pursuit of flourishing is, in part, conditioned and made possible by their own particular "nexus" (pp. 127–43). This understanding of the human good is the basis of "liberalism's problem" or the "central problem of political philosophy" (p. 2). The problem uniquely solved by liberalism consists in finding a "political/legal order that will in principle not require that the human flourishing of any person or group be given structural preference over others" (p. 78). The political/legal order must remain absolutely neutral to all of the various forms of human flourishing because no single form of flourishing is best for all (p. 147). Hence, the primary purpose of the political/legal order is to protect the possibility of all forms of human flourishing.

In order to guarantee that the political/legal order upholds the equal dignity of all forms of human flourishing it must be governed by an ethical principle possessing the following characteristics. The principle must be consistent with *moral pluralism* or the "moral propriety of individualism," *universal* or "applicable to all forms of flourishing," *immanent* or "present in any and every form" of human flourishing, *rationally compelling* or embodying "an agent-relative reason" for each and every individual to adopt the principle, embody *equality* or the equal dignity of each and every form of flourishing, and *possible* or a norm that all human beings "can in principle fulfill" (p. 272). The ethical principle that meets these conditions is a "metanormative" ethical principle. The metanormative ethical principle that supplies the solution to liberalism's problem must, therefore, be consistent with the individualized, agent-relative, self-directed, and social character of human flourishing (p. 93). This principle proves to be the "individual right to liberty" (pp. 93–94).

The political/legal order whose central and primary concern is achieving and maintaining liberty secures political and legal protection to a plurality of different forms of human flourishing without at the same time giving any single form of human flourishing "structural preference over others" (p. 78). The moral legitimacy of the right to liberty, however, ultimately depends on the nature of human flourishing itself (pp. 86–90). The possibility of participating in the human good presupposes the possibility of moral agency or self-direction and self-direction is the very essence of liberty (p. 90). Every person as a moral agent must enjoy the moral autonomy to use their practical reasoning to discover the manner in which the basic human goods and virtues can be "coherently integrated and particularized in their lives" (p. 80). It is only "through an individual's practical choices" that the goods and virtues of human nature become "determinate, real, and valuable" (pp. 80; 84). The right to liberty, furthermore, protects the possibility for individuals to make practical choices in a social context (p. 93). It permits each person a sphere of freedom—a "moral space" or "territory"—whereby "self-directed activities can be exercised without being invaded by others" (p. 90). Hence, the right to liberty supplies an ontological basis for the possibility of the moral individualism constitutive of diverse forms of human flourishing.

The moral justification of the right to liberty is grounded in the fact that liberty is indispensable for the life of moral virtue and hence for the actualization and manifestation of man's natural end. Human flourishing can come into being only through the free agency of each and every individual. Each and every individual must be free to legislate for themselves those norms that bring into being and constitute his or her own highly individualized form of flourishing because self-direction is the "central necessary constituent" of human flourishing (p. 87).

Self-direction refers to the "agency of an individual human being that is necessary for the operation of reason" (p. 300). The operation and exercise of practical reasoning is central to all forms of human flourishing because "effort is needed to discover the goods and virtues of human flourishing as well as to achieve and implement them" (p. 140). The goods and virtues of human flourishing must be made "one's own" through the deliberative choices and efforts of each. Self-direction is indispensable for this activity because the exercise of reason is an exercise of self-direction and an act of self-direction is an exercise of reason (p. 87). Reason and self-direction are "distinct aspects of the same conscious act." Together they constitute what Ayn Rand called "volitional consciousness" (p. 87).

Self-direction, however, to be exercised in an excellent manner, must be an act of practical wisdom or prudence. Practical wisdom is the virtue that "achieves, integrates, and unifies all the other ends that constitute human flourishing" (p. 275). Practical reasoning, properly engaged, is "the intelligent management of one's life so that all the necessary goods and virtues are coherently achieved, maintained, and enjoyed in a manner that is appropriate for the individual human being" (p. 147). Human beings, in order to live well, need both theoretical insight into the goods and virtues of human flourishing and practical insight into what is to be done at the "time of action" (p. 149).

The human *telos* consists in the actualization of human potentialities and capacities whose specific form is "individualized by each person's own attributes, circumstances, and interests" (p. 150). The individual must incorporate the goods and virtues of human flourishing into their own "nexus by an act of reason or insight," and this is necessarily a self-directed activity (p. 151). In fact, "constitutive goods and virtues of human flourishing are valueless apart from the virtue of practical wisdom" (p. 151). The human goods and virtues become valuable only in "relation to and because of the efforts of individual human beings" (p. 152). Hence, practical wisdom is the "central intellectual virtue for ethics" (p. 149).

The human good is grounded in human nature and in human freedom. Every human being has an "inherent potentiality" for his or her own "mature state." The mature state of an individual is the "natural end" and "moral purpose" of that individual. The natural end or form of flourishing proper to each individual is not itself "a matter of choice," however, but "a matter of human nature." In fact, human nature has "directive power for our choices" (p. 125). What is not a matter of choice, however, only becomes real, determinate, and actualized "through choice" (p. 126). Human beings are neither radically free nor radically necessitated (p. 62; see also p. 166). The activities that human beings "ought to pursue" are given by their nature but are nevertheless neither good nor real apart from "individuals and their choices" (p. 152). The reality and goodness of the individual's mature state presupposes the individual's self-directed exercise of their own practical wisdom. Human flourishing is both a self-directed activity and an expression of human nature.

Norms of Liberty is a defense of individualistic perfectionism. Its argument seeks to establish a "perfectionist basis for nonperfectionist politics." Individualistic perfectionism understands "human flourishing" as necessarily involving self-directed choice. The argument of *Norms of Liberty*, however, tends to abstract from the conditions of the possibility of human choice. Human choice becomes possible, according to Aristotle, by the presence of a disposition or condition of soul. An excellent psychic disposition comes to be present on account of actions done in conformity with the actions performed by one in possession of the excellent psychic condition. Human choice presupposes moral habituation which, in turn, presupposes education into what is by nature noble and base. Aristotle endorses an opinion of Plato's according to which it is necessary for the young to be educated to "take delight and feel pain in the things in which one ought."[2] Moral education reveals a difference between actions that merely conform to virtue and actions that are inseparable from a virtuous psychic condition. A virtuous psychic condition disposes the agent to feel pain in the presence of the ugly or shameful feelings and actions and to take pleasure and delight in the noble feelings and actions. The virtuous psychic condition capacitates and "inclines" the agent to pursue and choose what is noble and to avoid and reject what is shameful. If the agent were to choose the noble action on account of a prior rejection of a base action conceived as a real or possible alternative, that is, as something possibly good, then the agent, according to Aristotle, would belong not to the class of the virtuous, but to the class of the self-restrained. For this reason, the virtuous agent's choice *qua* virtuous cannot be properly understood as an act of will or of "volitional consciousness." The agent's choice proves to be a manifestation of a stable and abiding character that is informed by a conviction concerning what is "choiceworthy by nature" or beautiful. The moral agent *qua* moral is not in reality free to choose or pursue what he or she believes to be base or bad.

Virtue of character, according to Aristotle, is a mean condition between "natural virtue" and virtue in the "governing sense."[3] Human virtue in the governing or precise sense presupposes the exercise of practical wisdom or prudence as the authors admit and even emphasize. Prudence is defined by Aristotle as a "truth-disclosing disposition involving reason that governs action, concerned with what is good and bad for a human being."[4] The pursuit of the good and avoidance of the bad by those exercising practical wisdom cannot properly be understood as an act of volitional consciousness because the acts of the prudent follow from what is understood by the human intellect. What marks the activity of thinking that pertains to action as working well is "truth that stands in agreement with right desire."[5] In this context, Aristotle redefines choice or "deliberate desire" as "right desire" from within the horizon of moral virtue, and then as "either intellect fused with desire or desire fused with thinking" from the standpoint of practical wisdom.[6] It is the unity of desire and intellect that is the principle governing the activity of the prudent. It is for this reason that it appears to be impossible for the prudent to choose or pursue what he or she understands to be bad. "Nor is it possible for the same person to be possessed of practical wisdom and at the same time be unrestrained."[7] For, says Aristotle, it would be a terrible thing if, "when knowledge is present, something else were to master it and drag it around like a slave."[8] The pursuit of the good or self-perfection is not an act of "volitional consciousness," self-direction, or "freedom of choice." It appears rather to follow from an understanding of what it is that is the one thing needful for the practically wise. It is perhaps for this reason that Descartes, one of the modern thinkers, observes in the Fourth *Meditation* that knowledge eliminates choice while it enhances human freedom, and Thomas Aquinas, one of the medieval thinkers, seems to indicate that knowledge of the good is as determinative of the human will as the principle of non-contradiction is of the human intellect.[9] Aristotle's argument in the *Ethics* proves that the principle governing all acts of moral virtue is either the noble (books three and four) or the good (book six), but in neither case is a morally virtuous act an exercise of self-direction or "freedom of choice."

Finally, as indicated above, individualistic perfectionism is a form of moral pluralism. It teaches that there is "no single best form of human flourishing" but "only specific forms of human flourishing" that are "best for specific individuals" (p. 81; p. 137; p. 249). Rasmussen and Den Uyl move from the position that each individual's *telos* consists in the pursuit of the form of flourishing that is best for them to the view that "no form of flourishing is objectively or naturally superior to any other" (p. 147; p. 279). This latter view, however, in no way follows from its premises and is incompatible with the authors' own doctrine of teleological eudaimonism. Human beings possess an "inherent potentiality" to actualize the capacities, goods, and virtues of human nature. The specific form of flourishing appropriate for each individual is the standard by which to judge whether or not an individual is faring well. The standard used to evaluate the goodness of a particular instance of a specific form of flourishing can and ought to be applied to the forms of flourishing themselves. A form of flourishing that necessarily impedes the actualization of a capacity, good, or virtue of human nature would have to be judged inferior to another that did not do so. Aristotle, for example, argues that while it is excellent to practice virtue with regard to one's own affairs it is an even greater excellence to practice virtue in relation to others.[10] He implies that the public life of the politician or judge is naturally superior to the private life of the moneymaker or athlete. The public life of the politician or judge necessarily engages and actualizes a greater number of the human capacities, goods, and virtues than is possible to be engaged and actualized by a private man. It would appear that that form of human flourishing that required the possession, integration, and exercise of all of the capacities, goods, and virtues of human nature would be simply best. Such a form would manifest the nature of human nature to the highest possible degree of perfection. This form belongs to the philosopher.[11] In fact, it is the political philosopher who is the "master craftsman of the end to which we look when we speak of each thing as bad or good simply."[12] Rasmussen and Den Uyl's doctrine of teleological eudaimonism proves to be incompatible both with their teaching concerning human equality and with their understanding of human freedom. Their doctrine of individuality is incompatible with their doctrine of perfectionism. For this reason their attempt to establish the true ethical foundations of the liberal political/legal order by deriving the right to liberty from the duty to self-perfect or flourish is theoretically problematic (p. 65; see also p. 268).[13]

Notes

1. John Locke, *An Essay Concerning Human Understanding*, edited by Peter Nidditch (Oxford: Clarendon Press, 1975), II.21.55.
2. *Nicomachean Ethics*, translated by Joe Sachs (Newburyport, Mass.: Focus Publishing, 2002), 1104b12.
3. *Nicomachean Ethics*, 1144b15.
4. *Nicomachean Ethics*, 1140b5–7.
5. *Nicomachean Ethics*, 1139a30.
6. *Nicomachean Ethics*, 1139b5.
7. *Nicomachean Ethics*, 1152a7.
8. *Nicomachean Ethics*, 1145b25.
9. For example, in *Summa Theologica*, I-IIae, q. 92, a. 2.
10. *Nicomachean Ethics*, 1129b32.
11. See e.g. Plato, *Republic* VI, 487a.
12. *Nicomachean Ethics*, 1152b2.
13. This essay also appears in *The Journal of Ayn Rand Studies*, vol. 9, no. 1 (Fall 2007), and appears here (with minor edits) by permission.

13

Norms of Liberty: Challenges and Prospects

Douglas B. Rasmussen and Douglas J. Den Uyl

"It is important to reiterate once again how radical our position is: *we do not hold that the role of the political philosopher, any more than the role of the state, is necessarily to imagine his preferred society in some abstract and theoretical way as a prelude to reconstruction in the real world according to the theorist's plan or ideal.* That would make all political philosophy and every political philosopher perfectionistic. Rather, the political philosopher is concerned *simpliciter* with the appropriate rules or governing norms of political society. It must, at the start, be an open question as to whether or not the improvement of society is the theorist's standard for determining what rules are appropriate. In other words, that is a subject of debate and study within political philosophy and cannot be presumed at the outset, however common that assumption may be. Recommending the appropriate rules or norms for a society is not necessarily equivalent to recommending the ideal society or recommending that society should take on a particular look for the benefit of its members. Moreover, since we believe that societies, unlike individuals, do not have a *telos*, it cannot be said that the "purpose" of society (or the aim of the political theorist) is necessarily the "good" or well-being of the society. The aim may be instead, as we have argued, to

> provide a legal/political structure such that the well-being of those in need of such structures might be pursued."
>
> —*Norms of Liberty*, chapter 12, p. 326

The two of us have been working and writing together for three decades now. Our first joint publication of any consequence was "Nozick on the Randian Argument" in 1978. It has been a long, fruitful, and enjoyable relationship. We plan for it to continue for the rest of our lives. Anyone who writes about controversial issues hopes that someone somewhere will pay at least some attention to their ideas. We suppose we are no different on that score, though whenever we are together it is the ideas themselves—not their consequences, reception, or impact—that occupy our conversations. Still, whatever our hopes of being considered may have been, we never anticipated that a volume of essays would be devoted to our work, especially with the caliber of people who have given their time to this volume. We are frankly humbled and at a bit of a loss of what to say by way of thank you to all involved. The individuals writing here are people for whom we have the highest respect as independent thinkers and scholars in their own right. It is evident from the preceding essays that this volume is not the gathering of a fan club. Serious and substantive criticisms of our work predominate, albeit with a respectful tone of civility. We hope that our responses found below reflect a mutual respect and display at least some portion of the professionalism exhibited by the contributors. We thank everyone collectively for what seems to us a very interesting volume, and we thank each individually for the quality of his or her contribution and willingness to devote valuable time to it.

Two individuals deserve, however, to be singled out especially. The first is Fred D. Miller Jr. whose introduction to this volume is a version of an introduction he gave to the very first session of papers organized to criticize our work at a meeting of the American Association for the Philosophic Study of Society in conjunction with the American Philosophical Association. This meeting was followed by two other similar sessions, one at the

American Catholic Philosophical Association and one at the American Political Science Association. But behind all of these events stands Aeon J. Skoble for whom our gratitude is immeasurable. We see in this volume the visible fruition of his efforts, but long before the project we have before us was even in the works, Aeon was seeking out a number of the individuals who you find here and the venue for their presentations. Aeon is a fine philosopher in his own right, so it was particularly flattering for him to devote so much work to this particular endeavor. In the end we cannot say if we are worthy of the attention we have received here and for which we are most grateful. We can with certainty say that we learned from each and every one of these essays and enjoyed immensely the opportunity to say something in response.

Our comments will consist of three parts. We will reply to (I) those who raise objections to our argument and who attempt to show its inadequacy; (II) those who wish to apply or extend our argument in ways that we have not explicitly taken into account; and (III) those who ask what future there is in political philosophy for the sort of "foundationalist" argument that we advance.

I

Edwin England, who is concerned for the fate of political liberalism, provides a careful and broad analysis of our argument in *Norms of Liberty*[1] (hereafter, *NOL*). He raises some significant doubts regarding our argument. We will seek to allay these doubts and use our responses to them as the basis for approaching objections raised by other critics who offer a narrower analysis.

We state in *NOL*, "It is never sufficient in political philosophy merely to show that doing X ought or ought not to be done. Rather, it must also be shown why doing X ought to be a political/legal concern. It cannot validly be assumed that politics is simply ethics writ large."[2] Edwin England calls this our "uber-norm," and while we have no principled objection to this label, it should be clear that we neither consider nor argue that this norm is some transcendental condition for doing political philosophy. Instead, we base this norm on the prima facie distinction between two claims: (1) doing X is morally right or good (or wrong or bad) and ought (or ought not) to be done; and (2) doing X ought to be political/legally required (or prohibited).[3] England quite rightly notes that we make much use of this distinction, but he argues that we make too much of it. First, we do so by assuming that (1) and (2) are *not* identical, and to do this begs the question. Just as one cannot *assume* that (1) and (2) are identical, neither can one assume that they are *not* identical. Second, this ubernorm actually begs the question in favor of liberalism, because this distinction, though intuitively plausible, actually appeals to some pretheoretical judgments we have about the moral and political orders—judgments that already presuppose a liberal approach to political philosophy. This is, of course, the very approach to political philosophy with which the conservative or communitarian takes issue.[4]

England is mistaken, however, on both points. First, we do not assume that (1) and (2) are not identical (or ultimately not necessarily connected). Rather, we simply do not assume that they are identical (or ultimately necessarily connected).[5] This is all that is needed in order to see that one cannot go from (1) to (2) without argument; that is to say, one cannot validly *assume* that they are identical (or ultimately necessarily connected). Of course, this does not mean that one cannot make an argument that (1) and (2) are actually identical (or ultimately necessarily connected). Nor does it mean that one cannot make an argument that they are *not* identical (or ultimately not necessarily connected). As we note in *NOL*,[6] the debate about the type of the connection, if any, between (1) and (2) is the basic *datum explanandum* of political philosophy.

Second, the distinction between (1) and (2) does not require that one presuppose a liberal approach to political philosophy. In *NOL*,[7] we observe that Aquinas distinguished between demands of justice that are morally binding and demands of justice that are morally and legally binding. Aquinas was, of course, no liberal, and his own view of political philosophy can be seen as offering an argument for necessarily connecting (1) and (2) through an account of the political common good, but it is nonetheless clear that in order to make this distinction, one need not be committed to a liberal approach to political philosophy.

However, England is correct to claim that the distinction between (1) and (2)—and indeed distinctions in general—does not come without presuppositions. It must be based on something real. Distinctions without differences should not be countenanced. We agree. Indeed, we note throughout *NOL*, and especially in the "Epilogue," that it is a mistake to think that one can do philosophy, or any serious theorizing, without metaphysics.[8] We do not probe, of course, those depths in this work, but we do show how the distinction between (1) and (2) is grounded ultimately in our account of human flourishing, which we call "individualistic perfectionism." This view of ethics, which is of Aristotelian inspiration, shares many common insights with those ethical claims espoused by communitarians and conservatives. In *NOL*, we list these claims:

> that human beings are naturally social; that ethical relativism is an inadequate moral theory; that practical reasoning is not merely instrumental and is crucial to ethics; that the abstract universalism of ethical rationalism fails to recognize the role of the particular and contingent (for example, particular customs or traditions that happen to accrue to specific communities) in determining proper conduct; that abstract universal norms are of only limited use in guiding ethical conduct that relies upon situated norms and practices; that impersonal or agent-neutral moral theory can neither ground nor motivate moral conduct; that liberty cannot be defined or understood without an ethical commitment; that any theory of rights capable of motivating human conduct must ultimately be based on a conception of the human good rather than simply being a matter of right; and that rights are not ethically fundamental.[9]

Clearly, this is not an ethical view that advocates of liberalism have traditionally taken. However, this neo-Aristotelian view also holds that the breadth of the social character of human flourishing is much greater than Aristotle seems to have realized, because it requires that it be possible for there to be relationships with strangers—that is to say, with persons with whom no common values are as yet shared. There is no inherent limitation on the scope of human relationships. They are in principle open-ended or cosmopolitan. These realizations in turn require that an ethics of human flourishing give due consideration to those ethical principles that address issues that arise from the open-ended or cosmopolitan character of human sociality. Moreover, consideration of what institutions are required to implement these principles is needed. Thus, the sense of sociality that is espoused in our account of individualistic perfectionism goes well beyond that which is found in the notion of a *polis*.[10] It involves social orders that are large and diverse.

It should be emphasized that these social orders are composed of various levels of communities that involve complex, and sometimes overlapping, relationships. Such social orders might be best described as "civil associations,"[11] because they are not characterized by the pursuit of a single determinate end but rather by the backdrop or context they provide for the pursuit of diverse ends by the individuals and groups that make them up. This backdrop or context for the pursuit of diverse ends is provided by a "political/legal order" (or what is usually understood, though not necessarily, as a state). Thus, the distinction between claims (1) and (2) actually arises from the realization that the social character of human flourishing requires the possibility of social orders that extend beyond a polis and not from an antecedent commitment to a liberal approach to political philosophy. We do not, then, beg the question in seeing a difference between claims (1) and (2) or in understanding the central task of political philosophy as the search for the norms that might be able to connect them. Rather, we argue that individualistic perfectionism is the deep structure that not only justifies liberalism but also political philosophy in the modern sense.[12]

We have no truck with "justificatory neutralism." We do not think that political philosophy of any sort can be sustained without deeper views about ethics and human nature, or, if truth be told, reality. However, to reject justificatory neutralism does not mean or imply that the political principles that constitute liberalism must be in the service to what is good or obligatory. Liberalism is not a disguise for a particular ethical theory.[13] To grasp how this might be, it is necessary to reject the idea of equinormativity—that is, the idea that all ethical principles are of the same type or have the same function. It is possible for there to be ethical principles that function to regulate conduct so as to establish conditions that allow for the possibility of moral conduct. We call such principles "metanorms," and we distinguish these norms from those we use to guide conduct in the pursuit of good or in the performance of obligation.[14]

Our account of individualistic perfectionism shows how it is possible for there to be a need for ethical principles that are metanorms and in what these principles consist. It does so by showing how a conception of human flourishing that is objective, inclusive, individualized, agent-relative, self-directed, and social gives rise to a task that requires for its completion an ethical principle that is a metanorm. This undertaking, which we call "liberalism's problem," is constituted by the following set of questions:

> How . . . is the appropriate political/legal order—the order that provides the overall structure to the social/political context—to be determined? What is its ethical basis? Since the structure provided by the political/legal order will rule over all equally, how can the universalism of *political/legal* structural principles square with the pluralism and self-direction required by human flourishing? Hence, how is it possible to have an ethical basis for an overall or general social/political context—a context that is open-ended or cosmopolitan—that will not require, as a matter of principle, that one form of human flourishing be preferred to another? How, in other words, can the possibility be achieved that various forms of human flourishing will not be in structural conflict?[15]

Given our account of human flourishing,[16] we argue that a solution to liberalism's problem must meet the following interrelated conditions:

(a) it must not structurally prejudice the overall social context more toward some form of human flourishing than others—that is, it must respect the moral propriety of individualism;

(b) it must be universal or equally applicable to all forms of flourishing, that is, it must be social in the open-ended or cosmopolitan sense;

(c) it must be *concretely* present in any and every form of self-perfection—that is, it must be grounded in some common critical element that runs through any and every form of self-perfection (or its pursuit);

(d) it must appeal to some aspect of self-perfection in which every person has a necessary stake—that is, it must provide an agent-relative reason for a person to follow any principle that meets these other conditions;

(e) it must recognize the ethical obligation of individuals to pursue and achieve their own form of human flourishing—that is, it must recognize that different forms cannot be ranked independently of the agents that pursue them, and hence it must reject what we have graphically called "moral cannibalism"; and

(f) its requirements of human conduct must be ones that any and all human beings can in principle fulfill—that is to say, these requirements must be realistic or nonutopian.[17]

Ethical principles that meet all of these conditions are metanorms, and these principles offer guidance in the creation, maintenance, interpretation, evaluation, and justification of the political/legal order. Thus, we argue that both liberalism's problem and its solution are based in a neo-Aristotelian conception of self-perfection.[18]

For the most part, England understands that both the emergence of and resolution to liberalism's problem is vitally connected to our account of individualistic perfectionism. Nevertheless, he objects that liberalism's problem is actually only a parochial concern. He notes, "A ladder may be necessary to rid one's gutters of leaves, but one may instead choose to ignore the problem, tear down the gutters, or cut down the trees" (p. 20). So, analogously, why make liberalism's problem the central concern of political philosophy? Liberals may regard it as important, but so what? Why not simply ignore it or deal with other issues? Further, why may one not challenge the account of individualistic perfectionism? Instead of seeking to find a solution to liberalism's problem, one might reject some of the underlying assumptions. To wit: why must human flourishing be understood as we have described it—that is as, objective, inclusive, individualized, agent-relative, self-directed, and social?

There are a number of things to be said in response to this challenge. First, we know of no political philosophy or theory that can be considered self-evident. To the best of our knowledge, every one of them has some set of deeper supporting principles. Thus, it is always possible for someone to take issue with a political philosophy or theory by rejecting its deeper premises. Therefore, since this is an objection that applies to every political philosophy or theory, it cannot be judged as having any special weight against our view of political philosophy.

Second, if one does not assume that ethical relativism is true or that accounts of human nature and reality are undefendable, then acknowledging that political philosophy or theory is based on deeper principles need not be regarded as anything untoward. Rather, it might just indicate what England so rightly notes—namely, that the effectiveness of philosophical distinctions is dependent on some broader intellectual context. Indeed, to make more explicit what we stated earlier, we regard the entire attempt to do political philosophy without ethics, or ethics without philosophical anthropology and an account of reality, to be a mistake.[19]

Third, though our account of individualistic perfectionism is not complete—*NOL* is only a book in political philosophy after all—we do have quite a bit to say about individualistic perfectionism. We argue that it is quite plausible, that it has many advantages over competing ethical theories, and that the account of human flourishing applies to nonliberals. Moreover, not only do we spend one chapter developing our account of individualistic perfectionism but another chapter defending it.[20] Thus, the reader of *NOL* is not asked merely to commit to this deeper theory; it is a matter of arguments and reasons—many of which we will examine when we consider the concerns of other critics below.

England indicates that he is aware that we might respond to his charge about the parochial character of liberalism's problem in the foregoing manner, but he still insists that the distinction between normative and metanormative principles is limited in scope. It remains only a concern to liberals or those who share an ethics that gives rise to liberalism's problem. Our reply is however the same. If human flourishing is as we describe it, and if this applies to people, which includes nonliberals, then the need for metanormative principles is based on the nature of human flourishing, not some antecedent commitment to liberalism. Fundamentally speaking, liberalism's problem is a human problem.[21]

England is correct to suggest, however, that the next step in the process, or our next book, is to consider what the most satisfying ethical theory is. How does individualistic perfectionism stack up against its rivals? We welcome this examination and conceive of our future work in terms of addressing this issue. Regrettably, England notes at the end of his essay that even this process would not be free from the charge of circularity by the nonliberal. Yet, this seems to assume that political commitment is fundamental and that first philosophy as well as ethics is a matter of ideology. This is an assumption that we have challenged elsewhere[22] and will have more to say about towards the end of this essay. Regardless, we see no good reason to assume that such an examination of basic ethical issues must beg the question against nonliberal views.

Kenneth L. Grasso is appreciative of both our efforts to distinguish liberalism from an all-encompassing worldview and to provide it with a new deep structure. Indeed, he agrees with many aspects of the new deep structure that we offer. However, he has serious doubts about our argument in certain respects. Grasso expresses his doubt in the following claims:

1. Our account of "structural neutrality" is not that different from "liberal neutrality" and is thus vulnerable to the same objections that have been leveled against "liberal neutrality." We will call this the "Liberal Neutrality Objection;"

2. Even if "structural neutrality" is theoretically possible, it will allow in practice nonetheless for a bias against certain ways of life and thus will be destructive of certain forms of social life. We will call this the "Social Ecology Objection;"
3. Our conception of human flourishing is so "thin" that it is virtually no different than an agnosticism when it comes to relating the human good to particular individuals, and furthermore this translates (at least in practice) to just the type of relativism and skepticism that has plagued contemporary liberalism. We call this the "Tacit Relativist Objection;"
4. Our account of human sociality is not sufficiently sensitive to all of its dimensions. This is so because we hold that choice is the only common element in the social relationships necessary for the flourishing of individuals and because we hold that society, as a whole, has no *telos*. We call this the "Social Ontology Objection;" and
5. We implicitly assume that if there is a difference between the requirements of the moral order and those of the political/legal order, then individual rights are the link between these two orders. But this does not follow. We call this the "Non Sequitur Objection."

We will respond to each of these objections, but first we will begin by considering some comments that Grasso makes regarding liberalism being haunted by two specters—the specter of the polis and the specter of moral minimalism or skepticism. Then, we will start with the Tacit Relativist Objection and the Social Ontology Objection.

Grasso claims that much of Western political philosophy can be understood in terms of what Voegelin calls "the 'mortgage' of the polis" (p. 60). It tends to envision

> a rightly ordered polity as a small, intimate, homogeneous society, but more importantly . . . the goals of politics as being coextensive with the overall goals of human life; to see in the

> polity the ultimate milieu of man's perfection; to understand statecraft as soulcraft and to confer on the state an open-ended mandate to promote human flourishing in all its dimensions; and to . . . view politics as ethics writ large and insist that the proper relationship between politics and ethics is a direct and isomorphic one. . . . One thinks here, in short, of Western political theory's tendency to equate polity and polis. (pp. 60–61)

The power of this view cannot be denied, but some questions need to be asked: "Why did Modernity initially break away from this vision? Why was liberalism born?" and "What justifies, if anything, this break?" The first two questions are too complex to answer adequately here, but this much can be said. Due to many factors, but especially commerce, societies in Europe became less and less homogeneous, and so the very idea of a polis became increasingly irrelevant. But more importantly, the attempt to promote human flourishing (which was usually understood in religious terms) involved much of Europe in many bloody and long-lasting wars. Further, there was growing doubt about the effectiveness of trying to promote virtuous living by political means and greater confidence that a peaceful, orderly, and free society[23] might more likely be both attained and maintained by setting conditions that promote various forms of free exchange. In other words, statecraft became something other than soulcraft—politics was no longer conceived as the institutionalization of ethics—but rather as the means for protecting people in their efforts to "truck, barter, and exchange." Or, more bluntly put, politics became in actual practice concerned with protecting the possibility of people pursuing their own forms of self-interest consistent with others being able to do the same.

This does not, of course, justify moving away from the vision of the polis, and there have been many thoughtful people who have argued against such a move—from at least one version of Marx to MacIntyre to Taylor. Thus, the question remains "Is liberalism justified in breaking away?" This brings us to the second specter that haunts liberalism according to Grasso—namely, moral minimalism or skepticism. He correctly notes that moral minimalism and skepticism are problematic and that contemporary liberalism is foundering from an inability to either defend or understand itself. Moral minimalism or skepticism will not do. Yet, Grasso never asks why liberalism was (and still remains) tempted by such minimalism or skepticism. One answer is, of course, that it still understands itself as in service to a polis, and so if there is to be an attempt to make men moral, then to keep in touch with the realities of modern life morality would have to be something very thin indeed. Otherwise, nearly everything can come under the purview of the political/legal order.

There is, however, another answer—that is, that the conception of human flourishing employed by those who seek to implement it through political/legal means is grossly inadequate to the reality of individual, flesh-and-blood, human beings. In other words, it fails to represent adequately either the nature of human flourishing or what that implies—particularly as they pertain to the diverse ways in which individuals flourish. Thus, the temptation to adopt moral minimalism or skepticism also results from the desire to find some basis for affirming the ultimate moral importance of individual human beings and from the belief that an objective or "thick" conception of human flourishing works against individualism by requiring uniformity. Grasso does not discuss this answer, however, and the reason for this is the same as the one that supports his Tacit Relativist Objection.

Simply put, Grasso accepts the view that upholding the fundamental moral importance of the individual is ultimately incompatible with an objective or thick account of human flourishing. If our moral knowledge is robust, then one's commitment to moral individualism must be reduced. Accordingly, he thinks that to offer, as we do, an individualized and agent-relative conception of human flourishing is to offer a thin conception that borders on agnosticism and amounts virtually to relativism. Yet, nothing could be further from the truth. Human flourishing is a rich and complex activity that involves biological, environmental, social, and cultural factors. It is a way of living that entails the actualization of numerous individuative and generic potentials of individual human beings. Since a properly formed conception of human flourishing seeks to reflect reality rather than make reality conform to it, such a conception must begin with the diversity of individuals and the realization there exist many individualized forms of human flourishing. This is what we seek to do, and hence the conception of human flourishing that we offer is actually thick or robust.

If truth be told, not only does an individualized and agent-relative conception of human flourishing *not* generate a thin conception of human flourishing, but the opposite is the case. Conceiving of human flourishing as some monistic good, where individuals do no more than locate this good in space and time, is to make human flourishing quite thin. It limits human flourishing to only what can be conceptually specified with no room for the various ways in which it might be expressed. Such a conception makes an abstraction into a reality and makes the moral life no more than an exercise in rationalistic deduction from so-called generic goods and virtues with little or no role for the intellectual virtue of practical wisdom.

We need not here go over our account of the generic goods and virtues[24] of human flourishing, but we do wish to point out that we always argued that human flourishing is more than simply self-directed activity.[25] It is the self-directed use of human intelligence to discover, achieve, maintain, manage, and enjoy those generic goods and virtues that, when actualized, express this way of living. There is thus nothing about individualistic perfectionism that allows the individual, so to speak, "to get off the hook," when it comes to the demands of living a worthwhile life. The task of human flourishing lies squarely in the hands and minds of individuals, and its achievement is no easy matter.[26]

Yet, since the moral life as an actuality is both individualized and agent-relative, it cannot be something that is merely "read off" a generic account of human flourishing. It is with regard to this issue that Grasso seems to conflate concept with reality and to assume that if human flourishing is expressed or understood in a universal manner, then there must actually exist some common or universal form of flourishing that is identically present in each individual. He states, "What sense does it make . . . to assert that human beings possess a natural good if the content of this good varies so fundamentally from individual to individual . . . ?" (p. 69). This misunderstands how concepts function, because it confuses, as Aquinas puts it, the mode of our cognition with the content of our cognition—that is, it supposes that what is grasped through abstraction as common must actually exist in that manner as well. Interestingly, in spite of Grasso's professed allegiance to the Thomistic version of the Aristotelian tradition, he shows little awareness of its theory of abstraction, and thus he has not considered how it is possible for what is universal to be predicated truly of individuals and for the content of that predication to be individualized. Moreover, nowhere in his comments does Grasso take up our account of how human flourishing can be objective as well as individualized and agent-relative. Nor does he examine our criticisms of both "old" and "new" natural law theories.[27]

Grasso's statement in the previous paragraph also reveals an assumption about morality with which we have been taking fundamental issue. He assumes that moral knowledge is primarily and essentially for telling people what they ought to do in a concrete situation rather than people discovering what they ought to do in such a situation for themselves. There is a vast difference between giving directives to people to take a concrete action, for example, pursue a friendship with this person at this time and situation, and making a general claim about what is a worthwhile activity, for example, friendships are worth pursuing. The latter is the approach to moral knowledge that we advance, and, as already implied, it makes practical wisdom the chief intellectual virtue of the moral life of each person. For this approach, particular and contingent matters, but not universal and necessary ones, are the determinative factors of moral living. Though there is a place for universal concepts and principles, especially when it comes to providing a moral basis for the political/legal order, it is simply wrong-headed to think of the moral life as an activity of following a set of universal directives for concrete action regardless of the time, situation, or individuals involved.[28] It is in this regard that we think that Denis Sullivan's essay, which we will examine later, recognizes what is crucial about our individualized and agent-relative character of human flourishing.

Fascinatingly, the same misunderstanding of how concepts function also plagues Grasso's Social Ontology Objection. Regarding our account of human sociality, he states that

> [t]his account of human sociality, however, seems to exhibit problems that parallel those displayed by their accounts of human flourishing. Is it really plausible to say that although human beings are profoundly social beings by nature—that social life emerges out of our dynamic orientation towards the realization of our natures—each individual is so unique that it is impossible to generalize about the structure of social relations that should govern human life? How can this be reconciled with their insistence on a knowable human nature with natural needs and tendencies? If the network of social relations that collectively constitutes society issues from our dynamic orientation towards the perfection of our natures, how can it be said that society as such has no telos? (p. 74)

However, just as it is possible for us to speak of generic goods and virtues, which when actualized by self-directed conduct constitute human flourishing, so it is possible for us to speak of social relations that are vital to human flourishing. There are friendships of different types, family relations of various sorts, associations and partnerships for every concern, and clubs and groups of numerous kinds. These relationships, and others like them, stem from basic human needs and tendencies, but their particular forms are as diverse as the individuals that make them up and the contexts in which they exist. These social relationships are natural in the sense they are *for* the self-perfection of the individuals that make them up. However, their existence is still the upshot of human action,[29] and their particular form is the consequence of convention and artifice as much as biology and physical environment. Some of these relationships are internal to what and who an individual is, and some of these relationships are external. Neither atomism nor holism is true. Finally, these relationships, though not reducible without remainder to the individuals that compose them, still have no reality as wholes or substances over and above the individuals that ontologically sustain them. They have no telos other than what might be derived from the telos of each individual human being.

It is our view that these statements describe Aristotle's social ontology,[30] but we do not need to debate this issue, because we have always described our view as "neo-Aristotelian." Further, we think that Elaine Sternberg's essay, which we will consider later, underscores the non-atomistic character of our social ontology; so we will have little more to say regarding our account of it. Nevertheless, the point we want to make is just as Grasso errs in thinking our account of human flourishing is thin, so too he errs in thinking that our view of what social relationships are necessary for individual flourishing is based only on choice. On the contrary, virtually every constitutive activity of human flourishing involves a social dimension. This cannot be denied or ignored. Yet, because we emphasize that human sociality is open-ended or cosmopolitan and because we do not specify, beyond generalizations of the sort made in the previous paragraph, what are the necessary forms of social relationships, Grasso thinks that we treat social relations "as external, artificial, adventitious, and contractual" (p. 72). But this does not follow. As said, human flourishing is shot through with social relationships, but their exact form and role in the flourishing of an individual depends as much on the virtue of practical wisdom in dealing with the contingent and particular as any other feature of human flourishing. They are thus not something that can be simply deduced from the claim that human beings are social animals. Again, the concept does not dictate the reality. We will have need, however, to consider other aspects of this issue later when we consider the comments of David Thunder and Charlotte Thomas.

Grasso seems to be aware that the concept of the polis conflates the concepts of society and that of state (or political/legal order).[31] He also seems to be aware that this creates difficulties for anyone using this concept when engaging in political theory, but he nonetheless appeals to the idea of a political community as if it were not problematic. He complains that we reduce the basic questions of political theory to the relationship of the individual to the state. However, this is not true, or at least not as

Grasso intends it. As already indicated, we emphasize that human beings are thoroughly social animals and that it is a mistake to attempt to conceive of human flourishing as something achieved in isolation from others. Moreover, throughout *NOL*, but especially chapter ten, we note, "human flourishing must be always embodied in some form of community life."[32] When we speak of individual flourishing, we thus never deny that there are social relationships present. We are never for a moment assuming that there is not a vast network of social relations involved. It is never simply the individual, conceived of as some "atom," and the state.

Nonetheless, we are concentrating on the fundamental question of political philosophy—that is, what, if anything, legitimates the state (or political/legal order)—and we are not considering such questions as what are the forms of social life (institutions, conventions, etc.) that human beings need to flourish or how might they be sustained. Though we do not deny the importance of these questions, they are not our specific concern. They are only relevant insofar as they relate to the question of legitimation (of which we will see examples when we consider the Social Ecology Objection). Thus, we are engaging in political theorizing that distinguishes the individual, the social and communal, and the state from one another, and we are careful not to conflate one with the other. Further, we are using an ethics of Aristotelian inspiration to deal with the fundamental question of political philosophy, and though we are acknowledging the social nature of human beings, we are not assuming that what is true for us as social animals necessarily applies to our relationship to the state (or political/legal order).

Grasso does not appear to grasp this point fully. Indeed, at times he seems to miss it entirely, because he complains that we provide no account of the distinctive nature of the polity as one of the communities to which "our nature as social beings gives rise or its distinctive contribution to human flourishing" (p. 77). However, this is the very point at issue. If "polity" means state or political/legal order, comparing it to just another community among all the others that express our social nature misses something crucial—namely, the ability of this "community" to pass laws that apply to everyone within its jurisdiction and to use coercion to secure compliance. The question for political philosophy is what, if anything, justifies there being an institution with these abilities. Is statecraft for soulcraft or something else? In addition, when Grasso cites Jacques Maritain, who claims that the polity or state is more than force and laws, but also a "'heritage of . . . historical remembrances,' 'symbols,' 'glories,' 'living traditions and cultural treasures,' 'political virtues,' 'customs,' and 'unconsciously operating hereditary wisdom" (p. 77), he is not noting anything that is particularly distinctive of the polity or state. All of these are possible for the family, to give but one instance.[33] By treating the polity or state like all the other communities that express our social nature, Grasso fails, despite his claims to the contrary, to free himself from "the ' mortgage' of the polis" and grasp what is distinctive about political philosophy as opposed to social philosophy.

This failure to distinguish consistently between society and the state is also present in what we have called the Liberal Neutrality and Social Ecology Objections. Grasso notes that it may be difficult, if not impossible, for certain ways of life, for example, "traditional" forms of family life, to be practiced without the appropriate moral environment in a community. He argues that a political/legal order that is strictly limited to protecting individual rights might in actual practice "disadvantage" certain forms of flourishing and thus, despite our claims to the contrary, be systematically biased. However, this objection is based in part on confusing two questions: (1) "What kind of values, institutions, and practices need to present in a community in order to make possible or facilitate a certain form of flourishing?" and (2) "What kind of principles should govern the laws that will be applied systematically and universally to individuals and communities across society?" The answer to the first question is endlessly complex and depends on many contingent and particular matters, and any answer that is adequate for one form of flourishing may not necessarily be adequate for another. Indeed, this is the very question that shows "liberal neutrality" to be an illusory goal, and it is for this reason that we reject it.[34] But the answer to the second question, which we take to be but an abbreviated form of the questions that constitute "liberalism's problem,"[35] does not seek to deal with the various conditions that are needed to facilitate or make possible various forms of human flourishing. Rather, it seeks to find an ethical basis for laws that will not be, as a matter of principle, incompatible with various forms of flourishing.

Given our account of individualistic perfectionism, we have argued that only protecting the possibility of self-direction (which we clearly differentiate from self-perfection) can meet all the criteria for answering the second question, and the ethical principles that protect this possibility are individual rights. As we have noted, these ethical principles are metanorms. These principles are *political/legal* structural principles that determine the overall or general social context that secures the possibility of individuals pursuing their own forms of human flourishing. The point of these principles and the difference between these two questions (which also constitutes the difference between "liberal neutrality" and what we have called "structural neutrality") cannot be discerned if one conflates society with the state.

Since Grasso never fully comprehends how it is possible for human flourishing to be objective as well as individualized and agent-relative, he also errs in assuming that we need to meet the objections offered[36] by Sandel, MacIntyre, and others to liberal neutrality, when we have in fact rejected it as either a moral or practical goal for politics. He is not sufficiently sensitive to how our account of self-perfection undercuts the attempt to pursue liberal neutrality and defines the purpose of the political/legal order in terms of providing a solution to liberalism's problem. Indeed, if our account of self-perfection is correct, then contemporary liberal efforts via the state to secure for every form of flourishing the opportunity to exist are just as morally illegitimate as conservative attempts to legislate a social environment conducive for a form of flourishing regarded as particularly important for society, for example, the "traditional" family. Such legislative endeavors amount to the establishment of a sustained and systematic bias of the overall social context in favor of some form of human flourishing against others. They fail to meet the criteria for solving liberalism's problem.

Nevertheless, we are highly sympathetic to many of Grasso's concerns. We make it clear in *NOL* that having a political/legal order that makes liberty (as defined by individual rights) its paramount concern does not mean that there are not many things that people on their own in various associations and groups do not need to accomplish in order to make society worthwhile and decent. What we are objecting to is, of course, the assumption that beyond securing a solution to liberalism's problem this is a concern of the state. Yet, for the same reason, we are also rejecting the idea that the only things that need to be considered ethically are what the state does. We are insisting, on the contrary, that there is a large role for various associations, groups, clubs, and organizations in making society morally better. Moreover, there is a place for ethical philosophers—in political philosophy to defend the supreme value of liberty but also in social philosophy to call for changes in practices and institutions that are ethically objectionable. This is what we meant by claiming that we do not presuppose "a Hobbesian picture of man."

There are other issues involved here as well. While requiring compliance with individual rights is a realistic goal for the political/legal order, because it only requires people to refrain from initiating or threatening to initiate physical force, this does not mean that having a society that maintains and practices individual rights consistently does not require more than simply having a political/legal order dedicated to these rights. It is one thing to determine if what the political/legal order requires is realistic, and it is another thing to determine what it takes for the ethical principles that both justify and inform such an order to have social and cultural support. Since *NOL* is a work in political philosophy that is concerned primarily with the question of political legitimation, we did not spend much time addressing the issue of creating a supporting social and cultural order, but we did show an awareness of this issue's importance.[37]

Additionally, we have addressed in a recent essay, "The Myth of Atomism,"[38] an issue raised by Charles Taylor as to whether a liberal order can generate sufficient civic ethos to maintain itself. We think what we say there is relevant to concerns Grasso raises along these very lines. We state:

> Taylor fails to consider the possibility that something can have value to each of us as a function of our relationship with each other without thereby having to be an end for us. What belongs to us as a whole may only be the securing of the conditions or framework for the pursuit of goods (ends). Those goods we pursue might be the object of some enterprise, but the condition or framework for them is not, in itself, one such good. To consider the principles which secure the conditions for the pursuit of ends or goods (metanorms) as themselves an end is to misunderstand their nature. We may have to act that way toward securing those conditions, but if so, that would be a sign of some pathology in the conditions—the conditions have come under attack or are breaking down for some reason. In and of themselves, they exist not as ends but to make the pursuit of ends possible.[39]

A civic ethos that supports a society and culture that consistently practices the basic ethical principles that define and sanction the condition or framework of a liberal order is possible. This can be done, however, without turning the political/legal order or society into a common enterprise or confusing metanorms with norms. Individual rights can inspire a civic ethos. We are thus not precluded from having such an ethos.[40]

Towards the end of his essay, Grasso raises what we have called the Non Sequitur Objection. He notes that simply showing that the relationship between the ethical order and the political/legal order is neither direct nor isomorphic does not, by itself, show that the purpose of the political/legal order is to protect individual rights. This is correct. Indeed, the basic purpose of *NOL* was to address the question of what, if anything, connects these two orders. Particularly, our aim was to show that the "middle term" that connected these two orders had to be determined by what solved liberalism's problem and that it was by appeal to our account of human flourishing that a solution was to be found. We provided an overall, systematic account of our argument in chapter eleven and defended that account in chapter twelve. We were very careful not to commit ourselves to any of the bogeymen that Grasso raises—"the liberal soul," "freedom-at-any-price," or "radical freedom." We made it quite clear that our claim that liberty (as defined by individual rights) provides the solution to liberalism's problem was dependent on a deeper moral theory, that is, our account of individualistic perfectionism. Nowhere in the final section of his essay does Grasso, however, take up the argument we use to show how individual rights are the metanormative principles that solve liberalism's problem. Instead, Grasso raises objections that are appropriate for much current liberal theorizing but which are in no way applicable to us. He seems to think that our endorsement of individual rights as crucial for solving liberalism's problem is the same thing as saying that liberty is license or that it is the most important ethical value *tout court*. We explicitly reject these claims in *NOL*, but it may be that Grasso does not realize this because he assumes that all ethical principles are of the same type. He may assume that it is not possible for an ethics of self-perfection to generate a need of ethical principles of different types. He may not see the importance of the distinction between metanorms and norms. We are, however, speculating about Grasso's views regarding these matters and do not know for sure. We applaud Grasso's concerns, but we invite him to look more deeply at our argument.[41]

David Thunder's essay raises an important philosophical question that both he and we only allude to but which stays in the background of both our discussions of norms and metanorms and liberty: to what extent is the homogeneity of the ends of flourishing across agents a factor in the defense of liberty? Thunder's tacit thesis in answer to this question is that the more pluralistic the ends of flourishing are, the easier it becomes to put liberty as the central and primary political value. Thus, because we give pluralism so much weight (and thus homogeneity so little), liberty comes to have a central place for us. And because Thunder gives pluralism much less weight, liberty tends to become just one among a number of important values needed for human flourishing. The reason homogeneity seems to matter so much is that with less of it, it would be harder to identify and mandate standardized forms of conduct. The degree of pluralistic flourishing is thus the degree to which we fail to come up with successful generalizations about flourishing and thus must adopt the value of liberty as primary because only it seems to transverse all agents.

It does seem to us that the value of liberty is easier to *see* when homogeneity is diminished. We do not think, however, that a lack of homogeneity is primary and *essential* to our defense of liberty. Before making that case directly, let us start with Thunder's conclusion and work towards our case. We are accused at the end of holding that "whether flourishing actually or even tangentially occurs is politically of no relevance" (p. 38). This charge, as far as it goes, is quite correct, but its impact comes from the out of context—or perhaps question begging—manner in which it is put. Because the success, or lack thereof, of flourishing is so dependent upon the choices people make, and because politics serves only to provide a framework within which such choices can be made, it is true that whether people flourish or not is of no relevance to politics per se. But as liberalism's problem attests, politics is itself a tool of human flourishing and thus in that sense the success of flourishing is of concern to the political order—that is, politics exists because flourishing is the central human concern. Flourishing is not of concern to the direct ends politics seeks to secure, but it is of concern to the nature and purpose of having political arrangements in the first place. Moreover, in the Epilogue to *NOL*, we observe that metaphysically speaking we expect the good that is liberty to have positive consequences when put into action. That expectation seems to be borne out by the actual success of free societies. Therefore, in this other important sense we are not indifferent to the consequential success of the political order either.

Both of these points about consequences and politics can be made without any reference to the issue of whether the ends of flourishing for individual persons are few or many. What is critical about those ends is that they be chosen and be chosen by individuals. It is, then, not the plurality of ends that makes the difference here, but their exercise by actual persons who make them a part of their lives. Let us suppose, for example and for the sake of argument, that there are in fact only five ends needed for human flourishing—ends A-E. We can include, if we like, some of Thunder's favored ends (e.g., having a family) among the five ends. The problem with this way of conceptualizing matters, which also seems to be Thunder's, is that there is no argument for why these values or ends A-E are in fact *my* ends (or your ends, or another individual's ends). To say that it is because they are human goods and I am human is to simply raise the question all over again: Why are they *my* goods? The fact is that none of us is the generic entity "human," so we must find some way to say more than "these are human goods, I am a human, and therefore they are my goods." We must provide an argument that shows that being an end for someone involves a good deal more than being the middle term of a syllogism. We are more than placeholders. The essential way in which an end becomes an end for *oneself* is through an act of choice, within a context of possible choices, in light of one's own *particular* nexus[42] of values and goods. In this respect, we do not confuse the generic goods A-E with the sorts of goods actually needed for something to finally qualify as a good for *someone*. A-E are *not* actually my values or ends, nor can they be in that form, though they may be necessary building blocks of my values or ends. Once one sees this, one understands immediately that what is substitutable for Thunder under his way of conceptualizing the matter are individuals.[43] Whether I, or you, or the next person has, say, value C (e.g., having a family) is all the same, because the value or end is the same for each of us. On this conception of values or ends, therefore, generic goods cannot be substituted one for the other. They must apply, intact, to all the same way. By contrast, generic goods are precisely what are substitutable for us. That is to say, they can be mixed and utilized in various ways and to various degrees.[44] What cannot be substituted are the individuals who transform those generic goods into actual values.

Because of all this, one realizes that when speaking of finding a principle that reconciles the diversity of ends, it must be understood that the diversity comes not necessarily from the *variety* of ends there may be, but rather from the fact that ends, to qualify as values of relevance to virtue, are all individualized.[45] The tethering of values to discrete individuals is as much "diversity" as liberalism's problem needs. It is true that besides "diversity" in the sense of individuated, we also happen to hold that there are a wider variety of generic goods than may be recognized by the traditional Aristotelian. But our point here is simply to suggest that the primacy of liberty is not merely a function of the homogeneity issue, though it would be sensible to admit that liberty becomes all the more pressing if the ends that contribute to flourishing are various.

Finally in this regard, Thunder never takes quite seriously the order of the steps in which we make our argument. Because we take the individual to be so central to a proper conception of flourishing we do not begin with any a priori assumptions about the ways in which "society" might be utilized to ensure that flourishing is secured. In other words, individuals are not reducible to their societies so that restructuring societies is not ipso facto the reformation of individuals. That has to be shown as does the uses to which "society" might be put and the ends it is justified in pursuing. Consequently, our argument takes the political to be one form of social organization that is justified because it serves a *particular* purpose of *limited* ends in a context that takes flourishing to be our central obligation and pursuit. We believe we have given an argument as to why the ends are limited and why they cannot be expanded. Furthermore, we believe the burden of proof goes the other way: we no longer have to show why the ends of politics are limited as we have described, but rather others must show why they should be expanded further. We do not assume that it is obvious what politics is or should be doing simply because it has always done certain things.

Thus where exactly the political enters our argument makes a significant difference to fully appreciating that argument. For example, Thunder states that "To insist on the priority of liberty is to insist that *other* structural features of flourishing, for example, the property of not being addicted to heroin, are consistently trumped by liberty. But I find no argument in this book for this proposition" (p. 37). This claim could only be made by ignoring how our argument for the role of the political emerges (at a particular moment) from the ethical context in which it is set. Understood correctly, one would say that liberty "trumps" *politically* but not absolutely. It trumps politically because that is the nature of the solution to liberalism's problem. Not only do we identify it that way, but we also provide an argument for this in the book. The only way to claim that we do not is to forget the role of the political and its timing in our argument. For in other contexts, for example, the moral, liberty does not necessarily trump those other features of living a virtuous life. Our point here is also the answer to Thunder's closing question about the relation between negative liberty on the one hand and flourishing on the other—assuming that is a question of a political character. If it is, Thunder already knows the answer, because he accuses us of separating flourishing from politics. We just gave a response to this above. But if the question is a broader one, then the answer is the one just given—namely, it may not be. But it is important to recognize that negative liberty[46] as a political factor carries with it the characteristics of something essential to all acts of virtue itself, namely choice. In that respect, there is a deep and abiding connection between negative liberty and authentic human flourishing.

Susan D. Collins offers a subtle challenge to one of the core components of our doctrine, namely choice or self-direction. In effect, Collins asks what if choice or self-direction is not so clearly contributory to flourishing, as we seem to hold. Indeed, what would happen if we were to purge the sort of "will" language of choice and self-direction from center stage and instead saw the goods people pursue in terms of their social functions, patterns of habituation, or the values that the society in which they live tend to acclimate them towards? If we were to look at politics this way, so Collins seems to argue, we would see that not all forms of life are very encouraging of flourishing and some, which are quite necessary for a society to function, positively *dis*courage flourishing. An argument so dependent on choice or self-direction, such as our own, turns out to be vulnerable, Collins claims, to the reality that choice or self-direction may have little bearing on the actual lives of real people in real communities.

Her conclusion is not, however, pessimistic. Rather, given the current malaise surrounding liberalism, perhaps the kind of reflection upon it and emphasis on individual choice will itself serve as a habituating force that will contribute to the sort of flourishing that truly is appropriate for human beings. In effect, Collins seems to be suggesting that the sort of liberalism we advocate, even if it is a naïve expression of "an Aristotle made young and beautiful"—as opposed to the wiser, more correct, though "less beautiful, ancestor" (p. 111) Aristotle—is nonetheless salutary.

The philosophical issue here is whether virtue and flourishing require in *any way* an element of choice or self-direction or whether various forms of habituation, more or less subtle in nature, are sufficient to carry the whole burden of what it means to be virtuous and to flourish. If *any* element of choice or self-direction is necessary for, or central to, the exercise of virtue or flourishing, then our argument may still go through—however much the bulk of a person's actions are the result of processes of habituation. Indeed, if choice or self-direction is the rare component that transforms conduct into virtuous conduct and living into flourishing life, all the more reason to ensure the protection of the conditions that make that possible.

In this regard, Collins makes an important error in understanding our doctrine. Collins claims that "the authors so closely identify flourishing with the liberty of self-direction that it becomes hard to see the status or role of compulsion and coercion in moral education, human action, and politics" (p. 114). Of course, with respect to the last of these, it is not hard to understand the role of compulsion and coercion with respect to politics at all: their role in politics is completely and solely reactive—that is, compulsion and coercion are used in response to initiatory acts of coercion on the part of others. But that is not the main point here. The main point is that we do not in fact identify flourishing with choice or self-direction. We only claim that choice or self-direction is a necessary feature of actions which qualify as virtuous and thus for flourishing as well.[47]

There is certainly a good deal more to what it means to flourish or be virtuous than simply having the freedom to choose one's actions. Indeed, we stress this point because we do not want to fall into the camp of those who claim that respecting people's rights concludes the discussion of what is moral or contributory to flourishing. In morals then, free choice is critical but not very helpful in leading us to fulfillment. In politics, however, free choice is virtually the whole point.

The implications of the last point are important. In the picture provided by Collins, people are led to flourish or not by the roles they play in society and their forms of habituation within those roles. Society simply cannot provide flourishing roles for everyone, so some win and some lose when it comes to their possibility for flourishing. The question here, then, is the one posed above: Does choice play any necessary role in what counts as flourishing? If it does, then the reasons for its protection remain the same as we have argued. The fact that *a lot* of habituation needs to take place or that some roles throw up more impediments than others to achieving flourishing is of extreme interest when it comes to morality, but of very little interest when it comes to the political question; for we would still need to protect what is critical and necessary for virtue and flourishing however uncommon its presence.

On the other hand, Collins could be suggesting that choice or self-direction is not necessary for virtue or flourishing—appropriate molding and habituating are all that is necessary. We suspect that some version of this view—which generally is the view that individuals are pure functions of their society—is a direct challenge to our position. Even if true, it is not *logically* necessary that the state be the vehicle through which flourishing or virtue is achieved, and Collins is clearly someone who would not want to go that route. Still, if this case could be made, a number of steps in our argument would be less compelling or disappear altogether as reasons for our conclusions. We do continue to insist, therefore, upon the centrality and necessity of choice for virtue (without suggesting it is the whole of the matter) and thus its centrality to our political argument. We are not, however, impressed by the fact that there are people who need to clean our streets or remove our garbage. Our understanding of both virtue and flourishing is context bound—that is, it involves choices within a framework of possibilities based upon one's own particular circumstances and prospects. The job itself is less important than how it is integrated within a pattern of choices within one's own life. To say that, of course, is to make choice and practical wisdom central and necessary to any claim to virtue or flourishing.

A reflection upon the older less beautiful Aristotle is supposed to sober us up about our claims about the centrality choice. But again, even if the question is "vexed" about where, if at all, choice enters into the picture, so long as it must enter, the political argument goes through. The point is not conceded by Collins because, like David Thunder and others, her presumption seems to be that politics and/or society themselves have a purpose, namely to produce flourishing individuals. However, Collins, unlike Thunder, is a "realist"—politics can only go so far and we might as well recognize it. Thunder, by contrast, seems to believe that the right institutions can get large chunks of people within sight of flourishing. It is not a debate that concerns us, because producing flourishers is certainly not the aim of politics, and society, while necessary for the maturation of flourishing, has no purposes.

Charlotte Thomas' thorough critique of us from an Aristotelian perspective shares much with the criticisms of England and Collins. Like England, she wants to claim that our argument only goes through because of a prior commitment to liberalism. Like Collins, she wants to claim that the need for habituation in achieving and understanding virtue and flourishing throws up an impediment to our argument that a liberal political order follows from our commitment to an Aristotelian framework. In certain respects, at least, Thomas fleshes out the nature of these criticisms more completely than England or Collins. However, so as not to spend too much time repeating ourselves, we believe that our responses to England and Collins are also applicable to Thomas. Hence, we will not direct our remarks to all the points of criticism made by Thomas.

Thomas does add, however, an additional element not found in England and Collins by bringing up the question of external goods. Like habituation, external goods seem to be something that is necessary for flourishing but which can fall outside the scope of choice or self-direction. Indeed, external goods (e.g., food) may make choice or self-direction possible, since their presence may make it possible for one to engage in choice. It might even be said that they, rather than choice or self-direction, should be given the central role in what needs to be protected and secured for virtue to be possible. It is only our prior commitment to liberalism that keeps us from recognizing that positive rights to certain goods are required once one has made a commitment to a perfectionist ethics.

Before dealing with this question, it is important to correct a misperception on Thomas' part with respect to both habituation and external goods. Thomas says things like the following: Rasmussen and Den Uyl give "no clear reason for self-direction as a necessary condition for flourishing to trump habituation" (p. 50). The same could be said about external goods, that is, that we give no clear reason for self-direction to trump the provision of external goods. The problem here is that we *do not* say that self-direction trumps habituation or external goods absolutely (indeed Thomas quotes a passage from us to this effect). Self-direction is only a trump in the political realm.[48] When it comes to ethics, virtue, or morality proper, we expect self-direction to be working *together* with habituation and external goods.

The point is worth making because Thomas and Collins both see some incompatibility between habituation and choice suggesting that we must choose one over the other. Yet Thomas in her discussion of the lyre player actually indicates how they are compatible. For the decision to sit down and practice is not one devoid of choice. If one tries to habituate oneself to good piano playing, the repetition involved in doing so is not thereby outside the realm of choice. Indeed, it is not just the opening choice to practice that illustrates this, but also the *continual* choice to focus upon the results and nature of one's repetitive acts that also brings in the dimension of choice.

Thomas challenges us by asking the question: "Given the crucial distinction between self-direction and self-perfection, what objection would Rasmussen and Den Uyl have to establishing as a metanorm the right to the externalities requisite to self-direction?" (p. 53). It is not exactly clear to us why the section from *NOL* (pp. 303–12) is not sufficient to answer this question. Thomas quotes from part of that section (our discussion of the term "poor"), but leaves out the rest. The rest is, however, what answers the question. To reiterate quickly the point found there: we do not deny that there may be generic goods that are necessary for flourishing, even perhaps for self-direction. Yet, as we noted in our response to Thunder, there are no generic beings, only concrete specific individuals. This point is important because Thomas conveniently forgets to discuss how the external "generic" goods are going to be provided.

If we grant there are such goods necessary for flourishing, we confront the question of how to get those goods in their necessarily specific form to necessarily specific people. One way would be to coerce some people to give up some of their resources to serve others (or to coerce them to act in ways that produce those resources for others). Another way would be to ask them for help in providing those goods. This, by the way, is *not* a choice we face with the good of self-direction. By insisting that the metanorm on behalf of self-direction be secured, we are not thereby coercing some to provide a good to others, as we would be with the "external goods" Thomas advocates. Indeed, establishing the metanorm of protecting the possibility for self-direction does not coerce anyone to be self-directed or to give up some of their self-direction so that it may be added to that of others. At most, it responds to coercion by the use of force.

Providing external goods as a matter of natural rights by the state, however, necessarily is a form of coercing some to provide for others. We are not against this because we are liberals, but we are liberals because we believe we must be against this type of redistributionism. We must be against it because—as already noted—people do not interact with generic goods, but rather with specific goods provided by specific people in specific contexts. For this reason, we would actually agree with Thomas' statement, "It does not follow from the claim that human flourishing is highly individualized and agent-relative that it does not also have some intelligible generic shape" (p. 55), but we find it unhelpful to the problem at hand. Indeed, flourishing does have generic characteristics and needs. The problem is that the actual provision and exercise of goods is never "generic," so there is no way to provide those goods without structurally biasing the system in favor of some forms of flourishing over others.

Thomas (and Collins, and Thunder, et al.) is likely to object to this last claim on the grounds that the provision of generic goods cannot bias anything,[49] because by definition they are generic and thus the same for all. The biasing here, however, is in fact present when one moves from the generic to the actual, even if negative in character. Imagine that two people, A and B need exactly the same basket of goods to flourish. Suppose further that B has his basket full of those goods, but A is missing some for hers. To take some of the goods from B and give them to A clearly biases things away from B *structurally*. The system is supposing, in other words, that B's choices about what to keep and integrate are (a) not relevant to the goods in the basket being goods for B, and (b) that even if those choices are relevant they can be trumped by some other principle, namely the absence of those goods in A's basket. With respect to (b), to presuppose that any holder of a basket of goods "Q" with the goods "a . . . n" is not entitled to them if there is someone else in the condition of Qa . . . n-1 is in fact instituting a pattern of flourishing that ignores by design the choices and circumstances of the actual individuals affected. Thus, in this case, the bias goes away from B. Moreover, with respect to (a), the redistribution to A of some of B's goods could only avoid structural bias if that system assumes that B's choices and acts of integration of the goods is not particularly relevant to their being goods—an assumption that we argue is false. If those choices are significantly relevant for a . . . n being goods for B, then it is clear that the system is structurally biasing away from B. These points illustrate what it means to structurally bias the system, at least in the negative sense of biasing it away from some agent (B).

By contrast, the system we advocate, by its nature as a system (which thereby means treating people equally and without taking sides), must consider B's Q as being what B regards as resources he has chosen for his flourishing and thus as goods for B. Thomas herself agrees that the system is designed to protect the possibility of flourishing which minimally means agents making choices about how to integrate goods. To suppose otherwise, is to *presuppose* (i.e., structurally bias) that goods for B are significantly disconnected from his choices. Since we have assumed for the sake of argument that A's ideal Q is identical to B's, the structural bias in this case is negative (away from B). The problem, however, is only augmented if A's Q is not identical to B's. In that case, the agent's disassociation from his or her goods is even more pronounced. (Keep in mind we are talking about external goods here, not every good.)[50]

Let's suppose, however, that B has a surplus and will not "miss" the goods taken from him. Again, if this is the case, then we could try to convince B of this surplus or we can simply force him to give up the surplus goods. But only the former case retains structural neutrality. The coercing alternative again assumes that the goods in Q can be disassociated from B and still be goods. In sum, the structural bias requirement we insist upon is not (and cannot be) simply about respecting different lifestyles. There can be structural biases even among those opting for the "same" lifestyle in a very homogenous society. No doubt, people are drawn to redistributive schemes because they observe what seem to be so many others wasting their resources or having vastly more than they need or can use wisely. However that may be, the fundamental fork in the road is one of coercing an alternative use of goods or not. We believe that only the "not" answer is consistent with liberalism, but, more importantly, only this answer is consistent with the individualized character of the good and the perfectionist ethics that validates it.

Peter Vedder provides a fine summary of some of the main tenets of our argument. His criticisms are very much in the vein of Collins and others, though in some cases he is more explicit and in others less so about the character of the perceived failings in our argument. However, Vedder has chosen to ignore what the other critics emphasize, namely that we are not claiming to be interpreters of Aristotle, nor to be necessarily in agreement with him on all issues. Despite the fine summary, Vedder, unlike

Collins for example, is unwilling to evaluate us on our own terms, but must do so only through the eyes of Aristotle. This is fine, except that in Vedder's discussion there is no philosophical account of what makes something good and thus why we should accord with the understanding Vedder, speaking for Aristotle, has of it. The attitude displayed is one of "Aristotle says X is good, therefore we must believe it." That simply is not us, and it leads to rather silly comments later on (both on the part of Vedder and Aristotle) about how, for example, politicians necessarily have by nature the chance to live more flourishing lives than "moneymakers" do.

More valuable things are said by Vedder about moral psychology, and here is where one finds one of the two substantive criticisms of us. It is essentially the same criticism of us leveled by Collins, and our response to Collins applies here as well. The main difference is that where Collins treads carefully and slowing in distancing us from Aristotle, Vedder jumps in with abandon—he simply reduces our notion of choice or self-direction to a Kantian autonomous will. In response to Vedder, Collins, and anyone else inclined to understand "voluntariness," "choice," "will," or "self-direction" this way, we have made no such Kantian commitments in *NOL*. Furthermore, we go out of our way to suggest that we will not be making such commitments. We do not believe there are untethered and dispositionless will acts made in complete freedom from antecedent conditions. Indeed, our whole discussion of the "nexus" is meant to put such readings to rest. Moreover, we endeavored to use notions of self-direction in "common sense" ways, not packed with a lot of philosophical baggage, because we believed that ordinary usage (say, ordinary common law usage of choice and intent) was sufficient to complete the political argument.

At the same time, we certainly do not hold with Vedder, or Vedder's Aristotle, that there are these reified objective goods somewhere out there (and for some reason, "good"), with which, to enjoy or exhibit those goods, we must ally our dispositions to such an extent that we can think of doing nothing else. Both in terms of what makes something a good and in terms of the psychology associated with the exercise and pursuit of the good, our story would not be identical with the one Vedder tells of Aristotle. Still, Vedder, along with Collins, Thomas, and Thunder, make a good point that there is much more to do in discussing moral psychology, and that if we are not going to be Kantian in our use of "will" terms we need to do more. We plan to take the matter up on our next project. Still, as we mentioned in our response to Collins, we also do not believe a full unpacking of the phenomenon of choice will be devoid of "modern" elements. Nevertheless, we are certainly mindful of the classical Aristotelian and Thomistic doctrines of disposition and appetite when we think of choice or self-direction. Yet, from what we see here, we are not convinced that Vedder has gotten Aristotle right either. This is mainly because Vedder equivocates on the term "freedom" or "free," supposing it means "cannot" when in fact all he shows is that it means "will not."

The second substantive criticism of us has to do with our "inconsistency." Vedder nowhere makes it clear in exactly what this inconsistency consists, so we are at somewhat of a loss to respond correctly. It looks to us like our "inconsistency" is to be found in our relation to Vedder's Aristotle rather than with ourselves. If Aristotle is the standard and measure of truth, then of course any deviation would constitute an "inconsistency." In this respect, our crime seems to be that we do not hold that the philosopher (or political philosopher) represents the highest form of human flourishing which, if such were true, would contradict our claims in support of the political order which protects multiple forms of flourishing. If this is the charge, we plead guilty.

What Vedder actually says, however, is that "*Rasmussen and Den Uyl's* doctrine of teleological eudaimonism proves to be incompatible both with *their* teaching concerning human equality and with *their* understanding of human freedom" (p. 176, emphasis added). This statement suggests that Vedder has looked at things the way we do and found some inconsistency therein. No doubt our own self-interest blinds us in some respect here, but when we look at the matter what we see is that there is incompatibility between what we hold and traditional notions of teleology, perfectionism, equality, and ethical objectivity.

Though Vedder does a fine job in outlining just what these doctrines are in our case, they are not taken seriously in the end, as far as we can tell, but simply are measured against classic positions in the history of philosophy. We therefore do not see any internal inconsistency. Since the historically great philosophers possess superior minds to our own, it is perfectly fair to hold their teachings against ours and find us wanting, if such is the case. However, it is one thing to hold our efforts up to the conclusions of a great philosopher on similar topics and quite another to claim that one is inconsistent because those doctrines do not match those of some great philosopher. In the one case, presumably, defects are identified; on the other, all one has identified are differences with a presumption of mistakenness. Far be it from us to claim we see farther and deeper than such thinkers do; but that is not to say we do not see at all.

We have saved **Timothy Fuller**'s contribution for last in this section of our discussion because its challenge is both critical and prospective. Consequently, it represents a good transition from the mode of criticism to that of prospects. In the midst of Fuller's flattering compliments about *NOL*, one finds a number of pointed questions and implied criticisms. Among these are questions about our foundationalism, the degree to which our outlook is really Aristotelian, the place of teleology in our framework, the superiority of the Aristotelian framework relative to others, and how we understand the notion of "common goods" within our political theory. Implied in the way many of these questions are raised is either a suggestion of inadequacy on our part in giving enough discussion to them or the suggestion that our theory is likely to have significant difficulties in accounting for itself on some specific matter connected to the question. No doubt, we will have to plead guilty on both counts. Certainly, there is much left to do, and some questions may indeed carry with them special difficulties. Yet with respect to all those topics just mentioned, we believe that the responses we have given to others above on very similar issues are at least applicable to the issues Fuller raises, if not directly answers to them. Hence, we have chosen to say something about an issue Fuller brings up that is more prospective and speculative in nature and can thus provide a transition to our next section on prospective matters.

The issue is stated first by Fuller in the form of a suggestion that we should be "more attentive to the mystery of the human situation in which the aspiration for moral excellence is in tension with a polity that can defeat as well as promote it" (p. 135). Later on, we are told that:

> It appears that the authors do not accept the idea of an end, but there is nothing definitive in the arguments they bring against it. I think they are right, however, to say that a liberal regime constitutes itself in wary skepticism about how to settle this issue. Yet the liberal regime cannot exclude this issue, or those who would seek to settle it, because it appears to be one of the natural alternatives for reflective thought to consider. In this respect, there remains tension between the requirements of a liberal regime and the quest for wisdom. While we may not expect the authors to resolve the tension, it does seem that they presuppose its insolubility (p. 138).[51]

One way, perhaps, of putting Fuller's worry here is to formulate the question of whether the liberal regime *requires* agnosticism about there being a single telos for all persons. If there were to be such a telos, then liberalism's apparent allowance of actions contrary to those conducive to a telos we all in fact share would be tantamount to an endorsement of an agnostic attitude towards that good. That would be in tension with the recognition of the good itself. Moreover, the liberal regime would frustrate the pursuit of that good, at least negatively, by not devoting resources to its pursuit, and perhaps positively, by openly permitting resources to be devoted to ends contrary to that good.

It is, of course, something of a non-sequitur to say that because X permits A (or does not stand in the way of A), therefore X endorses A; but in politics this sort of inference may carry some weight because so much of politics influences behavior through its symbolic nature. Yet part of the issue here, at least, is whether the metanorms of a liberal order are, in the end, really a securing of the possibility for moral actions—and thus are *meta*norms—or whether they must be themselves regarded as shapers and directors of moral actions and characters. Fuller (and we suspect others such as Thunder, Collins, and Thomas) either ignores or simply refuses to accept the first possibility—that is, he does not take metanormativity seriously.[52] Rules of a political order must be, for Fuller, inevitably shapers of actions or characters. It does not matter how we regard them; that will be their fate in practice. What this means is that even if the metanorms start out as "rules of the game," they will eventually take on the characteristics of ordinary moral norms and be used to decide what qualifies as morally good and bad, right and wrong. Thus if those metanorms were minimally intrusive in character, the message is inevitably sent to those governed by those norms that the system is either agnostic about the nature of the good or encouraging of its alternative.

In response,[53] it is not that we do not believe that the metanorms might have an effect upon action or that those norms might not, at times, be confused with, or manipulated towards, more directive ends. It is rather that we believe the metanorms do not have to be taken as directives towards certain moral ends, that they should not be considered that way, and that people *need not* have to consider them that way—to which Fuller might simply disagree. Thus, we would maintain the distinction between norms and metanorms and hold that the liberal metanorms are not designed to surreptitiously point to some ordinary moral good but to define the conditions under which people might pursue such goods. It may be true that there is an inclination to collapse the distinction, but not only does it not follow that therefore it must be collapsed, but part of what it would mean to be "patriotic" or a "good citizen" in a liberal order would be to recognize and maintain the distinction.[54]

It might be true that homogeneity about the nature of the one true good for human beings may lessen the impact of liberal metanorms upon people's lives, because they may have less recourse to them in "boundary" disputes. However, it is also true that the idea of there being a plurality of final ends is equally appealing to contemplate as contemplating the idea of one final end. Therefore, a regime devoted to the one true end would be at tension with itself in the same way as the liberal regime is said to be in tension with the notion that there might be a single end. Looked at in this way, no regime can escape the problem of tension. The liberal solution (as we have described it), however, has the advantage of strongly distinguishing the political from the moral and thus indicating that the way Fuller wishes to look at the problem in terms of there being a tension is itself problematic, for it fails to make just this distinction between the political and moral. Making the distinction allows for the possibility that the issue of whether the good is one or many is not of central political concern and thus need not be a source of tension.[55] That is to say, the metanormative/normative distinction has the advantage of not just allowing, but actually taking seriously, both sorts of reflections about the nature of the good, because it does not muddy the question of the nature of the good with that of politics. Of course, in saying this, we have now raised the possibility that the real tension Fuller is pointing towards is between politics and morality per se, not the singleness of the moral good. This can indeed be a real tension and one our distinction is trying to manage. For the universalism required by politics is of a different order than the agent centeredness required by morality, as is the coercive character of politics versus the voluntary nature of the moral good, and the suitability of thin minimalist political principles compared with thicker norms needed for morality.

To say, however, that there is an inherent tension between politics and morality seems to move the problem in a direction away from where Fuller wants to move it. When one looks at the universalism, coerciveness, and appropriate minimalism of politics, one is drawn to the desire to separate politics from morality. By contrast, Fuller seems to be skeptical of any radical distancing of the two and seems to be objecting to just this separating tendency. In this respect we believe Fuller may not see—and we do not think he's alone on this—the full degree to which ethics for us is agent-centered, though his questions about our "nominalism" and "anti-foundationalism" suggest to the contrary that he does sense something of the direction we take.[56] Nonetheless, the questions Fuller raises about certain goods being common and incapable of inversion (knowledge is better than ignorance and that ordering can never be inverted to one where ignorance is better than knowledge) indicates that he may have a goods-centered approach to ethics rather than an agent-centered one as we have. As we have pointed out in a number of places, we are quite willing to talk about generic goods and believe they have an important and necessary place in thinking seriously about ethics. Nevertheless, these goods are not, as they certainly are for Robert George and John Finnis and perhaps Fuller himself, the starting place or ending place of ethics. Indeed, they are ethical "goods" only in a qualified sense for us. Rather they are more like tools the person with practical wisdom employs to gain ethical knowledge and thus intelligently direct action. The universality and power to compel others to their acceptance that these generic goods might possess are not of prime consideration in our agent-centered view, but they do seem to have pride of place in theories promulgated by the new natural law theorists (that is, thinkers such as George and Finnis) and goods- or right-centered theories generally. This is because these theories focus upon the goods and then apply them to agents. These theories thus measure the significance of those goods by the number of people to whom they apply and the degree to which the agent is to feel bound to the generic good. For us, because we are realists epistemologically and metaphysically about both human nature and the nature of things in the world, it is meaningful and valuable to talk in these general terms. But in the end, these generic goods derive their goodness as a function of the agent; they are not goods in their own right to which the agent's functions must adhere.[57]

With a goods-centered approach to ethics, the temptation is to identify the goods and then see if the political order either promotes or frustrates them. Under this way of looking at things, it will always be the case that the political order will be in the sorts of tensions Fuller worries about, because the political order will have to take some specific political direction in contrast to the necessarily open-ended character of contemplating the nature of the good. Any given regime will thus fall short, because there always will be a difference between someone's conception of the nature of the good and what goods are actually being promoted by the political order. By contrast, an agent-centered approach to ethics would tend to measure a political order not in terms of the goods it frustrates or promotes, but rather in terms of whether agency itself is protected, since goodness is a function of agency and not the reverse. By focusing on agency rather than goods, the central question of political theory is not what is the connection between the political and good, but what is the connection between the political and agency. A possible answer to this question consistent with the agency approach is that there is, to over-simplify in the interest of brevity, no direct connection between the political and the good at all, but only a connection between the political and agency. What the good is and how to promote or pursue it is another matter for another set of circumstances and institutions, because the problem of agency must take priority, since all questions of goodness are derived from it. If, under the agency view, politics *were* ever to focus upon the pursuit of the good, the case for that would be highly derivative from one that begins with the centrality of agency. One will notice in *NOL* that we treat issues of the pursuit of goods by political means in precisely this way. The goods-centered ethicist thus worries primarily about whether the political order has distanced itself too much from the good. From this perspective, there are some who want tighter and some looser reins upon that connection. The agent-centered ethicist, by contrast, worries that the political order will bring itself to promoting "the good," for from an agent-centered perspective the greatest danger we face is putting the anti-agency tools of coercion and universalism in the service or promoting some good or goods.

II

In his clear and tightly argued essay, **James Stacey Taylor** seeks to lend additional support to our neo-Aristotelian approach to ethics. He wants to develop further the idea of human flourishing as essentially a self-directed activity. He is particularly interested in our claim that "if self-direction is for the sake of the human good, then agency or self-direction is not radically free, as existentialists or voluntarists would apparently have it."[58] He notes that if this claim is true, then an important aspect of the so-called Continental approach to philosophy will have been undermined. He regards such a consequence as of no small importance.

Taylor begins by elaborating on an argument that he finds us implicitly making. Assuming that human beings have a telos and that self-direction is naturally for the sake of this end, then humans do not choose *ex nihilo* or, as we also state, "the end-oriented character of self-direction is not itself a matter of self-direction."[59] He observes that this argument depends on two assumptions—that human nature is teleological and that human beings cannot conform to their teleology by making radical choices. Noting that we believe a complete defense of the first assumption is part of a much larger project,[60] Taylor decides to concentrate his attention on the second assumption. He wants to provide a thorough defense of the claim "that humans cannot conform to their teleology by making radical choices" (p. 142). He does so by examining what he considers the main thrust of an existentialist response to our view—namely, that a teleological account of human flourishing does not preclude the possibility of radical choice.

Taylor starts by making a point that is in many respects similar to one we have used against those who interpret Ayn Rand's approach to ethics as being based on a so-called premoral choice to live.[61] He argues that the existentialist idea of the flourishing human being who constructs his own authentic will by engaging in radical choice is incoherent. He argues that a person's choices cannot be normative for that person unless they provide some particular reason for making them.[62] Yet, if one constructs one's will *de novo*, that is to say, if there is nothing beyond one's very act of choice that determines what one's will is ultimately *for*, then there is nothing that guides or provides boundaries on such a choice. However, if this is so, then there will be no reason for one to adopt the will one has constructed. Thus, such a creation would provide no reason for accepting the apparent normativity that is supposed to be drawn from such a will. "A radically free agent, then, might be radically free, but he would lack all self-direction, for he would have no *self* to direct" (p. 144).

The existentialist might respond that this argument fails to recognize that human flourishing actually requires making radically free choices, but Taylor dismisses this view of human flourishing. If radical choice is supposed to be "unbound by any considerations whatsoever" (p. 145), then it cannot be something that human nature "requires." Such a view of human choice must deny the possibility of humans having any definitive nature, but it does raise the question of how the relationship between human choice and human nature is conceived.

Taylor takes up this issue when he considers two other possible replies by the existentialist. These are: (1) making radical choices is actually constitutive of human flourishing and that is rock bottom; and (2) there are examples of people who construct a will for themselves but still have reasons for acting in the future. In response to the first reply, he notes that human flourishing is something that admits of degrees, but making radically free choices does not. One cannot be partially radically free. So, it does not seem that human flourishing is simply constituted by making radically free choices. Further, how is making radically free choices good for one? Flourishing is after all what is good for a person, and so if human flourishing just is making radically free choices, then how is this good for a person? How can choosing, regardless of what it achieves or expresses, be good for a person?[63] Taylor notes that without considerable argument on its behalf there is little reason to accept this existentialist view.

This is an important point. As we have noted in response to Collins, human choice or self-direction is vital to human flourishing being the very activity it is, but this is much different from saying that human flourishing just is choice or self-direction. What reason does one have to accept this existentialist view? Indeed, why would such a conception of human flourishing even be tempting? Though Taylor does not address this question, we would argue that the source of this temptation is the result of assuming that if there is something that self-direction is naturally for, then this orientation must be construed in terms of efficient or material causality and thus as contrary to self-direction.[64] The possibility that self-direction is the exercise of a power that belongs to a set of powers that makes a human being a living organism and as such must be understood in terms of a human being's inherent and overall potentiality for his or her mature state is not recognized by those who make this assumption. However, if self-direction operates in such a biocentric context (and we did provide in *NOL* some reasons for thinking that this is so[65]), then this assumption is most dubious. This raises, of course, the larger debate regarding that idea of natural teleology, but we welcome such a debate. We intend to take up this issue in detail in the future, because we have contended from the start that the basic questions of ethics and human anthropology cannot be handled without addressing deeper metaphysical questions.

Regarding the second reply, Taylor argues that the examples of people who construct a will for themselves but still have reasons for acting in the future are not the same as what the existentialist postulates. The basic difference is that the constructions found in these examples are not *de novo*. Taylor states, "The reasons given by the preference structure that he picked would be supported by other aspects of his preference structure that he did not pick. . . . It is not his endorsement alone that makes the reasons that flow from the aspect of his preference structure that he picks to endorse normative for him" (p. 147). This is a decisive point, but it is also revealing, because to say that human nature is definitive and not determined by choice alone does not mean that there is not a place for self-creation and self-definition. On the contrary, this is crucial feature of our understanding of the role of practical wisdom and the place of each person's nexus in our account of human flourishing.

We thus find this last point, as well as others made by Taylor, to be most congenial to the views we have advanced, but there is another point that we need to emphasize briefly—namely, that the ability to make choices that are not for the sake of our telos does not mean or imply that we are radically free. The reason for this is that there are many modes of causality involved. If we think only in terms of efficient causality, then every deviation from anything posited as an end would ipso facto indicate that it is not an end. However, there is much more to the story. As living organisms, humans have powers that have an inherent potentiality for their mature state, but the potentiality of these powers is not reducible without remainder to the potentialities that are found in the material elements that compose living things.[66] Since self-direction is one of these non-reducible powers, it too functions for the sake of maturity. Here is where formal and final causality play their role in self-direction. They explain the directive power that human flourishing has for our choices as something to which we are naturally drawn—as something our choices are potentially for—and thus why we are not radically free. Nonetheless, there remains something that an individual human being must do for him- or herself. An individual human being must initiate and maintain self-direction. Exercising human choice and reason is not something that happens to human beings; it is something they do. Here is where efficient causality plays its role in self-direction. This explains how it is through a fundamental failure to exercise both practical and speculative reason that human beings are turned away from their telos. In addition, this affords a basis for the idea that self-direction is the basic activity through which human reason makes human flourishing an actuality. There is very much more to be said regarding this topic, but this will have to be sufficient for now.

Denis Sullivan seeks to use the notion of agent-relative moral value developed in *NOL* to support a negative conclusion—namely, that irresolvable moral disagreement is not so common that it should raise doubts about the very existence of moral truth. We agree with his conclusion, and we do think that an agent-relative account of moral value offers a way of understanding moral truth that can be used to rebut moral skepticism.

We also accept two general claims that Sullivan makes about the position we develop. First, it is possible for an action understood as a dated and unrepeatable particular to be good even if that is never true of any other action. Second, it is possible for a description of a particular action that shows that action to be good to be applicable to another action and yet still not be sufficient to show that this other action is also good. Finally, we agree that even when it comes to judging actions that are wrong for someone to do, the basis for this evaluation is the complex of details of the actual act, not some general claim. Overall, we think Sullivan is correct to claim that "any citation of instances which supposedly show that what we generally believe to be good turns out to be bad, or what we generally believe to be bad turns out to be good, need not be seen as a disagreement with these beliefs" (p. 128).

There are, however, certain features of Sullivan's rich and thought-provoking argument with which we take issue or with which we are in doubt. In fact, it may be that our difficulty in most cases comes because we are simply not clear on what is involved. Nonetheless, here is a list of our caveats:

1. It is not correct to say that we argue that people should be left free to shape their own lives *because* ethical guidance should be left vague. While this claim—at least appropriately understood—plays a role in our argument for liberty as the paramount political value, the argument that we make is more involved than this. It also seems that what we say in response to Thunder is important here, but since Sullivan does not develop this claim, we shall not pursue it.
2. We do not reject universalizability *per se*, as Sullivan seems to imply, but only an impersonalist interpretation of it. We go to great lengths to show that agent-relative values can be universalized and used in arguments explaining why someone ought to do something. However, we also argue that unless one confuses the mode of cognition with its content, what is good or valuable is neither universal nor agent-neutral but individualized and agent-relative. We are thus not moral particularists who have no role for moral principles, but we also do not confuse principles or concepts with realities.[67] We will have more to

say on this point shortly when we deal with related matters.

3. Sullivan wants to use our account of agent-relativity as a "stand-alone position," but we are not sure that can be done simply by looking at how descriptions are used in justifying moral judgments. The underlying question is "Upon what are these descriptions based?" and it seems that this requires an account of what it is for a human being to be doing good or right. So, it seems that one has to appeal to something deeper theoretically than just how descriptions are used in justifying moral judgments.
4. Though we certainly agree that one can offer an abstract or general analysis of the morality of a human action, we would argue that it cannot be the primary object of moral analysis. It is the individual human being that is morality's ultimate concern. We thus start with the question "What is it for a human being to be good or to engage in right activity?" and from this we make moral judgments about the conduct taken. It is in this sense that we are virtue ethicists. Further, the moral evaluation of a particular action, as opposed to a moral consideration of it abstractly or generally conceived, cannot be adequate apart from that action's relationship to the other worthwhile activities and virtues that constitute an individual's human flourishing.[68] Yet, what is even more, making such evaluations requires practical wisdom.[69] As we noted in many places in *NOL*, practical wisdom is for us the central intellectual virtue, and there is no good or virtue practiced (nor evil or vice avoided) that does not involve it. So, just as we are not moral particularists neither are we ethical rationalists.[70]

Now, it may be these very points Sullivan is seeking to make in contending that judgments such as "Giving alms to the poor is good," or "Inflicting pain on human beings is bad" are vague and thus require, in Peirce's terms, "some other sign or experience" to complete their determination. However, as noted above, why does this apply to moral judgments? Why must they be, to use our terms, "individualized and agent-relative"? It is certainly possible to conceive of morality as a series of commands that one must follow regardless of how they relate to an individual's flourishing. Thus, while Sullivan is correct to view such ethical judgments as vague in the Peircean sense, more is required to support this view than this Peircean insight.

5. It also seems that the Peircean sense of what it is to be a "precise" general belief is not what we would regard as precise or determinate when it comes to a moral belief. If we consider, for example, what Aquinas regarded as the first principle of practical reason—namely that "goodness is to be done and pursued, and evil to be avoided"[71]—then it is precise in the Peircean sense. It is so because it leaves the actor free to choose from the set of good activities any good activity to pursue and from the set of evil activities any evil activity to avoid. Yet, what is actually the good activity to be done or the evil activity to be avoided cannot be determined apart from the considerations we noted in the previous paragraph. That is to say, the good activity to be done or the evil activity to be avoided cannot be determined apart from the activity's relationship to the other worthwhile activities and virtues that constitute an individual's human flourishing as well as the individual's nexus and the circumstances in which the action takes place.[72] So, it is not clear that the Peircean distinction between "precise" and "vague" beliefs, which Sullivan offers, works when it comes to the individualized and agent-relative character of human flourishing that we have offered.
6. Our agent-relative account of morality helps to overcome the claim that morality is generally beset with irresolvable disagreement because it shows that in many cases these beliefs are not about the same thing. There are moral truths, but they need not be universally applicable. To morally assess the conduct of one person is not necessarily the same as assessing the conduct of another.[73] This view fits nicely with Aquinas's belief that all true moral

beliefs are in principle acceptable by all, but this is not the same as holding what Sullivan claims—namely, that they are accepted by all. There is a difference between what it is for a belief to be true and what it is for all or nearly all people to come to accept a belief as true. The latter may be a sign that a belief has a good chance of being true, and once one rejects a Cartesian approach to knowledge, these beliefs may be the starting point in understanding in what flourishing consists—that is, what Aristotle called *endoxa* or established opinion. However, this does not mean that their truth consists either in coming to be accepted by all or in being a requirement for learning a language. Thus, we are reluctant to follow Sullivan's suggestion that Donald Davidson might be one to follow on these matters. Yet, much depends on what Davidson actually holds as well as the viability of metaphysical realism,[74] essentialism,[75] and natural teleology. These are extremely important considerations, but they must be left for another occasion.

We have no more caveats to list, but we finally would like to note one of the many helpful consequences of Sullivan's essay. It is one that he never considers—namely, that if individual rights are going to function as "trumps" on all other normative claims, they must do so as metanormative principles. Sullivan's essay clearly implies that individual rights could not have this overriding function if they were primarily for the pursuit of the good or the avoidance of evil. As we have noted many times before, it is only in solving a problem that emerges from an individualized and agent-relative account of ethics that they can take on their status as trumps. It is exclusively in light of liberalism's problem that individual rights can have the task of setting fixed boundaries on human conduct—specifically, of regulating human conduct in terms of what must not be done. If Sullivan is correct, then all other attempts to provide individual rights with this status are doomed to fail.

William Kline has made a most interesting argument for including trade among the list of things required for a flourishing life. Kline makes his case by arguing that the characteristics we apply in *NOL* to flourishing also apply to trade. In doing so, Kline points to an important part of human existence that has not received the attention it deserves for its contribution to human well being and the ethical life. Trading is often either disparaged or, as Kline points out in his opening paragraph, separated completely from ethical and social considerations. From our perspective, then, Kline's efforts here are to be applauded, for this is indeed a concept that needs resuscitation along Aristotelian lines. Kline does an excellent job in getting that work off the ground, and we appreciate his use of our own work in making his case.

Though we are in accord with Kline's efforts here, we also believe that one needs to step carefully in all of this. First, Kline tells us that "human flourishing is '(1) objective; (2) inclusive; (3) individualized; (4) agent-relative; (5) self-directed; and (6) social' (p.127)" (p. 151). In fact, however, what we say on page 127 of *NOL* is that these are interrelated features that apply to the human good, and by this we mean that they apply to those activities that constitute human flourishing. These six features are not criteria for determining what human flourishing comprises. Rather, they are a description of how the constituents of human flourishing are related to each other so that they make up the whole activity that is human flourishing. In other words, *these six features explain what kind of human good human flourishing is, but they do not explain what it is to flourish.* For example, human flourishing is a good that is composed of many worthwhile activities as opposed to simply one, or it is a good that is expressed through action, not passive or static. However, neither of these observations tell us just what are the activities (either generically or concretely considered) that need to be done by an individual if they are to flourish. The question then becomes one of whether "trade" is one of the constituent activities of human flourishing or whether it simply has (all or some of) the six features that describe the kind of good human flourishing is. If it is the latter, then that would not be sufficient to show that "trade" is a constituent activity of human flourishing. If it is the former, then upon what basis is trade to be considered a constituent activity of human flourishing?

Kline notes in a number of places, flourishing has a lot to do with judgment, evaluation and choice, but historically trade has been associated with the satisfaction of desires whether one gives any thought to one's desires or not. Is, therefore, the sort of activity that is characteristic of flourishing also the sort of activity characteristic of trade, and if so in what ways and to what degrees? Is trade good simply because the satisfaction of our desires is good or are there other characteristics of trade that factor in here? In our own account of things following page 127 we discuss how certain generic goods, through the exercise of prudence and judgment in the context of one's nexus, contribute to the meaning of a flourishing life. The generic goods (e.g., friendship, health, knowledge, etc.) help locate the components of flourishing, whereas the six features help one see (among other things) how those goods must be tied to individuals if they are actually to qualify as goods. Running throughout this whole discussion is the exercise of practical wisdom which is what, in the end, makes the whole process active. Our cautionary note here, therefore, concerns keeping in mind both the active and the component sides of flourishing or the human good. Here we worry a bit that Kline is too prone to seeing trade as a component of the human good, which is as a generic good. The hazard of speaking of trade (or anything else for that matter) as a generic good is that it is easy to lose sight of the active character of that good, even when analyzed in terms of our six features. With an emphasis on the goodness of X, one may be on the road to the sort of diminishment of the contributions of the agent to flourishing which we often complain are missing from so many ethical accounts. Such is perhaps not logically implied in placing an emphasis on the goodness of something, but doing so can have a tendency towards reifying the good and forgetting the agent.

Perhaps even more importantly, by not keeping in the forefront both the component and active character of the human good or flourishing, we believe that the normative/metanormative distinction could be threatened. For if the component goods of flourishing are emphasized at the expense of the active character of those goods, the metanorms would seem to exist for the sake of protecting goods, rather than to protect the possibility for their attainment. It seems a short step from there to the claim that the political order should be concerning itself with what sorts of goods are produced or achieved in society. Liberty would itself become simply a good, because with the active element of flourishing gone, there would be no other way to view it. That conflation would in turn mean that the political argument would be one of having to show that liberty was somehow a superior good to other goods when it comes to discussing the components of a flourishing life, and this is a form of argument we wish to avoid. But if liberty can also be considered an essential element in the process of the *activity* of flourishing as well as in its enjoyment (that is, in the exercise of its goods), the metanormative/normative distinction is much stronger and the political argument entirely different. We are not suggesting that Kline has traveled down this road yet or that he is unaware of the hazards involved in doing so. We offer these remarks as a friendly reminder that X falling under the six features does not finish what must be said about X to understand it as connected to human flourishing.

Another, and much related cautionary note, is what might be called avoiding the "liberal virtues" problem. Although it may be true that liberal orders might encourage some qualities of character more than others, or that a liberal society might flourish more if its citizens exhibit certain qualities of character, none of that has a bearing on the nature of our argument for liberalism. Moreover, although we believe that trade has been underestimated as a value to human flourishing, we would not want to be seen as suggesting that encouraging trading—or any other virtue for that matter—is the object of a liberal order, or that embracing the life of a trader is needed to qualify as a "good liberal." Kline does not make any such claims, so this cautionary note is retrospectively looking at the political argument given in *NOL*. As a prospective matter on what might be said in the field of ethics, we are happy to push with Kline the virtues of trade and explore what that might mean for an ethical life.

Finally, we need to make some comment on whether trade should be its own category as a component of the good life or whether it is sufficiently captured by other categories such as "sociality," "pleasure," or "friendship."[76] In general, we suspect that Kline is right: the historical lack of respect for trade means it deserves the sort of attention and emphasis Kline gives to it. But one is nonetheless compelled to ask the question of whether trade belongs as a separate entry on the list of "unqualified" goods such as knowledge, friendship, pleasure, health, sociality, and the like. In our understanding of "unqualified" in this context, we are talking about a generic good that, when considered apart from any agent or its role in any nexus, one would say that it is unqualifiedly good. Can that claim be made about "trade"? As Kline points out, trade might involve things that are either good or bad, so it would seem that trade in itself is somewhat neutral with respect to the good. That would be one issue to consider here. And if trade had as its end the satisfaction of desires, it would not be a good in itself, since something is not good simply because we desire it. It is not our view that desire satisfaction sums up trade, but it is an issue that would need some exploration. The other issue would be whether the good parts of trade to which Kline rightly draws our attention might already be captured by the basic list of final ends already promulgated. If so, trade, given certain assumptions or properties, would then become a subcategory of something like "sociality." Both of these questions are important issues for further exploration. However, trade may indeed have characteristics that make it, and it alone, a peculiarly *human* form of sociality and that would go a long way towards promoting Kline's thesis about the central contribution of trade to flourishing. Moreover, if we also remember Aristotle's insight that friendship or "philia" comes in many modes, which includes friendships of pleasure or utility, then Kline's thesis takes on even greater importance. In this connection we would probably say that it would be a mistake to focus on the Smithean notion of a *propensity* to truck, barter, and exchange. There may indeed be such a propensity natural to us (and not, for example, natural to the dogs Smith mentions in *Wealth of Nations* I); but what seems particularly humanizing about trade to us is the element of intelligence it requires of action.

Elaine Sternberg does a very thorough and careful job of detailing our own views on ethics and politics as well as those of David Weissman. In doing so, she highlights the ways in which our theory does not fall into some of the atomist traps that may characterize other defenses of liberalism. In this endeavour we could not be more grateful, for critics of liberalism and libertarianism often lump all the various defenses together. In addition, highlighting some of the differences between our approach and a communitarian one like Weissman's is valuable as well.

This last point, however, raises a question about the thesis Sternberg actually seeks to defend in her paper. Sternberg begins her paper by noting that Weissman's[77] "metaphysical challenges to individualism nevertheless do not touch the defense of individual liberty developed in *Norms of Liberty*" (p. 86). In a number of places later on, however, we are told that a specific principle of ours "seems compatible with [Weissman's] social ontology" (p. 96). These are rather different, and not necessarily consistent, aims for the paper to have. If these two aims are in fact compatible, it must be because of a form of argumentation that says that because Weissman and we have the same views on X, and we hold Q, then Weissman's attack on Q in the name of X cannot apply to us. That is a different form of argumentation than is suggested by the first aim of the paper which is something like we hold Q, and Weissman attacks Q in the name of X; but we are not subject to those attacks because (a) we have recognized the relevance of X, and (b) we have an understanding of X Weissman has not refuted or taken into account. In short, though we are convinced that we are not subject to the usual charges of atomism, we are not very convinced that the components of our doctrine really are compatible with Weissman's social ontology—at least in its metaphysical commitments. Similarly, we suspect that if Weissman were to read us, he would be no more sympathetic, even if he would be forced to concede that we are not atomists. The differences between us, we believe, would not rest solely upon opposing political orientations and conclusions. Let's spend a moment, then, looking beyond the political.

First, we are not very clear on what Weissman means by "self-sufficiency," and a lot seems to hang on how that term is interpreted. As presented here, Weissman seems to collapse a belief in separability into a belief in self-sufficiency. To believe in the former does not commit one to the latter, whatever "self-sufficiency" may mean. This is because self-sufficiency seems to be something one attains, whereas separability would seem to be a condition from which one might seek to arrive at self-sufficiency. Thus, unless one has some sort of strong state of nature myth, to claim that by saying individuals are separable one is thereby committed to saying they are self-sufficient would certainly be a mistake. But the opposite sort of conclusion that Weissman seems to want to embrace, also does not follow—namely, that because separable individuals are not self-sufficient we must thereby see (a) their characteristics as individuals as a function of some larger whole or system and (b) that the system thereby has standing in providing the degree of sufficiency individuals actually do possess. In the former case (a), it may be possible for individuals to possess substantive qualities which, when considered in isolation from others, are not of themselves enough for self-sufficiency of the individual or even for the full development of those particular qualities and yet which are still significant qualities of the individual in question. In the second case (b), "systems" do not thereby gain distinct ontological standing because of the weakness of the individuals that compose them. It may just be that the relations among the individuals in a system that contributes to their sufficiency is one that simply employs their individual powers more effectively than one that gains power through a collective joining of individuals and then distributes it down to individuals.

The foregoing helps point us to where we believe there is some real distance between us and Weissman at a metaphysical level, and thus why it is that our doctrines cannot be made "compatible." To put the point most simply, and in a way which certainly cannot be developed here, for us individuals are ontologically substantive and metaphysically primary units from which systems derive their nature; and those individuals are ends in themselves which in turn give any value to systems.

Weissman, by contrast, seems to believe that systems are the primary ontological units with individuals being derivative of them and with value for individuals being a function of the values systems impart to them. Our ways of looking at the world are therefore quite different and incompatible. Indeed, applying this discussion to (b) just above, systems would seem not to derive their sufficiency from collective individuals, but would rather be self-sufficient in themselves and then impart that sufficiency to individuals. In this respect, the self-sufficiency of systems for us is equivalent to the myth of self-sufficiency of individuals.

In places where she discusses agent relativity, self-directedness, and individuality, Sternberg quotes Weissman in ways that suggest compatibility with our views. From the nature of the quotations themselves, compatibility appears to be the case; but when one looks closer one finds no contradiction with what Weissman says and the fundamentally different orientation towards the ontology of individuals just mentioned. If we consider what Weissman states elsewhere in *A Social Ontology*, we find what he states to be quite consistent with the idea that individuals derive their value from the system. Moreover, these statements are consistent with the notion that there is a higher order of value than what may be realized through individual experience and action—namely that of the system. For example, Weissman says, "' We *choose* the objects of ultimate value. . . . We, by self-election, are good-in-themselves. This is a considered choice, one that is justified by experience and interest, as we value human beings and human flourishing for the good reason that we are humans who want to flourish."[79] For a "considered choice" to be something "that is justified by experience and interest" in no way requires any ontological primacy for individuals. Consequently, we do not find it strange that Weissman would say that each individual is a "good-in-themselves" (where Sternberg comments on the oddness of the expression), because in fact there is no individual that is a *his-* or *herself* and not a "themself" for Weissman. Individuals are loci of experiences and interests, but not sources of value or being for Weissman as for us. All this is why we remain sckeptical that there is much hope for achieving any real compatibility between us and Weissman on some fundamental matters of ontology.

We might mention here in closing another matter that is related to ontology but may not seem as significant at first. In her discussion of objectivity, Sternberg first cites us on objectivity and then says what we say "should pose no problem for [Weissman's] social ontology. He recognizes the existence of both 'core interests' and primary goods, and acknowledges health as an 'immanent norm'" (p. 94). Weissman may indeed recognize such things, but they are all at the level of the system rather than the individual. That was our previous point. Here what one should notice is that in Weissman's social ontology there is no need to have any commitment to teleology. The system need not have a telos of any sort, and with individuals deriving values from the system itself, teleology is not needed at the individual level to help define objective value. For us, by contrast, because teleology is at the individual level, it is going to keep "core interests," "primary goods," and "immanent norms" at the level of the individual and thus allow us our commitment to the primacy of the individual both ontologically and ethically. Of course, in this respect, and indeed with respect to most of what we have mentioned here, we have moved the focus significantly away from the political which was Sternberg's primary purpose in her paper. Our comments are thus not primarily criticisms of Sternberg's analysis, but rather an opening salvo to prospective work to come on the connections that may need to be explored when thinking of politics, ethics, and ontology.

III

Aeon J. Skoble does an excellent job of summarizing our view, and we have nothing to add to his summary. However, Skoble does raise towards the end of his remarks the interesting issue of whether *Norms of Liberty* has any prospects for persuading people. In general terms, the philosophical question is as old as Plato's *Gorgias* where the connection between philosophy and persuasion is explored. Like Plato, we would hold the view that persuasion is not the main point of doing philosophy—indeed, it may not be an end for philosophy at all. Yet the picture is somewhat muddied when it comes to ethics and social and political philosophy. Here the object is action, and Plato was certainly correct to suggest that persuasion precedes action, especially in moral and political matters. What the connection should be between philosophy and persuasion in these subject areas therefore remains an interesting question, though one too broad to explore here. Suffice it to say that we do not believe we are blueprinting a political or moral order when we write about these topics. The line from philosophical reflection on matters of ethics and politics to action is a circuitous one, and our continual references to the role of judgment, practical wisdom, and experience should suggest that philosophers may not even be the principal players in designing courses of action. We are, however, more comfortable in thinking about the persuasion issue with respect to our particular lives and projects. In this regard we have three points to make.

First, we think that we should just simply acknowledge some facts. We are not the sorts of philosophers whose reputation is such that high profile universities fall all over themselves to offer us positions among their faculty. Neither of us works at a leading academic institution that is known for its philosophy program. Nor have we had our works published by the most prestigious presses. So, it seems that we should just admit upfront that if persuasion is the goal, then in all likelihood the prospects are low. We mention this not in the spirit of self-deprecation or "sour grapes." Indeed we are often pleasantly surprised with how many people do know our work, both in the US and many other parts of the world as well. Saying that, however, is not the same as saying that when we publish something people feel they "ought" to read it if for no other reason than to keep abreast of what the most visible members of the profession are saying.

Second, we do not always approach doing philosophy in a manner that accords with the philosophical fashions of the day. As we have noted in many places in this essay, we do not think that political philosophy can function apart from deeper concerns, and these concerns go all the way to issues in metaphysics. Appeals to ordinary language, common sense, considered moral judgments, moral intuitions, basic narratives, and prima facie distinctions are all legitimate starting points, but they are not ending points. Such appeals do not stand alone or operate apart from a context that provides the basis for how they are understood and interpreted. Nor do appeals such as these create their own context. Indeed, their context is not itself a function of theorizing. Thus, we regard the task of the philosopher as examining what is the fundamental context for not only appeals such as these but for theorizing itself. We are dedicated to engaging in such a task, but this is, of course, not how philosophy is often done in this day-and-age. Thus, since we have chosen to be out of fashion, we have, in a sense, chosen to engage in an activity that currently does not increase our odds of being persuasive.

On the other hand, we do not think that this is an all-or-nothing matter. We may think that an examination of human nature is required to support an ethics or that a certain metaphysical position is vital if we are to have any hope of objectivity, but the exact connection between one area of philosophy and another is not a simple one. Drawing out such connections is a matter for investigation, discussion, and argumentation that involves exchanges with others, and it is a process where only the force of the better argument matters. There are many ways to skin the philosophical cat, and we would loathe being viewed as having a lock on the way such connections should be made. Doing so is part of what we believe it means to do philosophy; that the connections must be exactly as we have described them is not, however, itself a part of their description. We only hope that the reader will find the efforts we have made to be at least plausible.

Nevertheless, we think that a number of the principles or positions we use in ethics and political philosophy are ones that are in many ways similar to views held by others. There are, for example, many working in ethics who are interested in perfectionism and an agent-centered approach. Also, there are many working in politics that are interested in the importance of liberty. Finally, as a group, philosophers are not generally drawn to the idea that truth is completely beyond our reach and that everything is up for grabs. Thus even though our own view is that objectivity ultimately requires some form of metaphysical realism, our belief in the possibility of truth is not foreign to philosophers generally. In any case, this is one of the last issues to be addressed, not the first, and this view like all others must be part of the philosophical debate—not part of an ideological agenda.

Third, and finally, we intend to continue in our ways. We want to develop our account of individualistic perfectionism and consider related issues regarding human nature and reason. Ultimately, we even have things to say about what we like to call "Reality, knowledge, God, and the universe." These are the issues we think are important not only for the political vision we have, but for our own development as human beings. Because we see philosophy primarily as something one engages in for the sake of human flourishing, we think that Socrates had it right. Thus, as Skoble implies, we have from the beginning not been motivated by the goal of persuasion, as important as that is, but rather we have been motivated by the goal of understanding the central issues of philosophy. We think in all sincerity that such understanding is all—indeed, it is really everything—that a philosopher should aspire to achieve.

Notes

1. Douglas B. Rasmussen and Douglas J. Den Uyl, *Norms of Liberty: A Perfectionist Basis for Non-Perfectionist Politics* (University Park, Pa: Pennsylvania State University Press, 2005).
2. *NOL*, 283.
3. *NOL*, 85
4. To the extent that contemporary liberalism has adopted social engineering as a means to attaining its various ends, be they "equality," "social justice," or whatever, then it too shares the perspective of conservatives and communitarians on this issue. See *NOL*, 16.
5. We make no existential claim and thus bear no onus of proof.
6. *NOL*, 85.
7. *NOL*, 85.
8. This is what we take to be the fundamental import of England's

view of the effectiveness of philosophical distinctions.

9. *NOL*, 9.

10. See Fred D, Miller Jr., *Nature, Justice and Rights in Aristotle's* Politics (Oxford: Clarendon Press, 1995) for a thorough account of the *polis*.

11. Michael Oakeshott, *On Human Conduct* (Oxford: Clarendon Press, 1975), Chapter II, "On the Civil Condition," 108–84.

12. We take up this point again when we consider Kenneth L. Grasso's essay.

13. We discuss this point in *NOL*, especially in response to concerns raised by MacIntyre. See chapter 10. What we say here is also relevant to some of the concerns raised by Grasso regarding "structural neutrality," but we will have more to say about that shortly.

14. England recognizes that the right to liberty is for us a metanormative principle and that this is a kind of ethical principle. Yet, he says that its purpose is not normative, that it is *not* intended "to directly regulate" human conduct (this volume, p. 17). This is confused. Our position is that rights qua rights (that is, as metanorms) do not guide individual conduct in moral activity, but regulate conduct so that conditions might be obtained so that moral action can take place. Further, rights do not "trump" *tout court* but only in relation to solving liberalism's problem. We discuss this point again in many places below.

15. *NOL*, 271.

16. We treat the words "human flourishing" and "self-perfection" as synonymous.

17. *NOL*, 272.

18. We summarize this argument in a systematic fashion in chapter 11 of *NOL*.

19. As Etienne Gilson noted, "[B]y his very nature, man is a metaphysical animal." *Unity of Philosophical Experience* (New York: Charles Scribner's Sons, 1965), 307.

20. These are chapters 6 and 7.

21. As we note many times in *NOL*, we use the label "liberalism's problem" because liberalism has typically been the only political philosophy to appreciate the fundamentality and importance of this problem. We also note that liberalism has not always done so consistently. One way of understanding the general aim of *NOL*, then, is as an attempt to provide liberalism with a better understanding of itself and its foundations.

22. Douglas B. Rasmussen, "The Importance of Metaphysical Realism for Ethical Knowledge," *Social Philosophy & Policy* 25.1 (Winter 2008): 56–99.

23. There was also the sentiment that a polity that made virtue its aim was not as effective in providing for the defense of its citizens as one that concentrated on peace and order. See for example Spinoza, *TP* X, 5.

24. We argue that human flourishing is an inclusive, not a dominant, ultimate end and that it is constituted by basic generic goods and virtues that are valuable not as mere means to human flourishing but as expressions of it. Among these, we list such goods as knowledge, health, friendship, creative achievement, beauty, and pleasure and such virtues as integrity, temperance, courage, and justice. However, we do not regard this list as necessarily fixed or final, but as open-ended and revisable. Moreover, none of these goods and virtues should be treated as having either actuality or worth apart from an individual's exercise of practical wisdom. So, to appreciate adequately their role in our account of human flourishing they must be considered in light of the context we provide. See chapters 6–8 of *NOL*.

25. However, to say that human flourishing is more than self-directed activity is not to say that protecting or promoting human flourishing is the aim of the political/legal order.

26. This is not to deny a crucial role for culture, friends, family, and associates. We discuss this shortly.

27. See chapter 8 of *NOL*.

28. See Douglas B. Rasmussen and Douglas J. Den Uyl, "In Search of Universal Political Principles: Avoiding Some of Modernity's Pitfalls and Discovering the Importance of Liberal Political Order," *Seeking Common Principles of Justice: The Prospects, Challenges, and Risks of Universalism in a Divided World,* ed. Stephen Elkin and Stephen Simon (Forthcoming, University Park, Pa.: Pennsylvania State University Press, 2008).

29. Human beings create institutions, establish conventions, and create cultures. These are sometimes the result of design but not always.

30. See Miller, *Nature, Justice and Rights in Aristotle's* Politics.

31. See Fred Miller's discussion of how the concept of the polis conflates society and state. *Nature, Justice, and Rights in Aristotle's* Politics, 358.

32. *NOL*, 232.

33. Though even if it were the case that these factors only applied to the state, as opposed to families, communities, and voluntary associations, it would go no distance towards helping us decide the legitimacy of the rules that ought to be governing the state. No doubt the various museums to communism found in numerous "Eastern bloc" countries are a reminder of this.

34. We also reject it because "liberal neutrality" is generally thought to entail "justificatory neutralism," which we, as indicated in our response to England, also reject.

35. We explain this concept in our response to England above.

36. We do take issue, however, with the challenge communitarianism presents to liberalism. We consider MacIntyre directly, and Sandel indirectly, in *NOL*. Also, we take issue with Charles Taylor in a later work. See note 38 below.

37. See *NOL*, chapter 10, especially pp. 242–44.

38. Douglas J. Den Uyl and Douglas B. Rasmussen, "The Myth of Atomism," *The Review of Metaphysics* 59 (June 2006): 843–70.

39. "The Myth of Atomism," 855.

40. This also raises another issue—namely, how one understands the common good of the political community—but Grasso never takes up our discussion of this subject. We devote part of chapter 8 of *NOL* to this issue, and we discuss it as well in our earlier work, Douglas B. Rasmussen and Douglas J. Den Uyl, *Liberty and Nature: An Aristotelian Defense of Liberal Order* (La Salle, Ill.: Open Court, 1991), chapter 4, esp. pp. 131–71.

41. Grasso also accuses our account of human flourishing of ignoring the spiritual or religious dimension of human existence and thereby revealing a contemporary liberal bias. Yet, this is not true. Nothing we argue in *NOL* is incompatible with there being such a dimension. We even note (*NOL*, 212 n14) that we will have to leave for another occasion an exploration of the theological or religious implications of our view. What Grasso seems to do is to confuse our explanation of how human beings are causally responsible for their status as ends in themselves with the claim that human beings are responsible for their very existence. Though we talk about the importance of metaphysical issues in *NOL* and indeed allude to certain basic ontological and epistemological questions, we never take up the question of existence.

42. We define an individual's "nexus" as the set of circumstances, talents, endowments, interests, beliefs, and histories that descriptively characterize each individual.

43. In this regard, Thunder's views seem quite similar to views of John Finnis. See our discussion of his views in *NOL*, 185–96.

44. In *NOL*, we describe this as a process of weighting and balancing these goods in accordance with one's nexus and circumstances.

45. Put a little differently, human flourishing is inclusive *and* individualized.

46. We understand negative liberty to be the social condition secured by a polity that is dedicated to protecting and maintaining individual rights.

47. Exactly speaking, the relationship of self-direction to human flourishing is even more intimate than this. Choice or self-direction is not merely necessary for human flourishing to exist. It is necessary for human flourishing to be the very activity it is. See our discussion of the role of self-direction in human flourishing in chapters 4 and 6 of *NOL*.

48. It does so because it is the only feature of human flourishing that meets the conditions for solving liberalism's problem. We list these conditions above in our response to England.

49. In this regard, Thunder, Collins, and Thomas share the same premise as many contemporary liberals who seek to provide people with the "opportunities" for human flourishing.

50. There may be some goods, for example friendship, that are not divisible or capable of being redistributed or put in "baskets."

51. Fuller starts here with a worry about whether our account of human flourishing really allows for a human telos, but then he proceeds to conflate this worry with the worry of whether liberalism can allow for the existence of such a telos. In what follows, we respond to the latter worry, but what we have said already to others should suffice as a response to the former worry. In other words, we think we do show that there is a human telos applicable to all human beings, but this does not require that human flourishing must actually exist as some universal form that is identically present in each individual.

52. This failure to take metanormativity seriously is in part due to the failure to appreciate how human flourishing can be the telos for human conduct and at the same time something that is individualized and agent-relative. Not only do we explain how this is possible, but defend this view against basic objections. See *NOL*, chapter 7, 153–60. In addition, our comments above in reply to Grasso on this issue are relevant here.

53. It should be noted that versions of this issue were dealt with in chapter 12 of *NOL* under the headings of "Is the Concept of 'Metanormative Principles' Really Necessary?" 301–03 and "The Issue of Symbolism," 327–29.

54. We make this point in *NOL*, chapter 10. Also, our reply above to Grasso's worries about a civic ethos is applicable here.

55. Since our view of human flourishing is agent-centered (that is, human flourishing is inclusive, individualized, agent-relative, and self-directed), the question of whether the human telos is primarily one

single activity or many is answered by its relationship to each individual human being. Our point is that this question cannot presuppose that there is a universal answer.

56. This is not to suggest that we actually endorse such doctrines. We do not. But from some perspectives (for example, Platonism or an agent-neutral account of flourishing), we could look like we might be moving in that direction.

57. "Basic goods are for the sake of fulfilling individual human beings; individuals are not for the sake of achieving basic goods." NOL, 192.

58. *NOL*, p. 118

59. Ibid., p. 167.

60. Taylor does refer to Jerome C. Wakefield, "Aristotle as Sociobiologist: The 'Function of a Human Being' Argument, Black Box Essentialism, and the Concept of Mental Disorder," *Philosophy, Psychiatry, & Psychology* 7, no. 1 (2000): 17–44 in this regard. While we find many aspects of this essay to be helpful and important, we do not think that endorsing a biocentric basis for teleology is the same thing as adopting the perspective of sociobiology. We agree with Philippa Foot that it is one thing to use "function" and "good" to describe the life of an individual, which is a member of a species, and it is quite another to talk as if they apply to a species, One can endorse the former way of speaking without endorsing the latter. See *NOL*, 119 n19.

61. See Douglas B. Rasmussen: "Rand on Obligation and Value," *The Journal of Ayn Rand Studies* 4, no. 1 (Fall 2002): 69–86; "Regarding Choice and the Foundation of Morality: Reflections on Rand's Ethics," *The Journal of Ayn Rand Studies* 7, no. 2 (Spring 2006): 309–28; "Rand's Metaethics: Rejoinder to Hartford," *The Journal of Ayn Rand Studies* 8, no. 2 (Spring 2007): 307–16.

62. The reasons can be *ex post facto* but cannot be *ad hoc.*

63. This question is being asked in a normative, not a metanormative, context.

64. This assumption also lies behind the Kantian claim that morality requires an unconditioned and self-legislating will. See our essay, "In Search of Universal Political Principles: Avoiding Some of Modernity's Pitfalls and Discovering the Importance of Liberal Political Order," op. cit.

65. *NOL*, pp. 119–27 and 163–67.

66. Material causality is expressed through these material elements.

67. *NOL*, 153–58.

68. Nor can it be adequate apart from considerations of an individual's nexus.

69. As Aristotle states, "virtue or excellence is a state of character involving choice and consists in observing a mean relative to us, a mean defined as a rational principle, such as a man of practical wisdom would use to determine it" (*Nicomachean Ethics*, 1107a1–3).

70. *NOL*, 143–52.

71. *Summa theologiae*, I-II, 94.2.

72. "Practical reason properly used, which is the virtue of practical wisdom, is the intelligent management of one's life so that all the necessary goods and virtues are coherently achieved, maintained, and enjoyed in a manner that is appropriate for the individual human being." *NOL*, 147.

73. This makes our account of morality a version of pluralism but not relativism. But this must be carefully understood. See our comments on Isaiah Berlin's pluralism, *NOL*, 170–71, and our critical analysis of John Gray's, *NOL*, 173–83 and 244–50.

74. See Douglas B. Rasmussen, "The Importance of Metaphysical Realism for Ethical Knowledge, op. cit.," and Edward Pols, *Radical Realism: Direct Knowing in Science and Philosophy* (Ithaca, N. Y.: Cornell University Press, 1992).

75. See Baruch Brody, *Identity and Essence* (Princeton: Princeton University Press, 1980); Tibor R. Machan, "Epistemology and Moral Knowledge," *Review of Metaphysics* 36.1 (September 1984): 23–49; Douglas B. Rasmussen, "Quine and Aristotelian Essentialism," *The New Scholasticism* 58 (Summer 1984): 316–35; and Henry B. Veatch, *Two Logics: The Conflict between Classical and Neo-Analytic Philosophy* (Evanston, Ill.: Northwestern University Press, 1969).

76. See Douglas J. Den Uyl and Douglas B. Rasmussen, "Aristotelianism, Commerce, and the Liberal Order," *Aristotle and Modern Politics*, ed., Aristide Tessitore (University of Notre Dame Press, 2002), 278–304. Here we discuss, among other things, the different ways Aristotle understands friendship and how this can provide insight to understanding both commerce and the liberal order.

77. It is important to understand that we do not possess the in-depth familiarity with Weissman that Sternberg does. Our comments about what Weissman may hold, therefore, refer at best to some concerns we have as he is presented in her essay, and should not be taken as a claim to a greater understanding of Weissman or even as a disagreement with any of Sternberg's readings of him.

78. Consider the following: (1) "Assuming the system's survival as the point of reference, we say that each part is responsible to the others for such behaviors as would sustain the system. . . . These responsibilities are less than obligations or duties. They fall to individual[s]. . . because of the mechanical prejudice—the inertial identity—that favors a system's survival. . . . [T]his is all the basis required for natural obligation in members that can, do, or *should* perceive the value of perpetuating the systems in which they participate;" and (2) "For I who affirm my own value also affirm my responsibility to the systems that engage me." (David Weissman, *A Social Ontology* (New Haven, Conn.: Yale University Press, 2000), pp. 118 (emphasis added) and 298 respectively.

79. Weissman, *A Social Ontology*, 307.

Bibliography

Selected Works by Rasmussen and Den Uyl, Chronological

Den Uyl, Douglas J., and Douglas B. Rasmussen. "Nozick on the Randian Argument," *The Personalist* 59, no. 2 (April 1978).

Rasmussen, Douglas B. "Essentialism, Values, and Rights," in *The Libertarian Reader*, Tibor R. Machan, ed. (Totowa, N.J.: Rowman and Allenheld, 1982).

Den Uyl, Douglas J. *Power, State, and Freedom: An Interpretation of Spinoza's Political Philosophy* (Assen, Netherlands: Van Gorcum, 1983).

Rasmussen, Douglas B. "The Right to Project Pursuit and the Human Telos," *Reason Papers* 14 (Spring 1989).

Rasmussen, Douglas B. "Liberalism and Natural End Ethics," *American Philosophical Quarterly* 27 (April 1990).

Den Uyl, Douglas J. *The Virtue of Prudence* (New York: Peter Lang, 1991).

Rasmussen, Douglas B., and Douglas J. Den Uyl. *Liberty and Nature: An Aristotelian Defense of Liberal Order* (Chicago: Open Court, 1991).

Den Uyl, Douglas J. "Teleology and Agent-Centeredness," *The Monist* 75, no. 1 (January 1992).

Rasmussen, Douglas B. "Political Legitimacy and Discourse Ethics," *International Philosophical Quarterly* 32 (March 1992).

Rasmussen, Douglas B., and Douglas J. Den Uyl. "Reply to Critics," *Reason Papers* 18 (Fall 1993).

Den Uyl, Douglas J. "The Right to Welfare and the Virtue of Charity," *Social Philosophy and Policy* 10, no. 1 (Winter 1993).

Den Uyl, Douglas J., and Douglas B. Rasmussen. "'Rights' as Metanormative Principles," in *Liberty for the 21st Century: Contemporary Libertarian Thought*, edited by Tibor R. Machan and Douglas B. Rasmussen (Lanham, Md.: Rowman and Littlefield, 1995).

Rasmussen, Douglas B. "Community versus Liberty?" in *Liberty for the 21st Century: Contemporary Libertarian Thought*, edited by Tibor R. Machan and Douglas B. Rasmussen (Lanham, Md.: Rowman and Littlefield, 1995).

Rasmussen, Douglas B., and Douglas J. Den Uyl. *Liberalism Defended: The Challenge of Post-Modernity* (Northampton, Mass.: Edward Elgar, 1997).

Rasmussen, Douglas B. "Human Flourishing and the Appeal to Human Nature," *Social Philosophy and Policy* 16, no. 1 (Winter 1999).

Den Uyl, Douglas J., and Douglas B. Rasmussen. "Ethical Individualism, Natural Law, and the Primacy of Natural Rights," *Social Philosophy and Policy* 18, no. 1 (Winter 2001).

Rasmussen, Douglas B., and Douglas J. Den Uyl. *Norms of Liberty: A Perfectionist Basis for Non-Perfectionist Politics* (University Park, Penn.: Pennsylvania State University Press, 2005).

Den Uyl, Douglas J., and Douglas B. Rasmussen. "The Myth of Atomism," *The Review of Metaphysics* 59 (June 2006): 843-870.

Rasmussen, Douglas B. "The Importance of Metaphysical Realism for Ethical Knowledge," *Social Philosophy & Policy* 25.1 (Winter 2008): 56-99.

Rasmussen, Douglas B., and Douglas J. Den Uyl. "In Search of Universal Political Principles: Avoiding Some of Modernity's Pitfalls and Discovering the Importance of Liberal Political Order," *Seeking Common Principles of Justice: The Prospects, Challenges, and Risks of Universalism in a Divided World*, edited by Stephen Elkin and Stephen Simon (University Park, Penn.: Pennsylvania State University Press, 2008).

Den Uyl, Douglas J., and Douglas B. Rasmussen. "Retreat from Liberalism: The Human Capabilities Approach," *Libertarian Investigations*, edited by Susumu Morimura (Tokyo: Keisoshobo, 2008).

Other Works

Aquinas, Thomas. *Summa Theolgiae*, Question 91, in *St. Thomas Aquinas on Politics and Ethics*, trans. by Paul E. Sigmund (New York: Norton, 1988).

Aristotle. *Nicomachean Ethics*, translated by T. Irwin (Indianapolis: Hackett: 1999).

Berlin, Isaiah. "Two Concepts of Liberty," in *Four Essays on Liberty* (Oxford: Clarendon Press, 1958).

Cook, Travis. Review of *Norms of Liberty*, *The Review of Metaphysics* 61 (September 2007): 151–153.

Cooper, John. *Reason and Human Good in Aristotle* (Indianapolis: Hackett Publishing, 1986).

Finnis, John. *Natural Law and Natural Rights* (Oxford: Clarendon Press, 1980).

Foot, Phillipa. *Natural Goodness* (Oxford: Oxford University Press, 2001).

George, Robert. *Making Men Moral* (Oxford: Oxford University Press, 1993).

Golding, Martin. "Aristotelian Ethics and Natural Rights: A Critique," *Reason Papers* 18 (Fall 1993).

Gray, John. *Post-Liberalism: Studies in Political Thought* (New York: Routledge, 1993).

———. "Agonistic Liberalism," *Social Philosophy and Policy* 12, no. 1 (Winter 1995).

Hayek, Friedrich. *The Constitution of Liberty* (Chicago: University of Chicago Press, 1960).

———. *Law, Legislation, and Liberty* (Chicago: University of Chicago Press, 1973).

Hittinger, Russell. "Does Liberalism Need Natural Rights?" *Reason Papers* 18 (Fall 1993).

Jacobs, Jonathan. *Choosing Character* (Ithaca, N.Y.: Cornell University Press, 2001).

Klein, Shawn. Review of *Norms of Liberty*, *The Independent Review* 11, no. 3 (Winter 2007).

Kukathas, Chandran. *Hayek and Modern Liberalism* (Oxford: Clarendon Press, 1989).

Locke, John. *Two Treatises of Government*, edited by Peter Laslett (Cambridge, England: Cambridge University Press, 1967 (1690)).

Lomasky, Loren. *Persons, Rights, and the Moral Community* (Oxford: Oxford University Press, 1987).

Machan, Tibor, ed. *The Libertarian Reader* (Totowa, N.J.: Rowman and Allenheld, 1982).

———. *Individuals and Their Rights* (Chicago: Open Court, 1989).

———. Review of *Norms of Liberty*, *Philosophy of the Social Sciences* 36, no. 3 (2006).

Machan, Tibor, and Rasmussen, Douglas B, eds. *Liberty for the 21st Century: Contemporary Libertarian Thought* (Lanham, Md.: Rowman and Littlefield, 1995).

MacIntyre, Alasdair. *After Virtue: A Study in Moral Theory* (Notre Dame: University of Notre Dame Press, 1984).

———. *Whose Justice? Which Rationality?* (Notre Dame: University of Notre Dame Press, 1989).

Mack, Eric. "Rasmussen and Den Uyl on Natural Rights," *Reason Papers* 18 (Fall 1993).

———. "Moral Individualism and Libertarian Theory," in *Liberty for the 21st Century: Contemporary Libertarian Thought*, edited by Tibor R. Machan and Douglas B. Rasmussen (Lanham, Md.: Rowman and Littlefield, 1995).

Mill, John Stuart. *On Liberty*, edited by David Spitz (New York: Norton, 1975).

———. *Utilitarianism*, edited by George Sher (Indianapolis: Hackett Publishing, 2001).

Miller, Jr., Frederick D. *Nature, Justice, and Rights in Aristotle's* Politics (Oxford: Clarendon Press, 1995).

Norton, David. *Personal Destinies: A Philosophy of Ethical Individualism* (Princeton: Princeton University Press, 1976).

Nozick, Robert. *Anarchy, State, and Utopia* (New York: Basic Books, 1974).

Nussbaum, Martha. *Women and Human Development: The Capabilities Approach* (Cambridge, England: Cambridge University Press, 2001).

Oakeshott, Michael. *On Human Conduct* (Oxford: Clarendon Press, 1975).

Paul, Jeffrey. "Natural Ends and Natural Rights," *Reason Papers* 18 (Fall 1993).

Rawls, John. *A Theory of Justice* (Cambridge, Mass: Harvard University Press, 1971).

Sandel, Michael. *Liberalism and the Limits of Justice* (Cambridge, England: Cambridge University Press, 1982).

Skoble, Aeon J. Review of *Liberty and Nature, Vera Lex* 14, no. 1 (Winter 1994).

———. *Deleting the State: An Argument about Government* (Chicago: Open Court, 2008).

Smith, Adam. *Theory of Moral Sentiments* (Indianapolis: Liberty Fund, 1974).

Spinoza, Baruch. *Tractatus Theologico-Politicus*, translated by R. H. M. Elwes (New York: Dover Publications, 1951).

Taylor, Charles. *Philosophy and the Human Sciences* (Cambridge, England: Cambridge University Press, 1985).
———. "Atomism." In *Communitarianism and Individualism,* edited by Shlomo Avineri and Avner de-Shalit (Oxford: Oxford University Press, 1992).
Veatch, Henry B. *Rational Man: An Interpretation of Aristotelian Ethics* (Bloomington, Ind.: University of Indiana Press, 1962; Indianapolis: Liberty Fund, 2003).
———. *Human Rights: Fact or Fancy?* (Baton Rouge: Louisiana State University Press, 1985).
———. "Commendations and Queries *re Liberty and Nature," Reason Papers* 18 (Fall 1993).

Index

About the Editor and Contributors

Susan D. Collins is associate professor of political science and the Honors College at the University of Houston. Her research focuses on the political thought of classical antiquity. In addition to several journal articles and book chapters, she is the author of *Aristotle and the Rediscovery of Citizenship* and coeditor of *Action and Contemplation: Studies in the Moral and Political Thought of Aristotle*.

Douglas J. Den Uyl is vice president of Educational Programs at Liberty Fund, Inc. He has published books and articles in the areas of political philosophy, ethics, and the history of philosophy, including *Power, State, and Freedom: An Interpretation of Spinoza's Political Philosophy* (Van Gorcum, 1983), *The Virtue of Prudence* (Peter Lang, 1991), and (with Douglas B. Rasmussen) *Liberty and Nature: An Aristotelian Defense of Liberal Order* (Open Court, 1991); *Liberalism Defended: The Challenge of Post-Modernity* (Edward Elgar, 1997); and *Norms of Liberty: A Perfectionist Basis for Non-Perfectionist Politics* (Penn State University Press, 2005).

Edwin England, an administrator for the Educational Service Center of Franklin County, Ohio, currently coordinates Project KEY, a pilot program serving at-risk elementary and middle school youth in the Columbus City schools. He teaches ethics and political philosophy as an adjunct lecturer at central Ohio colleges. A graduate of Calvin College and Ohio State, he lives with his wife and two children in Westerville, Ohio.

Timothy Fuller is the Lloyd E. Worner Distinguished Service Professor of Political Science at Colorado College, working on modern political philosophy. He recently coedited, with Corey Abel, *The Intellectual Legacy of Michael Oakeshott* (Imprint Academic, 2005), and has written essays on Leo Strauss and Eric Voegelin.

Kenneth L. Grasso is professor of political science at Texas State University. A specialist in Catholic social thought and liberal theory, he is the editor (with Robert P. Hunt) of *Catholicism and Religious Freedom: Contemporary Reflections on Vatican II's Declaration on Religious Liberty*. (Rowman and Littlefield, 2006). His articles and reviews have appeared in a variety of journals including *The Journal of Catholic Social Thought, Interpretation, The American Political Science Review, The Catholic Social Science Review,* and *The Political Science Reviewer*. He currently serves as second vice-president of the Society of Catholic Social Scientists.

William Kline received his Ph.D. from Bowling Green State University. He has taught throughout the United States and Hungary including at Fort Hays State University, University of Toledo, Central Michigan University, Molloy College, and the Central European University. He has served as the director of the Center for Applied Ethics at Central Michigan, and as director of the Center for Business Ethics at Molloy College. He is currently the president of the Institute for Liberty in the Curriculum, which is dedicated to the study of liberty in undergraduate education.

Fred D. Miller Jr. is professor of philosophy and executive director of the Social Philosophy and Policy Center at Bowling Green State University. He is author of *Nature, Justice, and Rights in Aristotle's Politics* (Oxford University Press, 1995) and coeditor of many collections, including *A Companion to Aristotle's Politics*

(Blackwell, 1991), *Freedom, Reason, and the Polis: Essays in Ancient Greek Political Philosophy* (Cambridge University Press, 2007), and *A History of the Philosophy of Law from the Ancient Greeks to the Scholastics*, volume 6 of *A Treatise of Legal Philosophy and General Jurisprudence* (Springer, 2007). He served as president of the Society for Ancient Greek Philosophy from 1988–2004.

Douglas B. Rasmussen is professor of philosophy at St. John's University. His research interests are epistemology, ontology, ethics, and political philosophy as well as the moral foundations of capitalism. He has authored numerous articles in such journals as *American Catholic Philosophical Quarterly, American Philosophical Quarterly, International Philosophical Quarterly, The New Scholasticism, The Personalist, Public Affairs Quarterly, The Review of Metaphysics,* and *The Thomist,* and in many scholarly anthologies. He is coauthor (with Douglas J. Den Uyl) of *Liberty and Nature: An Aristotelian Defense of Liberal Order* (Open Court, 1991); *Liberalism Defended: The Challenge of Post-Modernity* (Edward Elgar, 1997); and *Norms of Liberty: A Perfectionist Basis for Non-Perfectionist Politics* (Penn State University Press, 2005).

Aeon J. Skoble is professor of philosophy and chair of the philosophy department at Bridgewater State College in Massachusetts. He is the coeditor, with Tibor Machan, of the anthology *Political Philosophy: Essential Selections* (Prentice-Hall, 1999) and author of *Deleting the State: An Argument about Government* (Open Court, 2008), as well as many essays on moral and political philosophy in both scholarly and popular journals. In addition, he writes widely on the intersection of philosophy and popular culture, including such subjects as *Seinfeld, Forrest Gump, The Lord of the Rings,* superheroes, film noir, Hitchcock, Scorsese, science fiction, and baseball. He coedited and contributed to *The Philosophy of TV Noir* (University Press of Kentucky, 2007), *Woody Allen and Philosophy* (Open Court, 2004) and the best-selling *The Simpsons and Philosophy* (Open Court, 2000).

Elaine Sternberg is a visiting research fellow in philosophy at the University of Leeds, and a visiting scholar in the philosophy department at the University of Florida, Gainesville. Her main work is in Aristotelian applied ethics and in political philosophy. The author of *Just Business: Business Ethics in Action* (Oxford University Press, 2000) and *Corporate Governance: Accountability in the Marketplace* (Institute of Economic Affairs, 2004), she is a fellow of the Michael Oakeshott Association, and is on the advisory councils of Public Concern at Work, the Institute of Economic Affairs, and the Globalisation Institute.

Denis Sullivan is professor of philosophy at St. John's University. His main interest is in ethics and the philosophy of mind. He has published in *Transactions of the C. S. Peirce Society, American Catholic Philosophical Quarterly, Religious Studies,* and the *Proceedings of the World Congress of Philosophy*.

James Stacey Taylor is an assistant professor of philosophy at The College of New Jersey. His main work is on autonomy theory, the metaphysics of death, and applied ethics. He is the editor of *Personal Autonomy: New Essays* (Cambridge University Press, 2005), and the author of *Stakes and Kidneys: Why Markets in Human Body Parts are Morally Imperative* (Ashgate, 2005).

Charlotte Thomas is associate professor and chair of the Department of Philosophy at Mercer University. Thomas works mainly in political philosophy and philosophy and literature. She also teaches in Mercer's Great Books Program.

David Thunder is Bradley Lehrman Junior Visiting Fellow at the Witherspoon Institute in Princeton. He is currently investigating the ethical and psychological foundations of social order, including the concept and practice of citizenship. His published articles include "A Rawlsian Argument Against the Duty of Civility" (*American Journal of Political Science*, July 2006) and "Can a Good Person be a Lawyer?" (*Notre Dame Journal of Law, Ethics & Public Policy*, Spring 2006).

Peter E. Vedder is an independent scholar working on the problem of reason and nature in Descartes' *Meditations on First Philosophy*.

www.ingramcontent.com/pod-product-compliance
Lightning Source LLC
Chambersburg PA
CBHW051253200926
51612CB00001B/30
9780739126929